A Diversity of Gifts:
Vermont Women at Work

A DIVERSITY OF GIFTS: VERMONT WOMEN AT WORK

D'ANN CALHOUN FAGO

THE COUNTRYMAN PRESS
WOODSTOCK, VERMONT

The Countryman Press, Inc.
Woodstock, Vermont 05091

Library of Congress Cataloging-in-Publication Data

Fago, D'Ann Calhoun, 1917–
  A diversity of gifts—Vermont women at work / by D'Ann Calhoun Fago.
    p.   cm.
  ISBN 0-88150-144-1
  1. Women—Employment—Vermont—Interviews.   I. Title
HD6096.V47F34   1989   89-15785
331.4'09743—dc20   CIP

Back cover photograph by Susan DeWitt Wilder
Cover design by James F. Brisson
Book design by Leslie Stevenson Fry
Map by Alex Wallach

Printed in the United States of America

All photographs by the author except for those of:

Mollie Beattie, courtesy of Tom Hark
Virginia Blackert, courtesy of Rita M. Malone
Suzanne Gillis, courtesy of Joan Knight Photography
Gertrude Horridge, courtesy of William Horridge
Lisa Lindhal and Hinda Schreiber-Miller, courtesy of Becky Lugart Stayner
Ellen McColloch Lovell, courtesy of Senator Patrick Leahy
Grace Paley and Deborah Lauro, courtesy of John Fago
Sister Janice Ryan, courtesy of Trinity College
Esther Swift, courtesy of herself
Dhyani Ywahoo, courtesy of Nina Miller-Levine

Some of these interviews were previously published in
Country Courier
White River Valley Herald
Vermont Woman
Christian Science Monitor
and permission to reprint is gratefully acknowledged.

DEDICATION

My deepest thanks to Celie Fago for her criticism, counsel and support in bringing this work to completion. I also owe a debt of gratitude to the women who sat for the portraits for their generosity, patience, and interest.

FEATURED VERMONT TOWNS

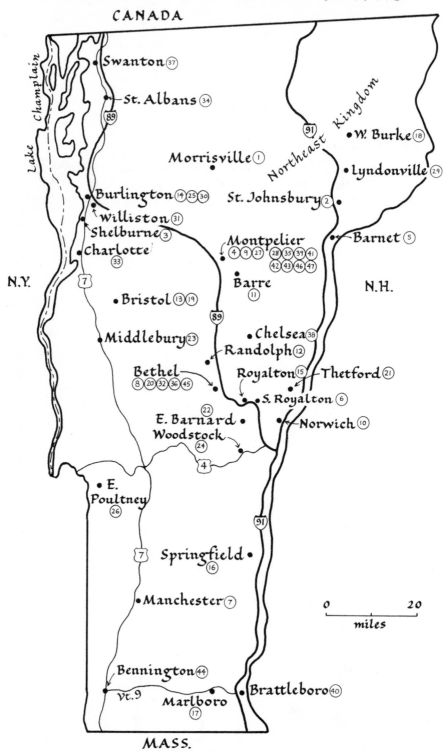

CANADA

Swanton ③⑦

St. Albans ③④

Lake Champlain

⑧⑨

Morrisville ①

Burlington ⑭㉕㉚

Williston ③①

Shelburne ③

Charlotte ③③

N.Y.

⑦

Bristol ⑬⑲

Middlebury ㉓

Bethel
⑧⑳㉜㊱㊺

St. Johnsbury ②

Northeast Kingdom

⑨①

W. Burke ⑱

Lyndonville ㉙

Barnet ⑤

Montpelier
④⑨㉗ ㉘㉟㊴㊶
       ㊷㊸㊻㊼

Barre
⑪

N.H.

⑧⑨

Chelsea ㊳

Randolph ⑫

Royalton ⑮ — Thetford ㉑

S. Royalton ⑥

E. Barnard ㉒

Woodstock ㉔

Norwich ⑩

④

E. Poultney ㉖

⑨①

⑦ Springfield ⑯

Manchester ⑦

0   20
miles

Bennington ㊹

Vt.9   Marlboro ⑰   Brattleboro ㊵

MASS.

CONTENTS

INTRODUCTION

*F*lying for the first time over country I'm accustomed to seeing at eye-level offered striking differences. The landscape below me appeared flattened; a design composed of textures, colors, shapes, and patterns of which I'm usually unaware. It was a view that also demonstrated connections ordinarily unseen.

Moving around the state, talking with women at different locations and situations, offered a similar perspective. Talking with women—across an executive's desk or a kitchen table; over the back of a cow or the bed of a printing press; in front of a judge's bench or a minister's pulpit; beside an expertly sawn pile of boards or in the cab of a bulldozer—revealed something, not only about the women being interviewed but also about the variety of successful ways there are for us to live our lives. It reaffirmed as well the continuous and frequently unrecognized nature of the connections that exist between us.

Some of these women were born in Vermont, others came with parents or husbands, and still others moved here as a result of their own work or inclinations. Some of the women are successful in what they've done; others in what they've managed not to do. Some were born in luxury and have used their gifts well; others were born in want, yet have multiplied their talents. Some started with emotionally disheveled and cluttered backgrounds but have shaped creative lives; others, with stable, balanced beginnings have had the compassion and commitment to help those without. Still, a struggle for personal independence has been common to most.

There were differences in attitudes concerning constructive ways of effecting change. And most felt that change was needed. Some believed that increased production of goods and services would result not only in more successful ventures for themselves but would positively affect "the good life" for others. Some were concerned about the uneven distribution of the world's goods and a too profligate use of the world's resources. Still others pointed out that while economic rewards have increased for women in some fields, there has been decreased support in others long considered to be female endeavors—childcare, nursing, social work, counseling, teaching, and care for the elderly.

Some of the women were interested in new forms for giving expression to a non-sexist, non-gender differentiated spiritual search, in the church or out. Many recognized the need for a deeper meaning in life, and for social values more expressive of reverence than of opportunism.

One of my own most affecting experiences in understanding the nature of reverence happened years ago. My mother-in-law held an egg towards the light for us both to admire. Balancing it gently but firmly between the thumb and forefinger of her wrinkled hand, her attention was concentrated on this simple object as she repeated softly, "Bella! Bella!" I was still young, she was then old. I was touched and instructed by the sense of reverence with which she approached not only food, but all the furnishings of her life; on one level, simple and uncomplicated; on another, as profound and significant as she chose to make them. As an artist, she possessed a gift for bestowing objects of ordinary existence with dignity and meaning; never as trifling and isolated events but as vital and integral parts of a larger reality.

That was years ago and my hands today mirror hers then. The world seems scarier in many ways, the reverence due all life even more crucial, and the relationship between all things more necessary to understand. Many of the women interviewed feel as I do, that if the values and direction of our society are to be restored, an important aspect of this revolution will be up to women. They believe our help is increasingly vital in developing a new kind of structure and means of communication; strong enough to include us all, nurturant enough to heal us, and practical enough to be put into place.

In the way an aerial view flattens our usual perception of the landscape, and strengthens our awareness of its overall design, I hoped to create a vista showing some of the ways women's lives contribute to the composition of our human scene. That we, as women, are now speaking more easily to each other, and attempting to eliminate some of the walls that competition and fear have built around us, provides society with reason for hope.

This project has lasted almost two years, and in that time I kept discovering more women I wanted to interview. But I had to stop somewhere. I cannot sufficiently express my gratitude to the women who agreed to sit for the portraits I made of them.

AGRICULTURE AND TRADES

LEPINE FAMILY

*T*he six-hundred acre Mount Sterling dairy farm has a story, one of courage, hard work, dedication, and family loyalty. For the last two decades it has also operated successfully within a matriarchal structure.

"We get up at four a.m. and milk around five," Gertrude Lepine said. "Milking takes three hours, then we clean up the gutters before breakfast. Ma comes down just before we finish milking to wash the utensils. That's her job and she takes pride in it."

Jennete Lepine added, "She comes down from the house every single day. When it's icy, she takes one step at a time; takes her about twenty minutes to get to the barn," she continued, hunching her own shoulders together, lifting one foot and putting it down carefully ahead of her before starting the next small step, showing the way "Ma" does it when it's treacherous underfoot.

"Twenty degrees below, whatever the weather, she always comes down to wash the utensils—takes tremendous pride in the job."

Gertrude added: "When the inspector comes Ma always wants to know later, 'did the inspector find anything wrong with the pails?'

"The answer is always 'no.' "

Therese Lepine completed the story. "The job takes her about forty minutes and then we all go back to the house for breakfast."

Imelda Lepine is ninety years old. Her daughters working the farm are: Jennete, fifty-nine; Gertrude, sixty-one; and Therese, sixty-three. Mount Sterling Farm is in "Mud City," a few miles southwest of Morrisville.

Other siblings live out of the state. An older sister, Marie, is married and runs a restaurant in Colorado; Andre, a brother, is a retired professor of vocational agriculture in New York; and Lawrence, the "baby," helped on the farm before he left to work in California.

Imelda Lepine is not as physically active as she once was, but she has always been, and continues to be, central to the organization.

Gertrude was definite about this. "Mom was always the dominant person in our family. She was the one who made things work. We wouldn't be here if it weren't for her."

We spoke in the "milking parlor" where some 65 cows, their registered Jersey herd, also play their part, twice daily, every day of the year. My conversation with the sisters covered the past, as well as the present; the people, as well as the animals; and the rewards of farming, as well as its perils. I was curious about the background of a family that came to this country in 1930.

When we began, the 140-foot barn was empty of its primary residents. They waited outside, more or less patiently, for the pasture gate to be opened allowing them reentry. And except for the swish of brooms and the scraping of shovels, it was quiet inside the barn and conversation flowed. The sisters spoke freely as they continued to work, stopping only occasionally to make a point, or change one of their implements.

"Pa built the barn in two sections, the first in 1945, and the other in 1950," Gertrude said, vigorously pushing a load of straw and manure ahead of her with a long-handled brush.

"We cut all the logs for it with a cross-cut saw. There weren't yet any chain saws."

"We've been on this farm since 1942," she recalled. "Pa found this place with 140 acres, and they wanted $1,200 for it. He had nine hundred dollars saved and put that down. We had a team, some pigs, and a few sheep. It badly needed a new barn and hadn't been farmed for thirty years.

"It's a wonderful farm and it has heavy, moist soil. But we've worked at this. All the land we use has been reclaimed, it was all grown up when we got it."

Over the years, as others farmers have left their farms, the Lepines have gradually increased their acreage to six hundred.

"We usually have about sixty-five milkers," Gertrude continued. "It's up a little now but sixty-five is usual. We also have surplus calves we're trying to sell; I've been putting ads in the farm papers.

"There's a lot of young stock too, twenty-seven calves, between a day and three months old; twenty-one bred heifers carrying calves, and eleven yearlings, open heifers, too young to breed. There should be about 120 head in all, but right now we're overstocked at more like 170."

At one of the stations a lone cow reclined and Jennete explained: "She won't cross the gutter—it may be a mental thing—or a slight fever. I gave her an intramuscular shot this morning."

"Jennete is our vet," Gertrude added, pointing out that calling a professional would cost at least forty-five dollars for the trip. Jeanette handles routine problems, but if an ailment shows signs of becoming serious a regular vet is called.

"We raise all our own crops, and the only thing we bring in is grain," she continued, explaining that silage, the fodder fed to the stock all winter, is grass with a fermenting agent added. This is cut on the farm during the summer.

"You have to be careful, though, the earlier it's cut, the more protein it contains and if cattle get too much protein they can die." She emphasized the importance of ongoing feed analysis and pointed out that theirs is done through the University of Vermont.

By now, Jennete was distributing silage to the feeding stations, forking it into her barrow from the bottom of the silo, loading and unloading it as often as necessary. The silo holds three hundred tons and the stock eats about one ton a day.

Smiling, as a good hostess ensuring her guest of the quality of the food to come, she picked up a handful of the dark, moist substance and held it before my nose.

"It smells good, not sour or rotten." And I had to agree.

"It's sweet and it analyzes very good," she said.

Gertrude added, "Everything is part of the farm income, even small things. Last year we cut about seventy-five extra tons of hay and sold it at twenty-five dollars a ton. We sell surplus calves, maybe a few heifers, but it's mainly dairy."

She calculates that their gross farm income will be about $151,000 this year. "Last year we grossed $175,000, but that'll come down," she added, pointing out that over one third of their income goes for grain and that grain prices, like other things, keep rising.

"We do our own haying, but there's new machinery to buy and repairs that have to be made. There's no end to the expense. It's not cheap to cut our own hay, but the hay price has doubled since a year ago, and anyway, you can't always get prime feed. Cows won't do well on poor feed, so we feel it's worth it."

Gertrude was the first daughter to devote herself seriously to farming as an adult. Old felt hat pulled down over her dark hair, worn blue jeans and a faded cotton plaid shirt, she is slender, of medium height and appears strong. She has the kind of clear blue eyes one expects to find in someone for whom observation of weather is not casual, but necessary to existence. It's hard to imagine Gertrude in a less elemental situation, and she appears to possess a soundness of judgment characteristic of people accustomed to weighing the influence of large natural forces against even the smallest details of their life.

"I've been farming since '53. When I quit teaching, my brother Lawrence was here with my dad and we opened up a lot of land. I quit teaching in my third year—it was during sugarin'," she said, a grin spreading across her face.

"I was teaching at Stowe Hollow and living here. It was April, and I couldn't stand it any longer. I liked the kids, and they liked me; everything was fine, but I just couldn't compare the two, farming and teaching."

"Gertrude manages, Jennete and I are helpers," Therese explained from the alley where she was sweeping. "Gertrude owns the farm with mother and Jennete has her own farm up the road."

"Therese was in Washington in Senator Aiken's office for twenty-odd years," Jennete added.

And Therese elaborated: "I was a Vermonter and born on the farm. But I became a secretary and worked with Lola Aiken in the Senator's Washington office. Didn't go down until 1954 and came home in 1975, when the Senator retired. I got to do some traveling and I met a lot of interesting people. Then I started helping out again on the farm."

Therese is a little shorter than the other two, with a closer resemblance to her mother. Her hair is trimly cut; she is also slender, but the crispness she conveys, in her jeans and shirt, is somehow related to a different quality of efficiency. She handled the heavy broom with alacrity and snap, but one could also place her before a typewriter if the script demanded.

"Jennete was an airline stewardess," Therese continued, moving the family story along in the cooperative fashion that seems to be part of a long established working relationship among the sisters and their mother. All share not only a sense of pride in the work, but a recognition and respect for each other as individuals.

Jennete straightened up, leaned against her shovel and explained. "When I used to fly I'd have two weeks off, and then I'd go back to the farm and work."

"I had some good years flying," she continued. "It was before jet planes—forty-two passengers and that was it. All first class, the big tourist business hadn't started. After that, flying lost the personal touch."

"I got to see other cultures and other places and I enjoyed it then," she said, but added quickly, as if determined to still any doubts on the part of her audience, "On the other hand, farming is a wonderful occupation as long as the body holds up.

"If I ever have to stop, I think I'll go into maple sugaring full time; there's something really nice about that too."

Jennete, like the others, is of medium height and slender. Like Gertrude, her work clothes also showed heavy wear but her previous experience in a different world has left its mark. Her hair is light and she wears it softly coiffed around her face. There is also makeup, unobtrusive but underscoring a kind of glamor that is integral to her personality.

Gertrude said that Jennete had run an antique market at her own place every Sunday for the past eighteen or nineteen years; she has only recently given it up.

"It was great," she said. "All kinds of people came. I never have a chance to go anywhere, but I got to meet all kinds of people."

But the Lepine sisters have far-reaching interests. Their house is full of paintings done by artists who have more recently become neighbors. Books are another important part of the furnishings and they appear to be worn, and well-read.

The sisters also share a quality of aliveness and a ready humor that can be traced to their mother, Imelda. My sense was that most discussions between the group, in the barn, in the fields, or in the house, would, more often than not, be of interest.

Gertrude narrated the family's history, from its origin in Canada to the move to a different country, language, and new life among strangers. Farming has been a tradition in the family, but it was maintained here at some sacrifice and with much of its success due primarily to the work and determination of its women.

"Mother was orphaned at three," Gertrude began. "She was raised by the Sisters. That's where she got her discipline, also her hatred of oatmeal and molasses. The Sisters brought her up and she was trained to teach.

"My dad came from a big family, two girls and twelve boys, fourteen of them. He spent some time at the Seminary and was always a wonderful penman.

"He was working on the family farm in Quebec which he bought after he and Ma were married. Jennete was only six months old when he sold it and headed for Vermont with his family, to 'the land of opportunity.' He found a little farm near Lake Elmore in 1930 and put down all the money he had."

"I didn't know a word of English when I first came to this country and I kept a French/English dictionary under my arm," Imelda had said, as we spoke earlier at the farmhouse.

She sat upright on a straight chair. Her eyes sparkled, and her expression was intent as she struggled to find words to explain the drama of this new life in Vermont, so many years before. In contrast to her daughters, her work clothes consisted of a housedress, neatly covered by an apron. While most of her time is spent in the farmhouse today, she is no stranger to the other kinds of heavy work required on a farm.

"We were new to that place when he got very sick. He had double pneumonia but he kept going until he couldn't go any longer," she said.

At the barn, Gertrude elaborated on the story, an account of individual courage and tenacity as well as kindliness displayed by rural people whose understanding of hardship surpassed their fear of newcomers with a different culture and a different language.

"Elmer and Elsie Jones lived on the nearest farm, and Elmer used to come over at night and sit up with our dad so Ma could get a little rest.

"Everybody was having a hard time then. There was no welfare, it was during the depression, and there we were, a family with six kids, no cash, very little food, a different language—and they repossessed the farm.

"The Lake Elmore people rallied around to help us. People brought food and canned goods from their cellars. I think the school teacher may have been in charge of organizing it all, but everybody was kind.

"After the doctor came he told my mother, 'I've done everything I can—there's no more to be done.' He didn't expect Pa to live, and he left.

"Ma gathered us all around the bed; we were on our knees praying—I can remember it now—and the fever broke. It was kind of a miracle. Another doctor treated him later, and he recovered, but it took a long time."

"Father had a wonderful brother," Gertrude continued. "He was a bachelor farming on halves on a farm in Sterling, about three miles from this farm. He got Father to come there. We moved up, and he moved on. He was a logger really, but he got my dad started again, working on halves with a businessman in town who owned the property."

But she remembers a long recovery period for her dad, during which it was impossible for him to work long hours.

"Mom worked hard to keep things going, to make things work.

After the kids were in bed she'd knit mittens at night and sell them for a dollar a pair. She sewed all our clothes, learned to work on the farm, learned to milk, and had a big garden. She'd drive down to the village with several cans of cream to sell two or three times a week, down over the hill in her buggy or on the sled."

They never owned this farm but were tenant farmers, working the land on halves. Gertrude pointed out that land barons were created during the 1940s, as many small farmers lost their farms, and businessmen from the neighboring towns bought them out. Big lumber companies also increased their holdings as the hard-pressed families sold out.

"I can remember the valley farms, lying unused and abandoned," she said sadly.

But farming was beginning to open up a little bit. And while the farm they were on was for sale, it was remote and their father never had a car. The children used a horse and buggy to get from there to grade school.

"That farm was sold at auction," Gertrude continued, "but my pa had managed to save nine hundred dollars which he put down on this place."

There'd been some good years, milk trucks were coming through and milk was bringing a better price, so he bought the first part of the Mount Sterling farm, where they are now, in 1942 for $1,800.

"Pa got a contract for the town garbage," she continued, explaining that in those days people fed garbage to the pigs.

"During World War II things were looking brighter and pork was selling good. We sold piglets and people came from all over the state to buy. At one time we had four hundred hogs, two hundred little pigs together—didn't always smell so good, but nobody worried much about that."

The barn had been swept clean by this time, manure and straw deposited outside, and feed distributed to all the milking stations. The sisters were spreading sawdust along the alleyways.

Gertrude stopped work, pushed her hat a little farther back from her forehead and said animatedly: "It's my pleasure to tell you that we've just bought the farm we were raised on. Bought it with a neighbor.

"We always had first refusal on the land and the day came when the owner was selling it—165 acres for three hundred thousand dollars to a man who was buying it for development. The owner called and said the deal was all set to go through but we had a day or two to exercise our right to buy it."

She explained that they had a neighbor who was also opposed to development, so the two families went into partnership and bought it together. The deal was closed that same weekend.

"Just to show you what's happened to prices," Gertrude continued, "This was the same 165 acres in Sterling that my dad went to work on halves. It was sold to Francis Clark for $1,100 in 1930."

By this time Gertrude had finished spreading sawdust, Therese went to open the pasture gate, and Jennete waited at the barn entrance like a country school teacher, monitoring the reentry of her students after recess.

The herd ambled in and the sisters moved in and around them, steering, cajoling, and making sure each cow was at her proper station with stanchions securely fastened.

Therese flourished her baseball cap at the back of a recalcitrant cow and commented, with no hint of sarcasm, "By the time we get it all cleaned up, it's almost time to start over again."

She might have been describing the work of the world.

RONNIE SANDLER

I do carpentry because I love the work," Ronnie Sandler said earnestly. "On my first carpentry job in New Hampshire several years ago, I put a dormer into an apartment building, and I still get a good feeling when I go by there, look up at that window and say to myself, 'I did that.' "

With an easy, independent, and assured manner, her short hair sprinkled with white, Ronnie Sandler was wearing shorts and had her feet propped comfortably on the top of her desk while we talked.

It was one of the hottest days of an unusually hot summer when I visited her in the St. Johnsbury office of STEP-UP, a training program designed to prepare women for apprenticeships in nontraditional trades. Ronnie is the director, and she explained that the purpose of the program is to familiarize women with a wider range of work; work that pays better than minimum wage, is more interesting, with a better future and more independence than the restricted opportunities open to many of them.

"We've just about finished our third year and as of today one hundred and twenty-five women have been trained. About eighty percent of them are working now, but we'll have better statistics later," she said.

As the circulating office fan coaxed hot air from one side of the small room to the other, we spoke of the kind of movement taking place within the trades, "one of the last bastions of male exclusionism." A colorful poster on one wall proclaimed: "Apprenticeships For Women, There's a Future In It." It was illustrated by photographs of capable and attractive-looking women working at several different trades: sheetmetal, mechanics, carpentry, and plumbing, among others.

STEP-UP was started as a model program when several state agencies got together three and one half years ago to take a look at an unfair work situation in existence for too long. The agencies included the Governor's Commission on Women, the Department of Education, the Department of Employment and Training, and the Department of Labor and Industry. They acknowledged that less than four percent of apprentices in the trades were women, and that even this small percentage was weighted by the inclusion of more customary "female" trades, like beauticians. This in spite of the fact that there is a federal law requiring that twenty percent of all people in apprenticeship programs be women.

"Other nontraditional careers like law and medicine have finally been opened to women through affirmative action, but the construction trades are the last frontiers of macho; this is the last barrier for women to break through," Ronnie explained.

The four agencies obtained funding from the federal Job Training Partnership Act to develop a model program, and that's when Ronnie became involved three years ago. Someone at the Education Department remembered her resumé and its unusual combination of education and trades. She was a college graduate with majors in both education and psychology, and she had also designed and run a pre-apprentice training program for women, teaching entry-level skills in the building trades, in Lansing, Michigan. She was an experienced carpenter as well.

Responding to the question she's frequently asked, "Do you have trouble finding enough women interested in this kind of thing?," she replied with a certain impatience: "The common thinking is that women would not be interested, and that's just not true. That's a real crock! After I started interviewing women I found that many of them had always wanted to work with things like this. Many said, 'I've wanted to do something like this since I was a kid.' "

Funding for STEP-UP has increased every year, and it's now expanding to a third site. The program is offered in Burlington and White River Junction in addition to St. Johnsbury.

The agency offers two sessions each year, one in the fall and one in the spring, with room for about ten women in each cycle. But in St. Johnsbury, sixty interested women showed up at the first orientation meeting, and there wasn't room for more than thirteen. "We always have more women interested than we can serve," Ronnie said.

There are federal guidelines based on income that women must meet in order to enter the program, but it's free to those who meet them.

"We also reimburse women for transportation and for child-care, but we're limited in who we can take; if we had some state money we could serve more," she said, explaining that if a woman makes four dollars an hour and has no children, she's making too much to be eligible. "You have to be poor—real poor."

STEP-UP includes a thirteen-week classroom training program; three full days a week, divided into three components. The first is in physical conditioning with upper body strength emphasized, along with cardio-vascular exercises and endurance. Ronnie stressed that most women haven't been trained to use their bodies properly, and need to learn how to use them more efficiently. She pointed out that this, in turn, gives the women more self-confidence.

The second element concerns developing their resources and is basically job getting and job keeping skills: interview techniques, resumé writing, and other useful information. They also address such particular barriers as mathematical handicaps and self-esteem, as well as consideration of the importance of obtaining good child care. Assertiveness training is included, as well as information about sexual harassment—what it is and what to do about it.

The third component emphasizes training; three hours a day for four weeks are devoted to learning skills within trade areas that include carpentry, welding, auto mechanics, sheet-metal work, printing, and plumbing.

"There are usually five weeks for carpentry, but the other trades vary from session to session and from site to site," she said.

"Of course nobody becomes a carpenter—or anything else—in forty-five hours, but the women get a basic understanding of what some of these things are all about. The kind of jargon used, the tools, and another thing that's very important—whether or not they'd really enjoy the work. We don't know, and the women don't know, they're activities that many of them never had a chance to experience before; but that doesn't mean they won't like it, or can't do it well, once they've had a chance to try it."

Ronnie stressed that this training is just the beginning: "In construction you learn on the job, come in as a helper, then work as an apprentice, then aim for master carpenter. But for women, this kind of orientation is crucial as a first step.

"Starting as a helper in one of the trades generally pays about seven dollars an hour, and within a year or two it's up to ten, twelve or fourteen dollars an hour, straight time; overtime is time and a half. But a secretary, after two years work, tops out at seven dollars an hour. Figure out for yourself which is better."

Ronnie's own background offered no particular clues to the vocation she would follow. "Pretty typically middle-class, it was expected that I go to college, but I never thought a lot about getting married. After my dad died, when I was eight, I saw the anxieties my mother had about work. She eventually remarried. But I guess I learned early that I wanted to be independent."

She grew up on Long Island; her father was a CPA, her mother "worked along as bookkeeper." Ronnie always liked outdoor "stuff" and was "kind of a tomboy." She went to high school and college, but took no vocational classes; none of the girls did. She liked little kids and thought she might as well become an elementary teacher because she believed she could always get a job. But the story was different when she graduated from Franconia College in 1971 with a teaching certificate. There were no teaching jobs because of a glut of teachers.

During this time, Ronnie bought a little land in Craftsbury and wanted to build a house. She decided to learn something about carpentry and took advantage of a course given at the nearby Morrisville Vocational Center. This training provided her with some techniques, jargon, and some background in tools. Since there were still no teaching jobs, she went to Maryland looking for work as a carpenter.

Ronnie found one job finishing off basements, but it was poor work so she moved back to New Hampshire and got a job as a flagger with a highway construction company, the first woman flagger in New Hampshire. About to get laid off during her second summer, she persuaded a friend who was a master carpenter to hire her and train her, and this led to five years of successful work. By the time she finished with him, she had "five guys working under me." Ronnie soon branched out on her own, had two other women helping her and spent the next year working independently.

Then came a possibility that couldn't be passed over, "the chance of a lifetime." Friends in Michigan persuaded her that there could be an opportunity to join the United Brotherhood of Carpenters and Joiners of America, and ultimately she became the first woman in the building trades union in Michigan. But it wasn't easy. "Michigan is a union state," she explained. "When I applied for my first job there as a carpenter, the guy in charge said, 'You mean a carpenter's helper, don't you, honey?' At first I got a typical run-around in the union. It took six months, but a friend who was an official in the Auto

Worker's and wanted to break the sex barriers helped to make it happen. I did it through connections."

After that she worked in the union as a trim carpenter in the Detroit area, and she got her journey "man's" card, but "it still wasn't easy," she said. "I decided I couldn't take production carpentry and the isolation of being the only woman in the union."

During 1979 and 1980 she designed and ran a pre-apprentice program for women in Lansing, Michigan, where she gained her background in training other women. Experience had taught her that not only was carpentry satisfying as an occupation, but along with it came a degree of freedom and independence that she enjoyed.

"I found that I could drive into a town, do a little networking at the YWCA or other women's groups, and discover where the work was. The pay is always good and it's a nice way to make decent money.

Ronnie moved back to New Hampshire and worked for a construction company. At the same time she did part-time consulting on women's vocational employment, an area in which she was becoming increasingly interested. With a still unsatisfied urge to travel, however, she packed her tools into her car and headed for California. After a five-month work stint in Nebraska, along the way, she reached San Francisco, and spent a year there working with her own construction company. A year in Monterey as a civil service carpenter followed until, becoming "bored with California weather," she headed back to New England.

Vermont was her next location, and again she formed her own construction company until she was hired to design and start the STEP-UP program in 1985.

"There are five on staff now, and there'll be three more starting in July," she stated with pride. "Each site will have a coordinator, a counselor, and a secretary. It's a comprehensive program, and has been used as the model for ten or twelve other programs around the country."

Historical precedents for women in the trades were established during World War II, when over three million were employed; women were credited with playing a major role in the ultimate victory. But when the war was over most were summarily turned out of their trades, and the practice was put on hold for several decades.

Ronnie explained that between 1981 and 1985, however, the number of women carpenters in the United States increased by 300 percent but this actually represented only an increase from 1.5 to 1.7 percent of carpenters overall. According to federal guidelines, women should represent at least 6.9 percent of the work force in this field.

"I'm involved with the National Tradeswomen Association, and we're planning a National Tradeswomen Conference in the near future. We've made inroads, but not nearly enough. It's still not easy, but at least we're building a support network. Women in the trades now have places where we can get together and talk; the hardest thing about it is the isolation and the harassment."

Ronnie admitted that she missed working with her tools, doing actual work with her hands. "I still do some carpentry work, and it's very satisfying, but I'm doing something here that I believe in, too.

"I believe it's important to increase the number of women in the trades. We've increased the number in Vermont now by threefold, but it's still not enough."

Leaning forward, feet on the floor, hands gripped together for emphasis, she said firmly, "I'm convinced that this is something that really empowers women, and I think we need that."

MARILYN WEBB

I've always thought of Vermont as more of a person than a state," Marilyn Webb said, "and two of the biggest influences on my life have been my love for Ascutney, where I grew up, and my love for the state around it."

While her allegiance has changed from Ascutney to Shelburne, the town where she now lives, her feelings for the state remain the same. Shelburne Farms, the organization for which she works, is an impressive example of what good land management and conservation of resources do in other areas.

Marilyn was president of Shelburne Farms, and served as its chief administrator and fund-raiser between 1972 and 1988. This unusual organization is based on a philosophy that is agrarian, environmental, and educational and was created to preserve and use the buildings, farm and woodlands of a large, historic country estate in ways that support this philosophy.

"Before I even met Alec [Webb, her husband] we had formed similar concepts regarding land management," Marilyn said. "We were both convinced there were practical ways of providing solutions to some of the widespread environmental problems we're facing today. He gave me the opportunity to contribute to plans for better land use at Shelburne Farms, where he was raised."

Marilyn played a key role in developing these plans, and her talent as visionary, supported by a pragmatic bent as planner, has been effective in their realization. She credits her childhood and adolescence in southern Vermont with influencing her ideals and actions today.

"My dad and I were always close while I was growing up. I was an only child, and he treated me like a son—took me hunting and fishing and taught me a lot about the woods and nature. I think it was my dad who laid the groundwork for the combination of farming and nature that's so important to me now," she recalled.

But the woods and farmlands of Shelburne Farms were threatened, only a few years ago, by rising land values and escalating property taxes caused by the industrial and commercial development that has consumed the best farmland adjacent to Burlington. The farm at Shelburne has been successful at resisting the market forces that threatened to destroy it and has become a legacy with lasting significance to the state.

Marilyn reminisced about the first time she was engaged in a political conflict regarding land management that affected her personally: "I was a senior in high school when Interstate Highway 91 was being planned, and it cut my town, Ascutney, right down the middle.

"The kids were tuned in and emotional about it. We were involved, and we thought this kind of planning was wrong. Highway men went around putting highway stakes in, and we went around pulling them out."

In relation to this she told the story of an elderly recluse, Romaine Terry, who lived alone in the "beautiful old gingerbread house" on the farm his family had owned for generations.

"He lived in the barn during the winter; it was probably warmer there. He was eccentric but the kids all knew him—and we respected him.

"When it became certain that the highway was going to take his place—and there was nothing more he could do about it—he went out to the barn and shot himself."

"I was really upset about this," she added quietly, "and it had everything to do with what I'm doing now.

"I believe in progress, but I also believe that human beings value continuity. We need it, and it has a lot to do with our feelings about the world and with what we eventually do with our world."

After high school, Marilyn attended Endicott Junior College in Beverly, Massachusetts, doing work in interior design. At age eighteen she moved to Burlington to take a job with an architectural firm, Burlington Associates, and was their first woman designer. She started their interior design section and did the interiors of several buildings at Johnson State College. Her first husband was an architect working in the same office.

Following her longstanding interest in conservation and better land-use planning, she did volunteer work at the University of Vermont under the biologist and environmental activist, Hub Vogelmann. Here she learned the disturbing facts about the environmental damage taking place within the state: loss of farmland, the difficulty of finding food unsprayed with hazardous chemicals and the devastating effect of acid rain. Her volunteer work eventually led her to Shelburne Farms.

Idylls have been created from less. The one-hundred room summer mansion built by Dr. W. Seward and Lila Vanderbilt Webb in 1899 in the village of Shelburne, overlooking Lake Champlain, with the blue Adirondacks looming majestically across the water, is dramatic. Summer concerts on the "big house" porch draw hundreds of people to spread blankets on the lawn and eat supper out of picnic baskets, as the sun sets behind the mountains and music pours from the verandah. But today this represents only a small part of what Shelburne Farms is about.

For three generations of Webbs, the 2,000 acre, beautifully landscaped estate, with its huge barns and stables reflected the leisurely summer pursuits of the rich and privileged. But death, taxes, rising land costs and J. Watson Webb's concentration on the adjacent Shelburne Museum created a crisis. The farm would have to be broken up unless ways could be found to preserve and use it in innovative ways, a challenge accepted and fulfilled by the present generation of Alec Webb's family.

A vital part of this transformation is educational. The Project Seasons Curriculum, involving elementary school children and their teachers, is an outstanding example. A curriculum guide for teachers was developed over a period of two years and declared an exemplary science program by the federal Department of Education, one of two in the country to be so recognized.

"Nobody else is doing what we do here with elementary school children, and we have between three and four thousand going through our program every year," Marilyn said. "I've always considered this one of the most important things that we've done here. This is where I feel I've made my largest contribution."

Based on the cyclic rotation of the seasons, the program emphasizes the changes that living things go through as a result of periodicity. It offers to teachers, as well as to their students, the experience of observing and studying with naturalists outside the classroom. The farm and woodlands at Shelburne Farms become the setting in which school children are able to observe and experience this process.

Another of the attractions at Shelburne Farms today is the "big house." The one-hundred-room building was recently renovated and made into an inn and a living museum. Marilyn assumed major responsibility for this project, which subsequently received the President's Award for Historic Preservation.

"Income from the inn can help support the rest of the program," she said, stressing that the emphasis placed on food at the inn reflects a serious attitude underlying the agricultural aspect of their organization.

She takes pride in the fact that most of the food served at the inn has been raised organically on the farm; this includes meat, vegetables, fruits, dairy, and bakery products.

"Food is basic to life, and more reverence is due the whole subject of agriculture. There's a tendency in the western world to think of farming as just another volume industry that manufactures food."

Marilyn's own parents ran a 1950s roadhouse when she was growing up, and she has vivid and exciting memories of it. She sees this as another similarity between her activities today and her own childhood experiences.

"Roadhouses were popular places in the fifties. They attracted interesting performers and audiences. There were good bands, singers, magicians—all kinds of acts. To encourage this kind of thing growing up in rural Vermont was important to me."

The duality of her adult life, between activities at the "big house" inn and the contrasting farm life taking place around it, also played a significant part in her own childhood.

"There was a neighbor's farm, just a few yards from where we lived, and from the time I was small I spent lots of time there shucking corn for pigs, working in the garden, feeding chickens, doing other farm chores, and I loved it."

"My grandparents had thirteen children, and at one time, they lived on a dairy farm," she said, "but my grandmother got into bootlegging during the Depression, sold the farm and bought the mayor's house in Springfield with her profits. She made money, loaned it out, became an entrepreneur—and loved it."

Her laugh included us both in a kind of unspoken understanding of the absurdities of most human posturing. It's a response that Marilyn makes, often as a way of relieving more serious pronouncements. Both her quizzical expression and the gentle laughter that follows what might be considered an outrageous idea, in some curious way allows the audience, of one or of many, to feel they've had some part in the birth of the idea proposed, and they're consequently absolved of the need to combat it. It is one of her most endearing characteristics as well as an effective communicating skill.

Throughout childhood, Marilyn spent many weekends with her grandparents. Her own parents, especially her mother, had a problem with alcohol, but there was always a strong support system available to her.

She recalled that her grandmother also took for granted that women were capable in business and made sure that nine of her children went to college.

"All the women had at least two years of business school and all of them did business with their husbands," Marilyn said, "and I seem to have carried on the tradition."

"My grandmother continued in her old ways after she moved to town," she added, her face lighting up at the memory, "scarf tied over her head, gold earrings, overweight, and always in straight cotton, floral print dresses—a real Russian peasant.

"Every Saturday she'd pack her big Cadillac with food: butter, sausage, bread and other things she'd made and take them around to displaced Russian people. The church was full of Russian immigrants at the time. I loved going with her and I have a vivid memory of seeing people, not only giving but receiving—easily."

Marilyn and Alec have two daughters, Anna, eleven, and Heidi, six. The girls attend school in nearby Shelburne Village. "Alec and I share a common idea about raising children. We both believe in the importance of physical as well as intellectual work, and we try to provide the girls with a balance between the two."

"For the children," she added, "living on the farm is like growing up in a small community. And even though it entails a certain amount of isolation for them, other things balance this out, like getting to see calves born, cows milked, and bread baked."

She mentioned two things of particular importance to her in combining a demanding professional job with the responsibility of a home and small children. One of these was an available and reliable sitter with whom the girls felt comfortable and who could be called upon in emergencies; the other was the nature of both her husband's work and her own. Much of this work, in both cases, could be done in or in close proximity to where they lived. While her husband's work is involved with overseeing the many farm activities, dairying, gardening and upkeep, it is relatively flexible. "This meant that Alec could relieve me when I needed to call on him," Marilyn said.

"Alec is the farm's general manager and in charge of its internal affairs. In this capacity he supervises the farming, cheese making, dairy, mail-order catalogue and marketing as well as the staff and staff meetings."

"I'm in charge of the external affairs, fund-raising, grant writing, public speaking, and things like that, although lately I've been very involved with the big house," Marilyn explained.

Managing the details, as well as the overall planning, for converting a crumbling, one-hundred-room mansion into a hostelry, with its historical integrity intact and its present comfort assured, has been demanding. For Marilyn there has also been the current fund-raising, with two million dollars already realized out of the goal of two and a half million dollars, necessary to support the Inn's restoration and the many other projects taking place on the farm.

"There are lots of different demands on me but my family life is what keeps me together," she said simply.

As a Vermont delegate to Bridges for Peace, Marilyn had recently returned from a trip to the Soviet Union when I spoke with her. This was the first organization to arrange an exchange between laypersons within the United States and Russia with the purpose of bringing people together to gain more understanding of each other and to talk about peace.

"No journalists and no government officials, just people talking together," she emphasized. "The Russians lost twenty million people during the last war, and it's hard to meet anyone there who isn't interested in talking about peace.

"Meeting with the Soviet Women's Committee was like a little United Nations. There were microphones and interpreters all around and women from all different fields. We discussed women's needs in practical terms and we discussed peace, and—since we were all women—this was also done in practical terms."

"I'm just coming to realize that nuclear war is the ultimate destruction. By reaching children early and teaching them about loving life, we have a better chance," she continued. "We must also teach them to understand and to respect the many different forms of life that exist on our small planet."

Marilyn feels good about the things that have taken place at Shelburne Farms over the last few years, but she's also aware of an important part of herself that's been neglected while working as an administrator. At some time, hopefully in the not too distant future, she intends to find time for things closer to her interior life, things that were important to her earlier, like painting and writing.

Guarded and analytical on some occasions, she can, on others, be open as a child and she speaks with unusual enthusiasm about her daughters' approaching adolescence, "I look forward to it," she said, blue eyes sparkling.

"I love the way you see the soul emerging in a teenager. I loved being a teenager myself—it was a time when I felt freer as a person.

But someday, before too long, I'm going to regain at least some of that spirit. And I'll have a different kind of strength to add to it."

[Since our interview, Marilyn has resigned as president of Shelburne Farms and is doing free-lance consulting for nonprofit organizations. She is redirecting her life to provide more opportunity for the kind of personal expression she missed as an administrator.]

Ann Ross

*I*t was a long bus ride from Louisville, Kentucky, to Montpelier, Vermont, but the anticipation of finding her boyfriend once she got here, and the expectation of a new life, made the trip for Ann Ross easier.

"The fellow I was living with was up here. I was supposed to wait 'til I was eighteen, but I jumped on the bus and came ahead."

That was in 1972. But the vision of a new life already in her head before she got here didn't exactly work out. Nonetheless, there was a quality of persistence about Ann, ensuring that when a different vision presented itself she was able to follow it. Today she is a master plumber and a member of the Vermont Plumber's Union. And although she's had to find her own way and open doors that few women had opened before her, she's now in a position to make choices.

"I've been thinking of going to college, learning to design heating systems, plumbing systems, gas systems, things like that," she said. "I've also thought about teaching mechanical engineering in a college, after I get my degree."

Prospects in Kentucky had not been bright. Ann and her boyfriend were working together in a poultry processing plant. Her adopted father, a used car salesman, had died the year before she left for Vermont; she and her adoptive mother, who "mainly played bridge," had never gotten along, so there was little to hold her there once her boyfriend of six years left.

Soon after arriving in Vermont, Ann found work as a low-level secretary in a state agency in order to support them both. The pay was $2.05 an hour, and there seemed little opportunity for advancement, but she claims it taught her some well-needed discipline. The future looked, if not bright, at least stable, and in order to make it more so, she decided it would be good to have a baby.

By the time the baby was born, she had acquired an old house in Marshfield with an assumed mortgage and no down payment, making it cheaper than paying rent. "I had to be up all night with the baby and up all day at work," she said. The child's father was home most of the time so she managed, but it wasn't easy. A quite different career opened up for her after a disagreeable and wet first night in the new house.

"I'd barely gotten to sleep," she said, "when I heard a loud noise in the basement. It turned out to be water under high pressure escaping from pipes in the cellar."

She called a friend who was a plumber, "a real sweetheart of a fellow." He came over and made an emergency repair with a rubber hose, promising to come back within two weeks and fix it right. But the same thing happened the following night, so when she called him, he came back with solder and pipes and proceeded to do the job.

"I ran upstairs and got a pad and pencil, went back to the cellar and wrote it all down—just what he did. We were both impressed by my interest, and I had a set of instructions for soldering pipes."

A small step, but significant.

Squeezed between the difficulties imposed by an infant at home and a poorly paying full-time job, Ann took another, larger step: she quit.

Before the baby's birth she had hoped the child might improve the relationship between its parents, but it didn't. The father was an alcoholic and abusive when drunk; home life was worsening, so she induced him to leave.

Receiving fifty dollars a week from unemployment, she lived and made mortgage payments of ninety-eight dollars a month. When this ran out, she received welfare payments, but when she asked her welfare supervisor to sponsor training that would enable her to learn an electrician's trade and get off welfare, he said, "No!"

Living in an area with many single parents, she began swapping simple plumbing repairs for baby-sitting. "I'd always been mechanically inclined, but the plumbing was possible because of the guy that taught me to solder.

"I was trying to figure out what kind of a job I could get when a friend asked, 'Why don't you go out and get a real plumbing job?' "

This was the push she needed and turned out to be a beginning.

When she saw an opening advertised for a plumbing job in Lyndon-ville, she took her two plumbing tools and went up to investigate.

It was a construction job, and she remembers that as she walked towards the building, several workmen standing at a picture window laughed. When she walked in there was silence.

"I understand there's a plumber's helper job open," she said. They indicated where the job foreman was, and she spoke to him.

The two talked for a few minutes, and then he said, "You're hired," adding as he pointed to her sneakered feet, "but not in those shoes." Pulling $50 from his pocket, he continued, "Take this and go buy yourself a pair of workshoes. You can pay me back after your first paycheck."

The work was on a combined senior citizen's center and low-income housing project, and Ann was making $4.50 an hour, more than double the pay at her former job.

"I was in charge of all fittings, unloading the delivery truck, or-ganizing the material and distributing it to the journeymen plumbers. It was good for me, and I learned what things were all about. It was quite an experience, good and bad," she said. "I liked the work, but sometimes I was confused about the way the men treated me."

As an example, she described using a mechanical saw to cut holes in a bathroom floor for the drain pipes to go through.

"It had a reciprocating blade, and the handle is supposed to be stable while the blade goes up and down. But the way I was doing it, the blade was stable and the handle was going up and down, and so was I. Everything was kind of a blur before my eyes, and it must have looked pretty funny. The young electrical apprentices on a scaf-fold just above me began making gorilla sounds. One jumped down and began approaching me, getting closer and closer, and making like a gorilla. Nobody was sure what he was going to do. All of a sudden the foreman came in, grabbed him by the collar and threw him up against the wall.

" 'If I ever see you doing anything like that again you'll get the (blank) out of here and fast!' he shouted, and everyone went back to work."

The construction job was completed in six months, and by that time, Ann was expecting another baby. She collected unemployment during her pregnancy, but the baby was born with meningitis and died after living only a few days.

Ann began looking for a job closer to home. There'd been a long commute to her last job, and she'd had to get her three-year-old daughter to day-care every morning by 6:30.

"She'd fall asleep standing up in the cab of the truck on the way over," Ann said, "and I'd pick her up again at four in the afternoon, after I finished work. I felt bad about how tired she was—how tired we both were. If you don't have a family or a spouse to help you, it's hard."

Nonetheless, she maintains that her daughter learned independence at an early age. "Grace taught me to be independent too," she added.

When a job was advertised for the position of water commissioner in Marshfield, Ann applied and was accepted. For two years she worked there while the town was having its sewage treatment plant built. Grace had day-care near the construction site, and the job was close to home.

It was a good situation, but the pay was low, because, while it paid $5.50 an hour, the town's budget didn't allow for a full 40-hour week. The village couldn't afford a full-time commissioner, so at the end of two years, she looked for another construction job.

One day in Barre, Ann passed a public building where construction was going on. She walked onto the job with her daugher holding her hand and asked to see the plumbing foreman. He was agreeable, and sent her to talk to his boss; she applied and got the job.

Along with the job, Ann took another important step and signed a contract with the state of Vermont as an apprentice plumber. This was a necessary move in climbing the plumbing trade ladder, but it required the additional burden of night school.

"The process takes four years, working forty hours a week, and going to night school two trimesters per year. But, I got the summers off from school," she recalled.

When the required work was completed, Ann received her license and later went on to sit for her journeyman plumber's exam. After that she received an immediate raise in salary. Her next goal was to become a master plumber.

"I sat for my master's and passed it too," she said, "and this meant that I was also capable of supervising jobs."

By this time, Ann knew that she never wanted to become a service plumber, on call night or day. "I wanted jobs that would stop at the end of the day," she said, "regular hours and no on call work at night. There were lots of big construction jobs going on at bottling plants, hospitals, computer factories, new restaurants, schools—things like that."

Ann asked for an increase in pay at her construction site job in Burlington; she was getting $8.50 and wanted $9.50. When the raise was denied she walked out, went to another site and was offered ten dollars, plus mileage. She was also in charge of the job.

From working where both union and nonunion plumbers were employed, Ann discovered that union workers made in two days what she made in a week. Working conditions were better on the union jobs, so she joined the plumber's union.

"The union checks your record carefully," she said. "If you've had any trouble with alcohol or other drugs, they don't let you join."

A $1,300 payment was required for joining, but the union offered an excellent pension plan as well as health insurance, all added on to the fifteen dollars an hour she was now making. Also the increase in her pay for one week's work paid the entire year's dues.

The repairs she had made on her original house helped it to sell for a good profit, and she has recently bought a larger house in Montpelier. "I'm having the work done on this one, and I have a woman contractor on the job," she said, smiling, "also a woman electrician and a draftswoman."

Weighing some of the disadvantages of being the only woman on a job, Ann said, "It's true that I got a lot of attention, good and bad, but I've always been able to get the job done. And it feels good to be independent."

But as a woman edging her way into a traditionally male field, Ann has encountered difficulties. Some men are protective, some agressively unkind: for instance, there was the old carpenter on her first job who invited her to "come on over here with me, honey, we'll go down in the basement and lay some pipes."

"There're a few now and again that wink at you—think it's their responsibility to flirt. But blue-collar men are constantly testing each other, teasing each other, and I was part of that. I learned that you have to let a lot of it just roll off."

"A few swear on purpose just to see my reaction," she added, "but I figure if I can't stand a little swearing I shouldn't be here. On my first job, I ate my lunch in the car, but at the next one, the men asked me if I was some kind of a snob, and that put an end to that. Most of us just eat lunch at our work station."

Measuring what appears to be a gain in acceptance, Ann says, "I'm probably more ill at ease now in a room full of librarians talking about the Dewey decimal system or something like that.

"Grace is now thirteen years old, and I was trying to teach her to solder the other day. But she doesn't want to get her hands dirty with pipes, she wants to be a vet.

"Plumbing takes physical energy and strength—lifting cast iron pipes and steel pipes. But you don't have to be big to be a strong woman. You use your head, use leverage. Still, your shirt size increases. I couldn't get my secretarial blouses over my arm after I'd been working for a few months."

There's nothing peculiar about Ann Ross. She was dressed neatly in jeans and plaid shirt the day we met, and we talked, sitting on the grass of the town green at the end of her work day as a contract plumber. She wears her hair short and explained the hazards of long hair in working around machines. A reserved, soft-spoken woman, she has a quietly confident manner and is keenly interested in her work.

Summing up her career in a few words, she said, "I picked trade out of desperation, but it got better and better and I don't regret it for a minute."

GRACE GERSHUNY

My husband, Stewart Hoyt, is the fourth generation of his family living on this land," Grace Gershuny said as we talked over tea in the house she and her husband built on their farm in Barnet. "I tell people I married him for his soil."

"I'm lucky to have a man with a good land base," she added with a grin. "The soil here has a nice texture, no rocks, and there's also a nice little growing climate."

Because of her admitted fascination with soil, and as co-author of a book about it, *The Soul of Soil: A Guide to Ecological Soil Management*, Grace might be accused of self-serving premarital calculation were it not that she and Stewart are dedicated to each other, as well as to organic agriculture. They share a quest for improved farming methods relating to better ways of handling soil, one of the mainstays of life.

They are also dedicated to a life-style that reuses everything possible in the belief that our society is overburdening its resources of air, soil and water with profligate industrial production. There is a principle involved, and their ambition is not to acquire more but to use more creatively what is already available.

"We built our house with used materials," Grace explained. "And our greenhouse is recycled from an old industrial greenhouse that we helped tear down and then put back up here. Stewart is a professional scrounge, and he brought back framing materials for the house when he was working as a carpenter on Cape Cod."

The house is well-insulated and uses both wood and solar heat.

The greenhouse opens onto their living room in its south-facing location, and the wood stove has hot water baseboard heaters.

As she continued her description of the way they built their house with an eye to conserving money as well as energy, she pointed out that the foundation is made with concrete posts. "It's much cheaper not to build a basement. We were able to do this ourselves and never had to have a bulldozer or a backhoe except for the water line. We started it in September 1984, got married here, but we couldn't move in until spring."

The house is an elongated hexagon that they designed together. Its orientation to the sun was an important consideration in their planning.

Grace and Stewart don't own the electrical conveniences that are standard equipment for many homes in our gadget-oriented society. Still, they're sold on the personal computer as an important tool in the information exchange vital to effecting necessary changes in our attitudes and methods for preserving our planet.

"The organic food movement has been burgeoning over the last few years," she said. "People are afraid of the chemicals used in producing the food they've been eating. But some people within the movement have a narrow vision of what organic really does mean. As the business of organic farming grows, there's a tendency to see it simply as 'business as usual.' But some of us see social change as an essential component of what *organic* actually means."

Grace explained that this includes the vision of an overall economy that is more democratic in its operation, with greater emphasis placed on social justice and cooperation as significant aspects of the whole.

"The word *organic* pertains to the interrelationship of all the parts within the fundamental structure of society or any other living structure," she added. "This is all part and parcel of what *organic* means. I get frustrated by continually running up against people who don't have a holistic vision of the world, who don't see that everything we do is connected."

She used the term *ecofeminism* in describing her philosophy, explaining that the word comes from a combination of *ecology* and *feminism*, and suggests a philosophical awareness of the environmental destruction taking place in our male-dominated society. Implicit also in its meaning is the importance of recognizing feminism as crucial for reestablishing balance in the world.

"My struggle, in working within an organic organization like NOFA [Natural Organic Farmer's Association] is in trying to find ways to make it accountable to all its members. Farmers don't have time for meetings; the people that are actually doing something green don't have the time to go, so there's too little emphasis on agriculture and too much on business."

Grace has been active in NOFA since 1975. She was a board member and a principal in starting the certification process in Vermont. She explained that when consumers buy certified organically grown foods they are assured of foods grown by farmers who adhere to exacting standards under a verifiable program of on-farm inspections, soil tests, and annual management reviews. Behind this is a farming method that keeps insects and diseases in check by the use of crop rotations, plant-derived sprays, resistant crop varieties and biological controls. They rely on soil fertility, built up by compost, animal manures and green manure crops, to help produce healthy plants.

"I developed NOFA's first certification," she said, adding that the organization hired her to set up the program and that they drafted guidelines for the organic certification program being used all over the world.

She clarified a major difficulty relating to the certification process itself, explaining that compounds whose effects won't be known for at least twenty years are steadily being introduced to the agricultural market, so that complete agreement as to their safety will always be difficult.

"Basically," she said, "I think farmers carry a particular burden of responsibility in our society."

She sees an ecological approach to agriculture as furnishing a basis for returning wholeness to our concept of the world: ecoagriculture and ecofeminism suggest the possibility of restoration of our planet through a renewed understanding of relationships.

"Ecofeminism is an intuitive understanding that everything is connected; it's a way of perceiving reality that is not based solely on concrete facts.

"Support for farmers in general is important, and all farmers need to stick together. Once you lose the skill of farming, it's as hard to regain as it is to restore farmland after it's been cemented over. Agriculture is a kind of art form."

"This has been the major theme in everything I've done," she added. "I've also come to believe that the planet is even more vulnerable than I thought it was."

Grace is a combination of evangelist, educator, and environmentalist. Her life is dedicated to living the things she believes in, despite their obvious financial drawbacks.

From college in New York, during the late 1960s, she went to Montreal and was food manager in a produce cooperative. She was influenced by the Rodale magazines, by Rachel Carlson's *Silent Spring*, and by the work of Sir Albert Howard, who wrote one of the seminal books on soil.

"When I started, I'd never gardened before," she said. "My first garden was on a half-acre covered with witch grass and sod. I harrowed and plowed, which was the worst thing for spreading the stuff, spent two weeks planting, lost thirty-five pounds and worked my butt off. But once my consciousness was raised about what I was eating, I thought I'd better grow it."

From there she moved to West Charleston with her first husband and for six years she worked with river bottom soil that was "amazing." She also organized a farmer's market in Newport that's still going strong.

"I've always had a strong, technically-oriented science interest. But I'm independent minded—couldn't hack the science institutions—and wanted to use my talent in a non-academic way."

As a child growing up in New York, Grace's background had little relationship to farming. "I was the child of an oddball family," she said. "My parents were always very independent system-fighters. Back then they were under the influence of E. F. Schumacher, the *Small is Beautiful* man."

"They were also adventurous," she continued, "and I got a lot of stuff from them. I was brought up with a mixed bag of agnosticism and Rosicrucianism—if you can figure that out."

It can be construed from this that her parents were also interested in ideas and looked in many directions for answers to problems they could see developing in society. In the last few years, however, her parents have moved to Newport, and their religious point of view has undergone a change.

"They're among the few orthodox Jews in the Northeast Kingdom," Grace said. "They're also involved in a lot of community things up here."

In addition to hours of actual farm work, Grace co-teaches a four-week course on bio-regional agriculture at the Institute of Social Ecology in Plainfield. She also teaches a course at the Community College of Vermont and writes about agricultural concerns for several farming magazines. She uses the word processor obtained from a Job Start loan for her consulting business. "This grew out of my long-term fantasy of being a farm consultant."

She explained that the Institute of Social Ecology, headed by Murray Bookchin, is trying to develop an ecological ethic. "It's an important part of my life, but the question is always how to make a living at it. Still, techniques are evolving that will help make changes in the way things are done, in machinery and attitudes, and these will eventually affect the living patterns of more people."

For instance, Grace is encouraged by a recent federal bill with funding to develop four regional research centers around the country for producing information on low-input farming (read *organic*). One will be centered at the University of Vermont.

"There's a lot of stuff going on, and there's growing emphasis on organic alternatives. One of my big goals is training, helping people to farm that way, and half my work is counseling," she said. "I get work occasionally from private people, farm evaluations, things like that, and I also work as an independent certifying agent, traveling around the country. More recently I've had requests that will take me abroad, and I would also like to do another book."

She received a grant recently from the state agriculture department for research in raising herbs that might provide market potential for Vermont farmers.

Stewart Hoyt has spent most of his life in Barnet, and knows the people and the community. He is a painter, as well as a farmer. Grace and Stewart are involved in community life in various ways; with the recycling center, school board issues. Stewart helped in the development of a gardening project that is still active at the correctional center in St. Johnsbury.

They sell their produce at the farmer's market in St. Johnsbury and to restaurants in the area. They're also part of the Vermont Grower's Co-op in East Hardwick, "a marginal operation that stores winter squash, beets and carrots."

One of Grace and Stewart's major concerns is their inability to get health insurance. "We can't afford it," she said, "and yet we need it in order to have a child—which we very much want.

"We're trying to work within the system, but the system doesn't recognize us. Sure, I have some anger, but I try to direct it in healthy ways so it's not internalized."

Grace Gershuny gives the impression of an essentially proud woman. She is not without humor but her serious side is more apparent. She has made a clear choice about the direction she wants her life to take, and she has her reasons for making it. At thirty-eight, she is unwavering in that choice.

"If you want something—and it's really important to you, it's up to you to prove it," she said simply.

DEBORAH LOURA

Stereotypes are tenacious, not easily changed; it's good for all of us to see one challenged and successfully defeated.

Deborah Loura, a stereotype breaker, seated in the cab of the loader or the backhoe she customarily runs, has not gone unnoticed as she goes about her work in downtown Bethel. Part of the road crew working on the new sewage system that involves heavy roadwork and the destruction and reconstruction of the main streets in town, she's caused more than a few heads to turn sharply, eyes focusing in surprise on the young woman maneuvering with ease one of the heavy pieces of machinery.

"The best thing about this kind of equipment is the way you can create with it," Debbie said the day of our conversation on her lunch break at the Black Forest Cafe, her fork poised over a green salad.

"It gets pretty hot in that cab," she explained, in response to my surprise at her light meal after a long morning's work. "I don't work up a big appetite, but I have a good breakfast before I start and a good supper later."

And while heavy equipment operators do not move their machines by pushing them physically from behind, with muscular rather than mechanical power, there is the general perception that a heavy machine needs a heavy operator.

Debbie contradicts this impression. She is slim, but appears strong.

Of medium height with shoulder-length dark hair, she wears her work clothes with style, and the graceful feather earrings she was wearing the day we spoke were not out of character. Her manner was straightforward and disarming as she talked about her job, generally regarded as exclusively within the male province. One senses an innate confidence in herself that's been tested and earned.

"My first work with heavy equipment was considered more or less of a joke. I was doing flagging for a construction company, and I didn't like it. When I said I'd rather learn to drive the machinery, they started me off. But they thought it was a laugh and that I would drop the whole idea, but I didn't," she said. "And when I left that job and was able to get work for another company, nobody laughed."

Questioned about her start in an occupation so traditionally male, she explained that about thirteen years ago she'd been very sick. When she was able to work again she wanted to be outside, but the only thing she could find was standing in the road and flagging at a construction site.

"I was there for six months and realized that flaggin' was *not* for me. Frank Whitcomb, the big contractor, had taken me on in Walpole, New Hampshire, where I was living at the time. 'No more flaggin', I said, so I became a pipe layer for him. He put me on a backhoe as kind of a joke, but it was no joke, I really took to it and I was good.

"I continued with the backhoe," Debbie continued, "did Whitcomb's small work, made tennis courts and used a Huber maintenance tractor-grader, same as they use in the street. I had a loader and a 'dozer and a little beaver tail trailer for hauling the equipment from job to job.

"I never stay with one job for over a year—two years tops," she added. "After a couple of years they begin taking you for granted, and the incentives to stay get fewer and further between; they don't worry so much about keeping you. But if you're good, there's always work at another place and you can earn better money by changing jobs.

"I have a loader and a backhoe that I usually run. It's a good job, busy job, and a good overtime job.

"In heavy construction the workers are like one gigantic family spread out in different states. Guys that have worked with you remember your work and want to hire you; they take care of you. I'm always learnin', but you've got to be capable."

She explained that an operator of heavy equipment is part of a team that works closely together. "Everybody knows their job and is expected to do it; they can't just call someone to fill in your place for a day or two. You can't call in and say 'my baby's got a cold,' or 'I've got a headache,' there's no room for that in this work," she said, pointing out that the superintendent of the job sets up a schedule indicating the progress that must be made each week. He has to be able to count on his crew for this. The state also sets deadlines that have to be met.

"Most jobs get finished on time," she said. "Those contractors have been around—they know what they're doing."

About continuing this type of work as the years go by, Debbie observed, "I would hope to be able to do it until I'm no longer physically able. I've seen men who've worked well into their sixties, even seventies."

"As far as this being unusual for a woman," she continued, "there've been a few men who kind of mistook my reasons for being there—but I set 'em straight pretty quick. If I have trouble with a man on the job I tell him that if that's what I wanted I'd have had it in the first few weeks.

"There're always a few peckerheads around, but believe me, it's not necessary to work this hard if I was just lookin' to have some quick fun. But I've never had it shoved at me because I'm a girl.

"I've always made it a point to work harder, and I like what I do," she said with emphasis. "I know there's a right way and a wrong way to do things—I figure the right way and do it."

"I'm naturally an outdoors woman," she added. "I also love my work, and I'm good at it."

She pointed out that she's made many friendships on the job, with women as well as men. "Anyone with a stable relationship," she said, referring to the wives or girlfriends of her coworkers, "usually becomes friendly when they get to know me; they know why I'm here."

Regarding the transitory aspect inherent in construction work, she said, "It's natural to move from job to job. Also I have a lot of companies that just write to me about coming to work for them. They do that if they figure you're good. And sometimes if I pass a nice place where construction is going on, I just stop and ask if they're hiring."

Debbie has worked for several different construction companies, among them Whitcomb, Park Construction, and Macmillan.

"Midway Excavators in South Hampton is excellent for giving women opportunities," she said, "but at Bridge Construction, I was the only female he ever hired; he didn't usually hire women for steel work."

During winters Debbie is a cement finisher and also does a lot of work in steel construction, erecting bridges and buildings because road construction is more consistently held up in bad weather. "You lose too many days because of the cold."

"Steel work is fun, but you work hard," she continued. "On bridges or on buildings when you're working high up, you're belted on and you can enjoy it—there's no need to fear height. But if I feel in my mind that I'm taking an unnecessary risk, I won't take it. From swinging those beams into place and tying steel, I looked like a linebacker for the Green Bay Packers by the time I finished there."

Regarding construction work for other women, Debbie pointed out that traveling goes with the job. The work in Bethel just happened to be close to where she lives, in South Royalton.

"They don't construct round and round your house," she said. "You have to go where the work is." This past spring she was driving 529 miles every weekend, going home and then back again to a job.

"A lot of women say, 'Would you teach me?' but then they say, 'I can't give up my family.' If you're an operator, you're expected to be there, you can't say, 'I need a day off, I'm having my period.' There's no such thing anymore. This operator works with a group of people—everybody knows their job and is expected to do it.

"Not too many women really want this kind of work," she added. "You have to give up family life—on the job at seven A.M.—work 'til six, five days a week and then there's the traveling. The job I really liked started at five in the morning," she said, "didn't quit 'til dark with not even time for lunch. I loved it! It was a challenge. Franconia Notch. We were building Route 93. I was there for two years, and I loved it!"

Debbie started young, working out the kind of independence that seems characteristic of her. Born on a dairy farm in Westminster, she got her start in learning to work hard. She left home early because of an untenable home situation.

"Left home when I was fourteen," she said, "got my first apartment when I was fifteen."

Debbie went through high school, working in the school kitchen afternoons and as a housekeeper at "the old folk's home" at night.

"At fifteen I was too young to be a nurses' aide, that wasn't until I was sixteen goin' on seventeen, but all the time I was doing whatever a nurses' aide would do. I worked at that old folk's home for three or four years and enjoyed working with those old people."

From high school, she went to Lyndon State College for a year and a half.

"Partied for the first year," she said, "then they called me in and said if I didn't bring my grades up to an A or B average I would have to leave. So I brought my grades up—and then left."

"I'm sorry sometimes that I didn't finish," she added, with a faint touch of sadness. "I worked with emotionally handicapped kids for two years as a teacher's aide, and I loved those kids. If I'd gotten my degree that's what I would've continued to do."

Family life is important to Debbie, but it hasn't worked out in the conventional ways. She and Paul Lord, the man she lives with, also a backhoe operator, bought land in Albany several years ago and are building a house there.

"We got it capped off last weekend, and next summer I'll take a couple of months off and build it," she said. "I know just what I want—and nobody else could get it that way." There's a saw mill only a short distance from their property where she buys the logs.

"We own a dozer," she added, pointing out that to own or to use heavy equipment you have to be able to do most of your own repairs.

Debbie has an eight-year-old daughter, Moriah—by a former marriage—who is with her at least every other weekend during the year and every other week during the summer. But because of the traveling and the nature of her work, Debbie is unable to keep her during the school year.

"My ex-husband and I have a good relationship now," she said, "and he's very good with our daughter, does all kinds of things with her and encourages her to read. I spend as much time as I can with her, bring her over to ride in the cab with me during the summer, and I also encourage her to read."

"She's always an A and B student and loves her reading," she said proudly. "We both tell her that life is a learning process."

Debbie Loura does not give the impression that she's out to "prove" herself as a successful *woman* in a *man's* field. What she seems to demonstrate is the importance of following and developing one's own inherent abilities without weighing these against societal generalities that have little to do with individual talents.

"I've always thought a lot about what my grandmother told my brother. She said she didn't care if he was a rubbish man, if he did the best he could.

"She used to tell him 'if that's what makes you go, then that's what you *should* do,' " Debbie said, "and I've always tried to follow her advice."

PROFESSIONS

ELLEN
HOLMES
MALONEY

"Women don't have mid-life crises," Judge Ellen Holmes Maloney said with a disarming smile, "we start off at mid-life."

I interviewed the probate judge at the old Manchester Court House, a small, white, brick building, with a dignity that inspires confidence and seems friendly. In a curiously overt way, it represents the kind of impression that used to be commonly associated with law. Talking with Ellen strengthened my belief that the possibility of strong moral purpose still exists in the contemporary practice of law.

Born in New York in 1939, and growing up for the most part on Long Island, she was raised in comfortable circumstances and had the good fortune to attend excellent private schools. She also graduated from New York University. "I think I had an educational advantage," she said, "and it makes a difference later."

Ellen was raised, however, to consider marriage and motherhood as the primary fulfillment of her life, with no emphasis on other vocational planning. Conventional wisdom still held that teaching and nursing were the most acceptable and suitable kinds of work for a woman outside the home, and it was assumed that either of these could be practiced without too serious a commitment. Not only did this thinking limit women's potential for broader occupational choice, but it seriously de-emphasized the importance of professional education and the nature of commitment required by both nursing and teaching.

Ellen married a clergyman whose ministry happened to be the South Bronx. They lived there for ten years, and her horizons were considerably broadened. Brought up with the values of a white, upper middle-class background that included limited tolerance for, or knowledge of, people of different cultures and circumstances, she was confronted with extremes of poverty, despair, and hope, unlike anything she had previously experienced.

"The South Bronx teaches you a lot about life, and I don't regret it," she said.

During this period, on the strength of psychology credits she had earned in college, she got her teacher's license and taught third grade to mostly Spanish-speaking children, continuing until she was seven months pregnant with her first child.

"In those days, pregnancy was cause for instant dismissal," she said with a broad grin. "Since they didn't know me well enough to know that I wasn't just getting fat, I stayed on as long as elastic could hold me in."

A daughter was born in 1963, a son, in 1965, and Ellen was at home with them for five years. In 1971, she was awarded an MA at the City University of New York. "For women contemplating educational preparation of any kind, I strongly recommend studying during those early childhood years; it's possible then to have a schedule that's more flexible in some important ways," she said.

"When the children were small, I became involved in starting a pre-school in central Harlem. It was a Montessori project, and the Berrigan brothers were a part of it."

The school's goal was to provide a supportive setting and an academic environment at an early age to children from poor and disadvantaged backgrounds. "We used reverse busing to bus white children into the school, including our own," she declared, "and it's still going." The motivating philosophy of the Central Harlem Association of Montessori Parents (CHAMP) was a belief in the effectiveness of parents working together to create a better social fabric.

During the same period, she did draft counseling as her contribution to the anti-Vietnam peace movement.

"I would mainly listen to young people, try to determine what they really wanted, and figure out a way to help them," she said. "Most were conscientious objectors."

When her husband died in 1971 and the church needed the rectory back, Ellen and her two children had no place to go. "As soon as he died our life there was finished; we had to leave."

Ellen could have returned to Long Island with the children, but the differences between her and her parents were now too great. Issues and opinions that had become important to her would have been met with disapproval. She had a sister, a graduate of Middlebury College, who was living in Dorset, Vermont, and since Ellen had always liked the idea of rural life, she moved there with her children.

"I spent the first three years doing all kinds of things. I was an apple picker, did construction work, auto mechanics, and even some roofing," she recalled proudly.

At thirty-five, she knew the time had come to figure out what she wanted to do for the rest of her life. "I wanted something that would be a challenge, also something that would be a service. Sounds sappy but I wanted something that would help other people."

While a career in medicine was one of her considerations, there was then an age barrier that precluded her acceptance in medical school. She also considered the practice of law, but there were problems: she didn't want to uproot her children again by moving to a place with a law school, and law school tuition was prohibitively expensive. Still, law appealed to her as an effective social tool.

Two events strengthened her interest in law. The first was the discrimination against her as a woman when she attempted to purchase a house in Manchester. The second, her discovery that Vermont was one of the last seven states where law could still be learned by apprenticing to a lawyer for a four-year period.

Explaining what happened in the first instance, she said, "The banks wouldn't give a mortgage to a woman, and I was damned if I'd have my father or any other man sign for me."

She bought the cheapest house in town for $16,000, a place that had been abandoned for eight years and, along with everything else, had saplings growing from the roof. Her work in the immediate future was clearly established: the rebuilding, with her own hands, of this shell into a home. But Ellen couldn't forget that she'd been unable to get a loan to buy a home simply because she is a woman.

"I was terribly disappointed later that the Equal Rights Amendment didn't pass, and I worked hard for it."

Returning to the subject of the house, she continued, "I was also led to do the work on my own house because of the construction challenge. I wanted to learn construction skills, and I didn't care if the work seemed 'unladylike.' I sensed that this would give me the feeling of independence that I needed."

Ellen also found an attorney who would accept her as an apprentice. David Putter, a former public defender (now a practicing attorney), was, at that time, the only clerk to Vermont's eight superior court judges. He had experience supervising the legal education of other clerks, and under his tutelage, she began her clerkship program in

1975. "I became a law clerk to the superior court judges because he was. As his clerk, I worked for the judges, and it was an invaluable learning experience. I later worked independently for them."

For the next four years her legal education followed a route that was the traditional method of studying law, before law schools were established at the end of the nineteenth century. John Adams, Thomas Jefferson, and Abraham Lincoln were outstanding examples of the process. There are disadvantages to this method, particularly in our age of specialization, where corporate procedures require lawyers trained for relatively esoteric and abstract fields. But she believes that clerking in a law office gave her increased insight into the actual practice of law, and also made possible a career that otherwise would have been out of the question.

"I did research for the judges, sat in on court proceedings and also repaired the judges' cars," she said, blue eyes sparkling.

Ellen has long since passed her Vermont bar examinations. She is now forty-eight years old, teaches a popular course in family law at the Vermont Law School and is on the board of managers for the Vermont Bar Association. She is also a member of their task force on gender bias.

For ten years, she has held the probate judgeship in Bennington County, an elective position. She also chaired a statewide committee drafting rules for probate procedure, which was then promulgated by the State Superior Court into law.

"It was a great committee," she said, "and we were able to complete the document in gender-neutral language. We were also able to set up the many forms so necessary in probate court, in language that a layperson could follow. We made them more accessible."

Ellen also maintains her own busy practice out of an office in Pawlet. Her work includes family law, real property, and domestic violence. She also represents several towns with real estate property and other municipal matters.

Active in spouse abuse legislation passed by the Vermont legislature a few years ago, she takes particular pride in an expansion of the act, that covers unmarried couples, as well as members of a victim's household, present or past.

Ellen was distressed by the lies and misrepresentations used as arguments against passage of the Equal Rights Amendment and felt that many women who opposed its passage had been misled as to its real intent. "There are also women who feel that it's wrong for men not to be the leaders . . . always," she said.

She acknowledges that there is some discrimination within the court system, adding soberly, "There's no question but that women attorneys, as well as women witnesses in general, are accorded less credibility."

"I'm convinced that most women who achieve success at their work are women with lots of energy. They've had to be," she said. "In most cases they've had to make their way over some pretty rough terrain in order to get there. The women attorneys I've come into contact with are all exceptionally hard-working."

"I was single for ten years," she added. "I think it gave me an opportunity to grow and develop, to get my career together, take care of my academics, and gather a more appropriate sense of myself."

"I'm married again now, to someone suitable to me," she continued. "He's a teacher, and he loves his work. We both work long hours, but we have things like hunting, fishing, and gardening that we love to do together."

Ellen Holmes Maloney gives the impression of a woman with clear, strong opinions carefully arrived at. She also has an underlying compassion which tempers, without impairing, her judgment.

Speaking about her work with other lawyers on spouse abuse legislation, as well as other work she's done with the Governor's Commission on Women, she stressed the importance of helping women feel they can make it on their own and develop positive feelings of self-worth. She explained that a woman with an abusive spouse can now get a restraining order without having filed for divorce, a condition that had to be met prior to the new legislation.

"Now an officer can make an arrest for abuse that constitutes a misdemeanor," she said. "Before it had to be a felony, and it had to be done in the officer's presence. Today a victim can show probable cause, which tells the abuser that someone can intervene."

If there is probable cause, a petition for relief from abuse is filed, an affidavit made; and the court issues a restraining order that may include four things: custody of the children, sole rights to the home place, restraint from further abuse, and restraint from further interference with her personal liberties.

Most spouse abuse is assault; if a man punches his wife, it is usually a misdemeanor and not a felony, in which case an officer could previously only have issued a citation. But now, in cases of domestic abuse, where the assault is still classified as a misdemeanor, the abuser is taken into custody if the victim can show probable cause.

"A batterer's dialogue is always predictable," she said, having heard it repeated by victims many times over. "It's pretty standard for him to say to the spouse he's about to batter, 'I'm going to have to punch your pretty face.'

"I have sympathy for women who're afraid to be alone, afraid of their own feelings of incompetence, who'll put up with almost any-thing in order not to be rejected.

"For myself, I figured that working on a house was a context in which I could be learning skills. Basically I wanted to become a com-petent person.

"Helping these women feel like a person of some account, to feel they can do things on their own, is an important first step.

"Sometimes as women, whatever we're trying to do, we feel we're out there all alone. We're going in a lot of directions that are new to us, and it's important that we help each other. In 1961 when my adult life was more or less beginning, I can remember being interested in the study of law. It was one of the three choices that I considered, and it was a rough time. I needed some kind of work, but I didn't have the courage at the time to pursue law. The other two areas were teaching or having children, and pregnancy won out."

"More and more of us today are going into law," she concluded, "and I'm convinced that its practice will be humanized by the presence of more women."

[Ellen's career turned another milestone in January 1989 when Gov-ernor Madeleine Kunin appointed her to the Vermont Superior Court, the first woman in the state's history to serve as a superior court judge.]

REVEREND JEAN STAFFELD JERSEY

*T*his is my first church. I only graduated in May, but I come from a family that were all ministers, fathers and grandfathers—a family business, you might say.

"My goal is to develop an atmosphere of trust and friendship within my church, but the masculine slant in Bible language, in which I feel myself excluded, is painful to me."

Jean Staffeld Jersey, rector of Christ Church in Bethel, is one of the two women who have been called to this rectory, and she spoke honestly about her feelings.

"This is hard to explain to men, or to other women who've not been bothered by this language thing. I faced that question every morning at the seminary; everyone I knew did, and I didn't know whether the problem would force me to leave—but I couldn't see myself happy outside the ministry."

"I'm trying to make my way carefully," she continued, explaining that she intended to proceed sensitively and slowly in enunciating to her parishioners the possibility of a biblical message more inclusive in its language.

"I don't feel it's a copout; it's a loving approach. The people in this parish have been very supportive, and they also have a strong commitment to women.

"I remember how difficult it was for me to change. I was frightened by feminist theology at first; it was a different way of being in the church. Language is a loaded issue."

Jean's route to her ministry has been indirect. In junior high school, she wanted to be a Congregationalist minister, but as the years passed, her desire underwent a subtle change; instead of becoming one, she married one.

She grew up in Lyndonville, Vermont, where her father was a Congregationalist minister. They moved to the town when she was six, and stayed until she finished sixth grade. "It was a wonderful place to be a child in, a great place to grow up."

But they had to move when her father enlisted in the chaplain corps during World War II. He left a wife and six children behind, became a troop transport captain on the high seas, met another woman and never returned to his family.

"He refused to have a divorce for a long time—didn't want to lose his assignment and his pension. He would have been summarily dismissed," she explained. "Mother was finally able to divorce him."

From Framingham where she lived with her mother and the other siblings, Jean went to Boston University. "I dated only seminarians, by choice," she said.

At the end of her second year, she met a Methodist seminarian, dated and married him. He was a Methodist minister for five years and then became an Episcopalian.

She remembers laughing at first when he said he was interested in becoming an Episcopalian. She thought of the social reputation the church had, of being class-conscious and appealing mostly to an upper middle-class congregation.

"I followed along, but at that time, I didn't appreciate the treasure this religious denomination would hold for me. I should have insisted on more knowledge from the Bishop who confirmed me. I only found out what the church was about later. And because of my experience as a minister's wife, I also didn't question the supposition that one half of the ministerial couple they required was unpaid.

"We were married for twenty-five years and had four children. I am a recovering alcoholic. He couldn't be the minister I wanted him to be, and it took me a long time to see the impossibility of living out one's own dream through someone else's, so we finally separated.

"By 1974, I'd been three years sober; I had an eleven-year-old son, and a series of jobs. I was trying to work something out about myself and what I wanted in life through changing jobs, and I eventually landed in the White River Junction area. My son graduated from the Thetford Academy."

When she came to Vermont, she considered going to seminary, but couldn't afford it. She had also promised David, her son, that he could finish high school in óne spot. In White River Junction she belonged to St. Paul's Church, and when she made the decision to go to Goddard to finish her college education, the parishioners were supportive.

She remembers repeating several times to a friend her desire to study, citing the obstacles. "Why don't you just do it anyway?" the friend replied.

"Sounds funny, but it was like someone had given me permission. It was what I was waiting for, so I matriculated in the Goddard program and completed my B.A. degree in one year. I would go there for nine days every now and then, and then come back home and work. It was a wonderful program."

Jean was remarried to a dairy farmer in Hartland in 1981.

After completing her bachelor's degree, she went to the Episcopal Divinity School in Cambridge, Massachusetts, the most radical feminist divinity school in the country. For three years she went down every Sunday night, came back every Friday afternoon.

"It was schizophrenic, it was hard, but it was wonderful," she said adding that she continued to be active in her home parish where she played the organ.

"This helped pay my tuition. The church people were supportive, and this partly helped put me through seminary. It felt good to be there, and it called me to account. School is an idealized place, but it's not life," she added wryly.

"It was a real luxury to study in graduate school, an intense place to be—radical, always out on the edge. Still, taking myself out of that and going home weekends on the farm was a dose of sanity. I'm not involved in the farm, but I have a huge garden. I love that, and the farm is in a beautiful spot."

After three terms in seminary, she decided to concentrate on feminist theology even though it scared her. She spent a year on this, and claims that it was an eye opener. Ideas were introduced that shook her entire religious base but it also taught her to remember how difficult it is entertain new ideas concerning one's religious beliefs—the risks, and the fear of losing everything. Nonetheless, there were always models, women who were strong radical feminists, yet able to work within the existing structure.

At the same time, however, she was unable to find role models in Vermont. In 1984 she interviewed women within the Vermont diocese who had been ordained and was discouraged. She found there were some women with the same feelings as she—but they were not functioning as independent rectors of parishes.

"The women I interviewed were ground breakers, but at a price.

The opportunities were not good. Some were paid five dollars an hour, some not paid at all. I found that, across the board, in all denominations, women were poorly paid."

Jean was ordained in 1987. She explained the process of ordination as a series of steps. The postulant for a diocese begins in the local parish and meets once a month with a committee made up of a cross section of people from the parish: men and women, liberal and conservative. She met with them for a year, which helped her clarify her own position. A general ordination exam is given across the country for all the postulants.

She was called to Bethel, to the Christ Episcopal Church, first as a deacon, and was ordained as a priest on December 16, 1987.

"It's a very unusual place. There's a great deal of support for women in this parish. I've been somewhat surprised. It has twice called women as rectors. It is also unusual in its makeup: many people who have been coming for years, and have retired here; many with urban backgrounds and also many people whose whole lives have been spent here."

When I spoke with Jean, she was excited at the prospect of being sent by her Bethel parish as an effective witness for Christ's Church to the Lambeth Conference of Bishops in London. She pointed out that at Lambeth there would be a critical forum for the role of ordained women in the Anglican church, worldwide.

"There's an after-effect of being a part of something like that, a great sense of empowerment," she added.

Ordained and laywomen from many nations are pressing for the recognition of women being allowed to witness at all levels of the ministry. The Wardens and Vestry of her parish favor the ordination of women, and the consecration of women bishops and feel that the United States should assume leadership in this cause. Adherence to the doctrine of apostolic succession to priesthood, which has recognized only males as rightful successors of the original apostles, has heretofore been an obstacle.

Jean explained that the bishops were to be centered in Cambridge; whereas women will be in neighboring Wye, but they will take part in the testimony given at the conference. She pointed out that women are not yet ordained to the priesthood in England, Australia and parts of Africa.

Since the Bethel parish is unable to support a full-time priest, she has a half-stipend position and is there on Thursday, Friday, Saturday and Sundays. Work as assistant to the director of The Human Services Council in Lebanon takes the rest of her week.

"This means that I'm learning about available social services in the area, which also helps me in my ministry. I feel very fortunate in the way this has come together."

Her primary duty in the Bethel parish is liturgical. She provides leadership in worship and offers sacraments to the congregation.

"I like to use the same liturgy, it allows me to soar. Now I can soar every week. I immediately loved the beauty of it, everything about it; it fed an aesthetic part of me that had been starved."

But the pastoral aspect is extremely important to her as well, and she laughed as she recalled being asked by the St. Paul's Committee if she would have a problem ministering to men because of her feminism.

"Women bring strong pastoral skills to the ministry. There's a *connectedness* they have to people and places. I've gotten even closer to it in myself. My feminism has only increased that. If anything, I'm more radical now than I was then."

Her animated expression became serious as she added softly, "There's a deep need on the part of many to be heard, and women may better understand that need. I'm thrilled by it. I would like to go every day to see people, men and women. That's how the gospel is spread. It's what we are in relationships, showing how much we love each other, the kind of loving community we can shape together. It is such an honor to be taken into people's lives, to have them show their lives in the way they do."

The sun was shining brightly through the windows of her upstairs office in the parish house. A Matisse print of figures joyously dancing together hung in a prominent place on one wall and seemed to bear witness to what she had been saying.

"I always had that hanging in my room at seminary," she said gently, "and I couldn't bear to leave it."

GLADYS AGELL

I started life as a painter and expected to go from womb to tomb with a brush in my hand," art therapist Gladys Agell said, as we sat talking in her spacious office in College Hall overlooking the Green at Vermont College in Montpelier.

"Some years later, married and with three children, I was still doing my painting," she added, "but after a divorce, since I'd never finished college, I figured I'd have to make a living, so I went back to school."

Now, seventeen years later, Gladys enjoys looking back on the route she traveled as she combined her art with a therapeutic profession. She is director of the master of arts program in art therapy at Vermont College, a lecturer, editor of the *American Journal of Art Therapy,* and the author of numerous papers in her field. She became active politically in the American Art Therapy Association (AATA) and eventually served as its chairperson.

"As with any psychotherapy, art therapy is a way to help people understand themselves in the hope that self-understanding frees them to make reasonable life choices.

"People tend to think we perform with bones, rattles and incantations, but it's basically using art materials of many kinds to make a visual statement. As a therapist, I look at the work done by a client, and then we both try to figure out what prompted the image he or she has made. Art is often a metaphor for life experiences that are sometimes obscure."

"In the program at Vermont College, we're trying to train art therapists who are careful, thoughtful clinicians," she said.

Art therapy was a new field when she started her training. There were no degree-granting programs and no national registry of professional art therapists. All these voids have been filled during the years she's been working; Gladys Agell played an important role in the process, and she is proud of it.

"This year I received the honorary Life Membership Award from the Association, the highest award you can get. I'm not a pioneer, but I am an early settler."

Sitting in her pleasant, high-ceilinged office, I was struck by the visual satisfaction it provided. Masks, paintings, and photographs were displayed on the walls; sculptures, magazines and piles of drawings took the hard edge off the necessary filing cabinets; there were books lined up on low shelves around the room and plants in abundance.

Down the hall are a well-equipped art studio and the offices of Gladys' full-time staff, Kathi Smith, program coordinator, and Carberry Neal, a faculty member who is coordinator of internships.

The art therapy program is unquestionably a well organized operation with a director who gives the impression of maintaining a firm grip on the reins. Her style shows itself in a talent for the unexpected. Her humor, dress and conversation, while suitable to a conventional academic framework, still manage to suggest unpredictability and a hint of stubborn independence.

Dress, for instance; on the day I was there, this small, trim woman with the short red hair adorned by natural frosting, wore a dark green outfit whose orange trim was repeated in the color of a simple pin near her shoulder. Her shoes were polished brown loafers. But luminous orange stockings contradicted her tailored and conventional image of academia.

Describing her transformation from painter to art therapist, Gladys said, "After deciding to go back to school, I went to N.Y.U. [New York University] to complete my degree. I took all the psychology I could and all the studio art courses.

"A friend of mine, who was a clinical psychologist, told me that a new field was emerging called art therapy. He suggested that because of my interest in people and also in art, I should look into it."

"So I also took art therapy courses, from the two foremost art therapists in the country at that time," she continued. "They happened to be Margaret Naumberg and Edith Kramer and they were pioneers. Elinor Ulman, the founding editor of the *American Journal of Art Therapy*, was another pioneer."

Gladys continued at N.Y.U. until she received her master's degree in art education. During college and after, she held a variety of jobs that included work in psychiatric hospitals and special schools. She was also involved with one of the first mental health programs in the country, in Rockland County, New York, where she lived in the 1960s.

She later worked at the Lorge School for troubled adolescents in New York City. At Pratt Art Institute she supervised internships for an art therapy program that was just starting.

Remarried in the late sixties, she and her husband decided in 1973 to move permanently to Vermont. They had a vacation home in Waits River and hoped to find a less frantic life here. Gladys also had serious plans to resume her painting in the studio that was part of their house.

"It was nine months to the day before I went back to work," she said. "Couldn't stand the solitude."

On a hunch, she'd previously put in an application for work at the Vermont State Hospital, and when its superintendent, Dr. George Brooks, called at seven A.M. one morning to ask if she wanted to come to work, she went.

She was chief of activity therapy, and trained employees who worked in the art therapy department. "I said I wouldn't take the job if I couldn't do clinical work as well, so in addition to being an administrator, I saw clients. I've always had at least two jobs."

Two important things happened during her years at the hospital; she found she missed doing the intensive training she'd formerly done at Pratt, and she also became chairperson of the American Art Therapy Association, a position she held for six years.

"At about the same time, I was asked to recommend someone to start an art therapy graduate program at Goddard. The friend I recommended didn't want it, so I took it."

Gladys was at Goddard for three years before moving the program to Vermont College in 1979. But she claims that the foundation for the program was laid at Goddard.

The recognition enjoyed by this field today has developed primarily within the past decade. Gladys attributes this to actions taken by the American Art Therapy Association in part during her tenure as president. AATA was responsible for the approval process of training programs and standards for professional registration which, in turn, have influenced the professional quality of its practitioners. The *American Journal of Art Therapy*, in publication for twenty-six years, predated the AATA and played a major role in the development of the field by establishing a forum for isolated art therapists throughout the United States and Canada.

She said that when the *American Journal of Art Therapy* indicated it might have to cease publication she persuaded Vermont College of Norwich University to buy it.

"For years it was magnificently edited by Elinor Ulman, and it would have been a great loss to the profession if it closed its doors."

Summer is the busiest time for the art therapy program at Vermont College. There are at least forty students on campus for classes and field work and an adjunct faculty of eight other members. The entering class generally numbers about twenty students.

"The program has attracted students from all over the world," Gladys said, peering at the framed photographs of graduating classes grouped on one wall. "They've come from Switzerland, Brazil, Israel, West Germany, Costa Rica, all over Canada, Alaska and Australia."

A unique part of the plan is that students are on campus only during the summer, with the rest of the year spent in professional situations. During the fall and winter months, Gladys or another faculty member travels to oversee the students and their supervisors.

She explained that people are going through the program more slowly now, often taking two years instead of fifteen months. Most have the responsibility of supporting themselves while they're in school, and many are raising a family or are single parents; some are starting second careers. Most are people who wanted to paint or do something in the arts, and all have well-rounded art backgrounds.

Explaining the range possible within this field, Gladys said: "Art therapy is used effectively in cases of sexual abuse, for both children and adults. It can be an important way for people to begin relieving themselves of past experiences. It's also used in treatment for substance abuse, limb impairments or a loss that has created traumas. You name it, there are all kinds of uses."

A curious characteristic of the field is that it includes very few men. "Money has a lot to do with it," Gladys explained. "Considering the kind of dedication and training required, the wage scale in the early days was low. Men tended to become administrators in mental health, or go into private practice. But opportunities for decent salaries are growing."

She is unconcerned that only about six percent of the practitioners are men. "I would like to see the field become a women's field, with power and prestige. That's why we put so much pressure on students to make it a class act," she said firmly, "to be not only good clinicians

but also to talk and write about what they're doing. Get more recognition among their colleagues in the mental health field.

"I started out thinking I'd spend my life with a paint brush in my
hand, but it's still difficult for women painters to get recognition and
a lot of painters have to make a living doing something else."

"In this field we look for people who are strong in visual arts," she
added. "Not everybody can use art-making as their sole livelihood,
and art therapy provides a remarkable means for combining talents."

ELLEN FALK

I don't ever use textbooks," said Ellen Falk, third grade teacher at Norwich Elementary school. "I don't like textbooks."

"Science is observing; teaching science to children has everything to do with getting them accustomed to *looking*," she continued. Ellen explained that the current project was a study of birds and that the class started with nests. My attention was directed to a table on which a variety of bird nests had been assembled, each with an identification card. She described the way the children started a unit of this kind.

First came discussion and comparison of the different sizes, shapes and materials used in building the nests of various birds and where the different kinds of nests are to be found. Several large posters along one wall displayed illustrations of many New England birds in their characteristic environments, plus individual pictures of these birds.

"I say to the children, 'Look at these birds. Pick one of them to study and tell me some things you would like to know about the bird you've chosen.' "

She gave as an example one child who picked the hawk; "I already know the size," he said, "but I want to know what he eats."

Another said, "Oh, it's me and the chickadee, we have two things in common—we can't settle down, always on the go, because we have lots of energy! But I'd like to know what she does with hers."

While the children had left by the time I arrived, the excitement and sense of their presence still remained through their work.

"Each child is asked to make a commitment to finding out all she or he can about one particular bird; look at pictures of the bird, tell what's happening, describe the sort of things she'd like to know about the bird she's studying. The child is also asked to build a nest at home, using whatever materials he can find to approximate the bird he's studying."

"Look at the nest carefully," she tells them, "the kind of material used to build it, is it soft? Is it wiry? See how close you can get to building one like it." Without hesitation she added: "I like for parents to become involved too, this gives a child the feeling that what she or he is doing is important."

At the beginning of each year, Ellen tries to identify parental skills and plan ways of using them during the school year. Parents can contribute a range of skills, but in her view, all have importance, from the simplest to the most sophisticated, and it's good for the children to see them working together within the context of what is being studied.

In Ellen Falk's classes the children are never sent to an encyclopedia for material, because the information included there has already been compiled. Instead, when a subject is being studied, she finds several books and makes them available. The children use index cards for taking notes, and each card may contain only one paragraph. Not only does this practice teach them about paragraphs, but later, when they write up the material, each paragraph will have been organized.

"Paragraphs are quite hard at this age," she said. "The cards help them learn to organize their thoughts."

She pointed out that it's unusual for children to do reports in the third grade. "I have a high standard, and I don't want them to think it is easy. I also don't want them to become discouraged. Interest is the key. I have children of high ability and some of low ability. It's a good cross section, but what they all have in common is strong interest."

Her classroom is richly furnished with materials: books, posters, paintings, magazines and objects—all relating to what is being studied, all proof of her avidity and skill at collecting useable resources. She also makes video tapes of special programs on nature and on other countries or on any other subject that she sees on television and that relates to future study.

Many units are researched during the school year including, among others, local history, birds, mammals, trees, insects, tall tales, Mexico and Indians. When they start the unit on trees in April, before the leaves come out, Ellen takes the children outside to the schoolyard where each child adopts a tree.

"Start simple," she tells them. "Develop it, tell what you see, don't name it yet, just tell what you see, then go deeper." She shows them pictures of buds and how they grow. "Match your tree's buds to the right one in the picture; is it alternate or opposite?"

By the time the leaves are out, the children start to classify the trees. Each one must be identified, and she has many books on tree identification. Bark rubbings follow.

"There's a basic curriculum that we follow, but the way you approach it is up to you," she explained. "It's the resource material that makes the unit come alive. The work must be hands-on for children of this age; it can't be too theoretical."

"Art is very important in anything I do with the children," she continued. "As one of the ways a child responds to an idea and as a way of making different cultures come alive." She feels that both the factual and the creative processes are necessary to thought, and makes sure that this combination is observed.

With the completion of each project, Ellen takes it a step further and duplicates all the work the children have done, including their illustrations. The reproduced material is divided into individual books, so that one goes home with each child. The books include: *Original Tall Tales, Olden Days Stories, Bird Stories of All Kinds, Mammal Studies, Food Around the World.*

"I'm a great believer in Piaget and the definite stages in child development. When a unit doesn't work I know that I've gone too fast, or if a unit isn't successful, it's my fault."

Ellen grew up and went to school in Czechoslovakia, in the city of Prague. She and her family were in England during World War II and came to this country in 1946.

"I have a Montessori background, but my interest in teaching children sort of evolved," she recalled. "I took note of the Montessori philosophy and outlook and thought a lot about how I wanted to impart knowledge. It is wonderful and interesting and hard, but I believe that children rise to high standards if they're set for them."

"I have no good memories of school in Czechoslovakia whatsoever," she said. "I'm a very intuitive, creative person, and my education there was oppressive. It was only later that I experienced the excitement of learning. We brought up our own children to have a love for it. I firmly believe that if children have that, their life is shaped."

Ellen's former husband is a professor at Dartmouth College. With obvious pride, she pointed out that their children are both teachers, her daughter and son-in-law in the Strafford elementary school, and her son, an M.D., in college.

Before coming to the Norwich area in 1963, she and her family lived in Minneapolis where her husband taught in a university. But during the years her children were small, she felt it was important to be with them.

"You should give them time first, and later you can give them material things. If there's a choice, I don't feel that it's right to have strangers with different values bringing up your children. Many women don't have to work and yet they still do—and the children are quite unsettled. I feel that definitely. I think you need to spend these early years with your children."

"However, if something is important to you, you find a way of doing it," she added. She became interested in teaching as a career, and as her children were growing up started courses in Minneapolis. She received her master of arts from Antioch College after moving to Norwich.

Outside the classroom, Ellen Falk might give the impression of formality and reserve. Yet her appearance also affords a clue to the magic she works with children. There's nothing about her to suggest a temperament capable of kicking off her shoes and "romping with the kiddies." There's nothing casual about her appearance: nicely coiffed gray blond hair, softly tailored knit suit, a subtle hyacinth with a slightly darker silk blouse underneath and jewelry that consciously projected the mauve tones of her outfit, yet it suggests an exquisite sensitivity to color. The environment she creates in her classroom also suggests a personality singlemindedly directed toward alerting children to the potentials of a multi-faceted world.

There was total conviction in her assertion that she "prepares the environment where children will be spending their school time, so that they'll be stimulated by it—so that learning will be exciting.

"It is also important to me that each child feels good about herself or himself. I care very much for each child and I am very much geared to the individual child."

At the end of our interview, when asked if I might photograph her with some of the children's work, a look of real dismay spread across her face.

"Oh, but it's the children we're concerned with, photograph their work, or come back and photograph them, that's what is important!"

LINDA ABBOTT

*P*eople sometimes ask me why I didn't become a physician—'why just a nurse?' " Linda Abbott, R.N., commented. "That says a lot!"

"I've always enjoyed the sciences. If I'd wanted to be a physician, I could have been," she added without hesitation. "I happen to like the high touch of nursing, that's what got me. I felt I could make a difference in the lives of people I'm in contact with, I can affect more people in what I'm doing."

Linda is one of four R.N. staff supervisors at the Central Vermont Home Health Agency (CVHHA), located in a large building off the Barre-Montpelier Road. The building's architecture, like that of the discount stores neighboring it along the strip, is of a style best characterized as neutered rectangular flat. Yet despite its impersonal exterior, one's impression undergoes a transformation upon entering the CVHHA office space.

An immense room, it is partially divided into cubicles providing semi-privacy for some of the more than one hundred employees working there: registered nurses, therapists, homemakers, home-health aides, supervisors, secretaries, clerks and others, some of whom are there for only a fraction of their working hours.

The reassuring sense of human scale in this otherwise formidable space was hard to account for. Simple friendliness was part of it and evidence that people with real feelings worked in the different cubicles was another. In every space there were objects reflecting personal tastes: plants, posters, photographs of children and families, lively ceramic dishes, a colorful quilt on a wall. Somehow these touches, in combination with the professional and efficient services associated with the organization, indicated an exceptional overall policy and the commitment shared by the people working there.

But the most telling part of the agency's work takes place outside its walls; much of it in caring for children and adults within their own homes. Some of the assistance provided within the twenty-three towns it serves are: personal care of patients, some recently released from hospitals; clinics; screening programs; physical and speech therapy; childbirth education; a Hospice program; a homemakers program; and visits to elderly and disabled persons needing help to remain independent.

"We handle many different kinds of problems in Home Health," Linda explained. "The patient is not just an individual in a hospital bed, but someone whose whole family must be considered and worked with. People at home and under stress need a lot of support; they also need teaching if there's special treatment involved. Social, as well as medical problems, go hand-in-hand in the home."

Linda Abbott is enthusiastic about her work and enjoys discussing it. She proudly described the range of services covered by the agency, and she understands its importance to the community. She is also concerned with a major problem in nursing and its consequences for the future in this important field.

"Nurses are sensitive to the word *training*. We prefer to call it *education*. For years it was *nurse's training* but that hardly begins to dignify the educational background we need. Nursing has become a science in the twenty years I've been practicing. There's a different level of sophistication in health care today."

She pointed out that nurses are required to do technical things now that are altogether different from what was allowed only a few years ago. People are sent home from hospitals "quicker and sicker" than ever before and are still in need of professional attention.

"We're the ones who are there. We pick up changes in conditions of patients at home, and we're aware of what's going on. The doctor may not see someone for as long as a year, and we're the ones who translate her or his condition to the physician."

And while the need for nurses with good medical/scientific backgrounds is increasing steadily, salaries have not kept pace with educational expectations. More and more nurses are going into other occupations, and fewer people are choosing to enter the profession.

"Salaries are beginning to improve now, for the first time in years, but we can't find the nurses. Lots of schools of nursing have closed, and it's frightening because there are not enough other educational institutions taking their place. I don't know what we're going to do in ten years."

As more and more people look away from conventional medical, hospital or convalescent home care to effective care in their own homes, finding nurses will be increasingly difficult, from the standpoint of both comfort and healing, as well as expense.

"As the traditional way of going into nursing is decreasing," Linda continued, "there are more adult learners becoming interested in the field, and different kinds of programs are being developed to educate them; things like weekend and satellite programs. But this is not keeping pace with the growing need."

She is also concerned that the American Medical Association is pushing for a program for registered care technologists, which is primarily a program for teaching hospital aides.

"People with a limited background can make beds, run errands and bathe patients; but to assign them the responsibility for a patient on an eight-hour shift is inappropriate. Patients in hospitals today are very sick, and they need someone who is tuned in to subtle changes and who can handle emergencies."

Linda attributes her own beginning interest in nursing to an aunt who is also a nurse. "I really looked up to her and respected her. She was the sort of person I wanted to be like. I wonder sometimes if it goes back to the sense of nurturance that women are supposed to have.

"But of course there are men who can be just as nurturant," she added quickly, "and men are finally being given permission in our society to be more caring. To see a father pushing a baby carriage on the street isn't that unusual."

Linda was born in Burlington, Vermont. Her father was a math professor at the University of Vermont (UVM) and is now retired. Her mother is a writer and presently working on a history of Richmond.

"I'm about as local as they come," she added, pointing out with pride that her 101-year-old grandfather and his family come from the Brookfield area and go back many years.

"My interest in science showed up early. My mother once found mice in my bed; they'd escaped from a cage in my room, but she made sure afterward that the cages were securely closed. I'd been running the mice through mazes while I was in high school."

After receiving her degree in nursing from UVM in 1966, Linda worked for three years in Burlington as a Community Health Nurse and psychiatric coordinator for the Visiting Nurse Association (VNA) in Burlington. She continued with the VNA in childbirth education and almost twenty years ago, when she was pregnant with her own daughter, taught the first Lamaze class given in that area. "By the time I left, in 1974, there were six or ten classes every week."

She spent another year at the Lund Home for pregnant and troubled adolescent girls and was supervisor of their house staff, teaching childbirth education and preparation for parenting with the resident girls.

When their daughter was three, Linda and her husband decided to spend the next year visiting Europe. "The three cf us had a marvelous time camping all over the continent," she said.

Returning to the U.S., they moved to Boston so she could obtain her master of science in nursing. With that completed, she worked at the Children's Hospital Medical Center as their clinical specialist in developmental and behavioral pediatrics. This important step in the development of her career was made possible when her husband decided to become the primary caretaker for their daughter during the three years they spent in Boston.

"I can hardly say enough about the support my husband has given me over the years," she said. "Nursing today is geared toward treating the whole person, and this makes different emotional demands on us as nurses.

"I have a beautiful marriage, and we're each other's best friend. It's made a big difference in my work," she added. Her husband is the registrar at Norwich University, and they've been married since 1965.

From 1977 to 1980, Linda worked for the University of Maine at Presque Isle developing an associate degree nursing program.

In 1980 the family moved back to Vermont, and for five years she was the clinical instructor to freshmen associate degree nursing students at Vermont College. She then worked as a coordinator of satellite nursing education to off-campus satellites in Newport, St. Johnsbury, Springfield and White River Junction for the associate degree and baccalaureate nursing programs. She went back as clinical instructor to associate degree nursing students for two years before taking her present position.

"It's an extraordinary agency here; the quality of care is very good," she said. "I've worked in Burlington, Boston, and a large district in Maine, and I'm convinced that this is exceptional.

"The pay scale for home health agencies is less than at hospitals, but ours here is good compared to others, and we have excellent benefits."

As in many publicly funded organizations, nurses at CVHHA must spend about forty percent of their time on imposed paperwork required by health insurance, primarily Medicare, but the agency is working hard to reduce that figure. "We can't just provide the care but must *prove* that we did. We've had to increase our staff to keep up with the paperwork and have had to raise our fees due to staff increases."

A stack of paper forms she showed me represented about five hundred visits a month; the supervisor must review them all. "It's a challenge, but it's also frustrating. We don't question documentation, but it's the extent of it that's disheartening. Nonetheless, the nurses are willing to do it because it gets the patient better care. It's the sort of thing you have to do in order to get the important work done."

There was a common observation I heard frequently from people working in areas of public service. Social workers, child care providers, teachers, as well as nurses—all work in fields that have for years been primarily associated with women—and all are underpaid in relation to many other jobs. Still, they're all jobs that demand not only education but also extra time and extra ingenuity when they're well-done, and yet all are underappreciated. Even so, these are areas of work that society desperately needs.

"People need to be recognized and respected. We need to feel as though we're making a contribution that counts. But society says 'we pay people we appreciate,' and all around us we see highly-paid jobs that are relatively trivial, in terms of education and commitment. I think it's a question of values and where we place them," Linda said.

"Old attitudes towards nursing, much like they were towards teaching, that any *woman* can do it if she has no better skills—are no longer compatible with what is required—not that they ever were," Linda said. "Low salaries are still the rule, and the many more options open to women today have made a major dent in the numbers of people going into the profession."

The commitment required for successful nursing is possibly no different in degree from that necessary to other professions, but there's an extra demand. Working with people in vulnerable physical and mental states must be based upon highly developed skills, but if human responsiveness to the individual is kept safely behind a technological facade, one of the vital ingredients to successful health care is missing.

"Still, from observing my aunt so many years ago, I began to feel that I really wanted to serve my fellow creature. This seemed to be what being a nurse was all about, and that feeling hasn't changed. As far as my own life goes, I've found what I was looking for."

CAROLYN
TONELLI

I started law school when I was thirty-five and got my degree when I was thirty-eight," Carolyn Tonelli, Randolph attorney, said proudly, "but now, after hanging up my diplomas in my own office, I can finally say, 'I really am a lawyer.' "

Carolyn joined another attorney, Karen Miller, in April 1988, but not before spending time, after her degree, acquiring a broader knowledge and application of the law. Her first job was with the judges in the state district court (criminal court) and superior court (civil court). Although clerks to the judges are generally hired for only a year, she was invited to stay an extra year as chief law clerk.

The twenty-four judges throughout Vermont have only eight law clerks available to them.

"Being a judge is a lonely job, since they can't talk to anybody during their day in court," Carolyn said, explaining that the law clerk also serves as a sounding board and research assistant. The judge depends on the clerk for investigating legal precedents. "It gave me an opportunity to become acquainted with, and to work with, all the judges in the state."

"I also read the law," she added, explaining that people are hired just out of law school for this work because of their generalized knowledge. "It's a marriage between the judge's experience and the fresh information of the clerk."

After working for the judges, she spent the next two years working for the man generally considered to be the best trial lawyer in the state, Richard Davis of Barre.

"It was an exciting time, but I was working long hours and isolated from my family. Besides, I've always wanted to work in the town where I live, to be part of the community."

Finding her way into the legal profession was not a straight course for Carolyn Tonelli, and chance played a part in leading her into a profession that suits her well.

"My whole entry into the world of education was late," she said. "At high school, in Philadelphia, there were five hundred and seventy girls in my graduating class, and only twelve went on to college. I wasn't one of them."

"It was primarily a training ground for low-level jobs in big corporations," she added, pointing out that she came from a blue-collar, anti-intellectual background, with no expectations of college built into her future.

Out of high school and into a clerk's job with a large corporation, she had the good fortune to have a boss who recognized her potential and felt compelled to give her strong advice.

" 'Get out of here and get yourself some education,' he said. 'You're too smart for this!' "

Taking his suggestion when she was twenty-five, Carolyn began college at Temple University in Philadelphia. "When I started there, I thought I'd died and gone to heaven! I was like a sponge, I soaked up everything there was to get and loved it! The world opened up to me."

Because of her innate confidence and enthusiasm, she spent little time worrying over gaps in her own background; she understood that an important part of her purpose in being there was to fill those gaps. She described an English honors program in which other students were several years younger and from some of the best private schools in the country. Most had broad backgrounds in travel and other cultural experiences.

"The professor was my age, and he put me down in the classroom several times. I felt intimidated, so I went to see him and told him that as far as I was concerned two of the most important things in the world are intellect and knowledge. 'Both of us have intellect,' I told him, 'but you have more knowledge, and that's why I'm here, so my knowledge can be nurtured by yours.' He never put me down again, and I ended up with an A plus in his class."

Before starting her senior year, there was a hiatus in Carolyn's education. She fell in love with Thurmond Knight, a young physician, and married him. Since he was starting a practice in a rural area of Vermont and she wanted to be with him, her own graduation was sidetracked.

The couple moved into the vicinity of Randolph, where there were hospital facilities for Knight, and Carolyn became interested in farming. Self-sufficiency became her goal, and she used some of her abundant energy taking courses in agriculture at Vermont Technical College, and raising cows and pigs. In 1977 a daughter was born, and she had to reevaluate her thinking and her plans.

"After Chelsea was born, I did a turnaround. I was thirty-two, and it became clear that I had all this energy and that she had become its major focus. I realized I had to get back on a stronger track for myself or I'd be raising one neurotic kid. I considered going into psychiatry, but law was more manageable. Helping people solve problems in a more limited framework suited my personality, and law school was also nearer than medical school.

"From my first day there, I knew I'd made the right choice, and no one was happier than Thurmond when I started. He knows I'm a person of enormous energy, and it meant that the heat was off him, and Chelsea."

Firmly supported in the endeavor by her husband, Carolyn went back to Temple University in 1980 and finished college. She graduated *summa cum laude* and was ready to enter Vermont Law School. She maintains that going to school and having her family was the perfect combination for her. "They balanced each other out. I believe that in a solid relationship, anytime a woman enters the world a man enters the home. Thurmond has a closer relation to Chelsea now than would have been the case if I was always at home and he was always at work. This way, we've both shared her care in very practical ways."

She thinks that it's now her husband's turn to take a sabbatical from his work, to do something he's always been interested in but never had sufficient time to pursue. Courses at New Hampshire College are enabling him to build and repair wooden musical instruments.

"He's always been interested in music, and he likes doing things with his hands. It's a good combination. So for now, it's my turn to be the main support of the family."

Talking with Carolyn about her experiences within the legal profession, I was struck with the combination of qualities she brings to it. She has a genuine interest in people, and she responds to tense situations with humor and a fine sense of where legitimate lines need to be drawn. Incisive, as well as forceful, her tendency to make quick judgements is tempered by an innate sense of compassion.

"Law has helped me to become more objective. By temperament I don't work that way—I'm Italian! But I've learned that my gut feelings can be wrong. You have to first look at the facts, the objective evidence.

"It's been a conservatizing education, but I'm convinced that the Socratic method of examining both sides of a subject works. I sometimes mourn the loss of my swift judgments about things, but now I'm persuaded that there are always two sides to every story."

She also believes that the Constitution covers everything she does in law. "It's the only way we have for controlling the real power in our lives, the *big power* that could otherwise have too much authority over us."

Pointing out that a lawyer's business is not all litigation, she stressed the importance of counseling and helping people manage their affairs. Her philosophy towards litigation is that there is generally a reasonable compromise. If a case goes to court, there's always a winner—and a loser. If it is mediated or settled, however, everyone comes away with something. "It's not really mediation so much as negotiation."

Carolyn believes that the development of the law in the last twenty-five years has created new entitlements, rights, and regulations that people didn't have before. Protective in their intent, they create more legal mazes. She agreed that there is validity to the complaint that only the rich can hire lawyers to navigate all the technicalities for them. Defense of individual rights is part of the philosophical basis of this country; nonetheless, she stressed, of all the legal problems that arise, only about five percent ever go to court.

Carolyn raised another subject: people sometimes can't understand how she can represent someone with whom she doesn't agree or sympathize.

"Due process doesn't stop when you're accused. Take sexual misconduct, for instance. If someone has a defense, it should be heard. I can't say, 'I don't do rapes,' as if I was saying 'I don't do windows.' I don't just take easy cases," she added sharply, "I'm not capable of drawing those lines very well.

"But if I do take a case, I also have to feel I've done everything I can do. If I miss something, somebody can go to jail. I've spent some sleepless nights about this, and I work my butt off making sure that I've done everything I can."

Carolyn believes that the Fifth Amendment and its technicalities are important to us all. In presenting evidence, for instance, if the police make an improper search without a warrant, even though they find damaging evidence, it would be suppressed because it was improperly obtained. "This is something that protects us all. It means that the police can't go into your home, or mine, or even a suspected drug home in the middle of the night without a properly obtained warrant. Otherwise, whatever they found would be discounted as evidence."

I questioned Carolyn about differences in the difficulty of practicing law for a man and a woman. "I couldn't say," she answered, "since I know it from only one perception, but personally, I don't feel any disadvantages in being a woman attorney. In the first place, I don't approach my work as a *woman* but as *me*. I don't consciously think about it too much. It's probably there, but I never feel discriminated against. I don't get bent out of shape if I think someone is treating me differently because I'm a woman, I just do my job."

Carolyn Tonelli does not seem to have been burdened by a weak self-image and seems never to have lacked confidence. She is personally attractive and vivacious with curly dark brown hair, expressive brown eyes and a flair for style.

While financial security was missing in her early background, one cannot help but feel that there was some kind of important nurturance that supported her sanguine expectations from life. She also has a brother with a Ph.D. in microbiology and a sister with an M.A. in social work.

"I've never felt inferior—wasn't burdened with that. If I'd let every affront affect me, I wouldn't have a nerve left in my body. You have to know what you want and go for it. But I'm pretty tough and I confront things."

Summing up what seemed to be her basic approach to law, as well as to life, Carolyn told a story. It had to do with a judge she'd never worked with before and who was probing to discover any acute feminist sensitivities she might have regarding her job. "He asked how I would feel as a woman if I were asked to go for coffee for a judge at the end of a hard day," she said. "I answered that if somebody really needed a cup of coffee, I'd get it."

"However," she continued, "I would also expect the same response if I were the person who needed the coffee. I think it gets down to more of a human question than a gender thing."

But she described another judge who remarked, on first hearing her name, "Your husband must be Italian." When she explained that she used her maiden name, his face fell and his disgusted reply was, "Oh no, one of those!"

Judicially speaking, she said, they got along well together and he respected her work, but there were obvious gaps in his understanding of women's points of view and subjects they simply couldn't discuss. He was puzzled about why there was resentment when he used the term *girl* in referring to a *woman*. Her reply was, "Just don't do it! It makes me mad."

She also told the story of a client from out of state who called on her to straighten out a real estate deal he had botched. At one point in a phone conversation, he blurted out: "I can't deal with women. From now on you should talk to my wife! You women are good at managing these things."

"I praised him for being open about it. And I understand that these men who have a hard time dealing with women are really frightened of us.

"I have a very high regard for the law," she concluded firmly, "and I believe that one of its most important functions is to help us get beyond personal prejudices."

DHYANI YWAHOO

W herever we are," Dhyani Ywahoo said, "it is important to keep the right perspective, to be mindful of what is around you."

Prepared by her elders since childhood to carry the ancestral wisdom of the Ywahoo lineage, Dhyani Ywahoo is clan chieftainess of the Ani Gadoahwi, and a member of the traditional Etowah of the Eastern Tsalagi (Cherokee) Nation; she is also the twenty-seventh generation to keep this wisdom alive. In a century characterized primarily by rapid change, this is an impressive span of continuous history.

To share this knowledge with a wider community, she was directed in 1969 by the Native American Elders to found the Sunray Meditation Society. She was instructed by her grandparents to do this in Vermont, since the mountains here were the sites for many traditional and sacred ceremonies. Sunray has since grown to be an international spiritual society dedicated to planetary peace with headquarters in Bristol, Vermont.

In her teaching and writing, as well as in her conversation, Dhyani Ywahoo restores images and power to many words whose ancient representations have been limited and tamed through contemporary usage. Words like: fire, wisdom, heart, medicine, circle, Earth, energy, balance and peace. Woman's role in aiding the return of balance to the earth, and to all life upon it, is one she emphasizes.

"As women, we need to work with our hearts and minds together seeking for ways to nurture a world of peace. We must be courageous in cutting away the illusions of scarcity, racism and sexism."

"Prejudice has many guises," she added, "and the way we react reveals our state of mind. If anger is our reaction, then we ourselves have been caught in this prejudice. Too many times women have thought that our empowerment comes through anger. Change must come through the heart."

She is concerned about the situation that has existed in contemporary society for the past four thousand years and emphasized that women have allowed their power to be weakened, put down. She pointed out, however, that women in Native American culture have traditionally played decisive roles within the family and the tribe. Ywahoo's grandmother and her great aunts were strong influences in her own development.

"They were the most powerful women I have ever known and were women of color. My grandmother, Nellie, had great insight, with a mind so big and a heart so vast that people came to her for help from all over the world."

She told the story of her grandmother who, "six feet tall and beautiful, with the gifts of clarity and confidence," left a country background in South Carolina and, with only a third-grade education, became a successful buyer and seller of stocks, bonds and real estate in New York City. She was also responsible for the well-being of more than 150 people whom she fed and clothed.

"We need to think of the needs in our local communities," Ywahoo said. "Invest in things that are beneficial to it. My grandmother always upgraded everything; if she bought a property, she would improve it, make it better for people. She used to say that in the act of giving, you see the spaciousness of your own heart, and this opens the door to more giving."

She explained that her grandmother used her gifts of clarity and of confidence to the fullest and that she was personally involved in everything she did. But though her sons were well-educated, their gifts were different. They were unable to continue what their mother had started.

"My aunts and great aunts," she continued, "did remarkable needlework, and their empowerment came through crafts. To make beautiful things is an expression of unity with the vastness of space and matter. What you yourself can do is not important if it does not show itself to others." Ywahoo pointed out that projects undertaken by Sunray members are concerned with ecological issues, Native American rights, pure water and pure food. Developing community gardens is one way they work together with other people in their communities in sharing the responsibility for renewing and transforming life on Earth.

"If someone says to me, 'I live in the city, how can I grow anything?'" she continued, "I say, 'Do you have a windowsill, or a roof?' There's always someplace where you can grow something, and if we give something to Earth, Earth gives something back to us."

Because of her visits across the country once a year to other Sunray Regional Councils, there were three years when Dhyani Ywahoo planted no garden.

"I didn't feel right about it," she said. "Now we put the garden in before we leave Vermont, and someone else stays home and weeds it."

Another example of her concern with the practical, as well as with the ideal, was her experience as a single parent. Living in a town on Long Island as a young divorced mother, she found herself responsible for raising three children on her own.

"The women there came together and formed a food coop," she said. "We shared many social concerns, got a Head Start program going and cooperated to improve everyone's quality of life."

About the same time, during the mid sixties, she realized that it would be cheaper for her to buy a house than to pay rent. On paper it made perfect sense, but her bankers refused to give her a mortgage. Finally she convinced an officer from the federal government's Office of Economic Opportunity to use his influence with the bankers. As a result, she was one of the first single women in New York State to get a mortgage in her own name.

"Then as now," she said, "we women need to establish our own parameters and not be caged by the limits that others have established for us—bankers or anyone else."

Dhyani's experiences as a student counselor on Long Island and later at a state university in Old Westbury, Connecticut opened her eyes to the deteriorating family relationships in western culture.

"I had no idea that people had such bad thoughts about their parents," she said. "In the eyes of Native American teaching, the breakdown of the family is a violation of an inner wisdom, of the spirit of everything that unites us."

She expressed concern too about an attitude toward children that she feels is too pervasive, both at school and in the home.

"In general, children are rushed through things, not given a chance to find things out," she said. "It is an issue of the kind of patience needed for the development of creative consciousness. There is too much pressure from the concept so pervasive today that 'time is money.' Time is other things as well."

"What kind of society is it that lets our people become homeless, living on the streets and in the parks?" she continued. "There's something out of balance in a national view that withdraws money from feeding and educating our children to spend on weapons and wars. Why isn't the system set up to prize these families, to help them in their need and to recognize their value?"

On her visits to Sunray Regional Councils across the country, Ywahoo traveled by car with her husband and their small child.

"I'm a mother the second time around," she said, explaining that her other children are now grown.

"My daughter and I were pregnant at the same time," she added with a smile of pleasure. "It's like living two lifetimes. The first time, when I was raising my first three children I was trying so hard to be a *good* mother that I may not have enjoyed all the beauty there is in small children."

It was on these trips across the country, almost five years ago, that she first became aware of the homeless people, living in cars beside the road. "These were families that had worked for years, paid their taxes, paid their dues; and as a society, we have let them down."

As a way of sharing, she pointed out that Sunray participants, in all of the regions where they live, make a feast once a week for people in need. In Vermont they have also furnished food for the holidays and provided toys for children.

She sees a hopeful sign in the talk of some new business-minded people who mention the possibility of sharing profits with their employees, developing decent daycare centers at work, and other such programs, but so far thinks these have only had token application.

"Women have taken big steps in business," she said, "but too often in the process they've taken on the attitude of their oppressors . . . the nurturing aspect of women is held hostage to profit."

The concept of wholeness of vision, and the healing that results, is one Dhyani Ywahoo stresses. She sees a strengthening of the family unit as necessary for reinvigorating communities, and regards vital local communities as an essential foundation for a balanced society.

"People are lonely," she continued. "I believe we all need a focus, and some sort of spiritual practice. It is important to be able to talk with others about our inner vision."

Ywahoo explained that the traditional Cherokee national structure is based on ten clans, each with its own leader. The Sunray Meditation Society is established on this basis.

"We have ten regional councils," she said, "Each geographic region has an ongoing Peacekeeper Mission, and each town has its own council. There are 710 main trustees, one from each region, and they all get together once a year. There are also quarterly reports so that everyone knows what's going on."

The Peacekeeper mission and its study program is a part of the Sunray School of Sacred Studies. In the autumn and winter terms, there are two-day intensive weekends in each term and three monthly meetings thereafter. Multi-media materials are used in conjunction with the studies. A spring tour *intensive* with Dhyani Ywahoo is held at other regional councils and is available for those who have successfully completed the autumn or winter term of study. There was a summer program in 1988 in Vermont during July and August. This was attended by Native American and Buddhist teachers, as well as a special gathering of Native American Elders.

Weekly meditation meetings, to which visitors are invited, are also held in Vermont as well as in other parts of the United States, Canada and western Europe.

The teachings can neither be bought nor sold, but are to be considered a sacred gift to be received. In order to accept this gift, the student first makes an offering, and the Sunray Community responds through the sharing of its teachings and practices. Course donations are applied to the logistical and administrative costs, such as the protection of sacred places and the support of Native American Elders.

"We caretake each other," Ywahoo said. "All over the world what's needed is spiritual healing, and even if someone is sick, we use spiritual medicine. If there's no improvement we look for the best physician in that area, but we try spiritual medicine first."

"The teaching tradition was passed through our family," she continued. "We have a set of meditation and spiritual practices that are followed and that I was taught from early childhood. We're also recognized as a church by the IRS."

Meditation is used to achieve *stillness* of the mind, and concentration on breathing is an important aspect. The best times for meditation, according to Ywahoo, are from five to seven in the evening, eleven P.M. to one A.M., five to seven in the morning or eleven A.M. to one in the afternoon.

"Confidence," she said, "is very precious energy, and the stillness achieved through meditation can help us to recycle it. Our faults can be used as compost for the growth of better ideas."

Ywahoo said that for many people there is a deep resonance for Native American practices. Sunray is also a recognized center of Tibetan Buddhism.

"The teaching is the same," she said, "only the ceremonial forms are different."

"The world is a reflection of our thought, and we are its caretakers. Nothing should be wasted," Ywahoo continued. Becoming conscious of the dream is an important aspect of their practice. She also described a childhood memory that concerned the way her family separated all the fishbones at the table, carefully putting them aside into one pile so they could be put back into the river—to bring more fish.

"It's the same as giving seeds to the earth, and the earth giving back food for us to eat. It's an ongoing reciprocal process. It's rewarding to know that everything can be recycled."

She spoke about recycling in Vermont as one of the most profitable new directions that could be followed today. Discovering ways of solving this problem would be establishing a better relationship between ourselves and our Earth and is currently being considered at Sunray.

"Our breathing helps us to perceive the great circle of being. It is giving and receiving," she said, "exhaling and inhaling, and is the only certainty in this life. We need to acknowledge and use the beauty of breath."

"Women, as a rule, breathe far more shallowly than men," she continued. "They should feel the breath deeply through the belly, shallow breathing comes often from fear."

"We think women are empowered anyhow," she said. "We need to remove the veils from our eyes, but innately we **are** empowered. We need to place more focus on our own accomplishment, not in competition with the ideal, or with someone else's expectations for us, but on what we can do in our own lives."

She recalled a dream she had as a child of only five years. To her, it was a prophetic message about the nature of land use and development taking place today. "There were huge metal animals," she said, "and they were walking across the mountains, devouring the land."

Her recent book, *Voices of Our Ancestors,* is based upon her understanding of traditional Tsalagi teachings, instructional stories and games. Its intention is "to strengthen individuals' relationships with their families, communities, nations, and the land: the Earth herself."

"What is needed is spiritual healing," she said, "and there is something for all of us to do. As human beings we are all genetically related, and we need to ask ourselves, 'What do we want to happen? What is our ideal for our family, our town, our country, our planet?'"

"Working toward that end, the Cherokees have always told a story that illustrates the necessity and purpose of a good leader," she continued, getting up from her desk and acting out the motion involved.

"We see the good leader as a walking stick who helps us to travel over rough terrain," she said, her hand closed around the imaginary head of a cane, bending forward as though her weight was being supported, "but with a good leader it is always the citizens who guide, not the walking stick."

SISTER JANICE RYAN

I'm in the process of becoming a citizen of the planet," Sister Janice Ryan, president of Trinity College in Burlington, said quietly. "I'm very clear about that mandate in confronting the two choices ahead of us."

"We can continue in the overwhelmingly suicidal and divisive manner in which we are going, or we can truly develop a sense of hope and compassion in meeting the challenges of governing our planet."

She followed this sober pronouncement with a pragmatic observation that revealed the balance that is her striking characteristic.

"I also believe that you do what you can each day, and then get a good night's sleep."

Although the truth is simple, carrying out this maxim requires a faith of profound proportions, another of her attributes. While she spoke seriously of things that concerned her, she also laughed heartily and gave the impression of a predominantly happy, strong and enthusiastic person.

"Trinity College is sponsored by the Sisters of Mercy," she explained, "and they take three sacred vows: poverty, chastity, and obedience."

"I've added a fourth, a special commitment to the uneducated. We've made it our mission to use our resources here at Trinity so people can get their degrees, in spite of the time, or the money, they have to spend.

"We made this commitment in 1969, opened our Adult Continuing Education in 1972, followed this in 1979 by adding weekend college and in 1983 started our evening degree program. In 1988 we opened the doors of every program to make it a truly cross-over education. We now make it possible for students to put together a degree program based on the time they have.

"I am hopelessly fond of the 1,200 Trinity students," she continued. "Half are full-time, eighteen-year-old women, the other half are older women and men, part-time degree-seeking students who fit their classes into the kind of schedule they can work with.

"The core of it is affordability—access to education—and we've increased tuition aid to our students over four hundred percent."

A group of pictures, carefully framed and hung on a wall of her office, added color and imagery to the motivation one senses behind Sister Janice. At one end is a composite of three pencil portraits: Mahatma Ghandi, Martin Luther King and Dorothy Day. Next, an icon; a symbolic representation of Dorothy Day; beyond that, an exquisite, small, paper cutout of a landscape; then a dramatic black and white print of struggling figures; and finally, a composite of four pencil portraits of the four Sisters murdered in El Salvador several years ago.

She explained that the struggling figures related to the plight of blacks in South Africa, and she had taken the print from a newspaper.

"To me it represents the plight of people all over the world; I liked the way it symbolized this, and I had it framed."

The small landscape was a memento of the five weeks she spent last summer with a family in Bogota, Columbia. On the night before she was scheduled to leave, the husband failed to return home; the family was distraught because they had reason to believe that he now was among the *missing persons.*

It was about three in the morning, and while the night had been grueling, the hostess wanted Sister Janice to take back with her a reminder of the place and of their time together. She took scissors and construction paper and soon had cut and assembled the beautiful little landscape that was later framed and hung in a place of honor, with the other special pictures.

Her resumé includes positions of importance in national and state activities and reflects her overall interest in education, especially of people who need help. The positions include: co-chair of the Commission on New Initiatives, National Institute of Independent Colleges and Universities; member, Governor's Commission on Vermont's Future; executive committee, Campus Compact (A Coalition of College Presidents for Promotion of Public Service); chair, Federal Initiatives Task Force, Campus Compact; member, American Council on Education's Governmental Relations Commission; chair,

Association of Vermont Independent Colleges' Governmental Relations Committee; and chair, Vermont Developmental Disabilities Council.

The titles, like leaves on the surface of a swiftly moving stream, indicate velocity and direction of the water but little about its depth and source. The story of her life adds more.

"I was brought up on a farm off Route 36 in Fairfield, Vermont, the oldest of six; three girls and three boys. My mother and my father both came out of agriculture. My mother was Veronica Maloney, third-generation Irish from County Tipperary.

"I went to school in a one-room school house and was the only one in my grade for six years. I did a lot of tutoring, and I also read a lot."

In 1950 she was a freshman in high school, and the school bus system in the state was poorly developed. The custom was for some of the girls in rural communities to live away from home and attend school in the larger town where they boarded.

"This came about for me when my father met another farmer at a cow sale. The other farmer had five girls, and the two men spoke of the high school problem for their daughters. They agreed to send their girls to Burlington so they could become boarders at a private academy there, Mount St. Mary's.

"That's where I met the Sisters of Mercy. I entered the order after I graduated from high school in 1954."

Her introduction to Dorothy Day, the liberal Catholic theologian and newspaper editor, came through a high school great books course that introduced her to the world of ideas.

"I was fortunate to have an excellent education in high school," she added emphatically.

In the Mercy Order, the general practice was for the novitiate to have two years of college after high school and then work with a mentor for the next two years. From 1956 to 1966, she also taught elementary and junior high school in Burlington at the old Cathedral school, a Catholic parochial school with nine hundred students.

"Among the student body there was diversity in everything but color. Students came from all the different parishes in the county, from the very poor living nearby, to the well-to-do attending from other parishes."

In the summer of 1961, she was given a *little charge*. She was sent to a college in Minnesota to study mental retardation so she could return in the fall and take over the religious program concerned with this problem. In practical terms, it meant she would continue her regular teaching duties but could spend her time after school and her weekends on the other assignment. She had reservations, but obedience to the direction of her superiors in the order prevailed. The effect of this experience significantly shaped her future.

"The result of my immersion in working with children and youth with mental handicaps was that I came back and organized college students from UVM [the University of Vermont], St. Michaels, and Trinity College as teachers. It also raised new questions in my mind about what it means to be labeled, *mentally retarded.*"

She received her baccalaureate at Trinity College and then worked for an M.A. in special education at Boston University during the summers of 1963 to 1966.

Coming back to Trinity as a member of the faculty, she served as assistant professor of special education from August 1967 until 1974 and set up their teacher's education program. She also established and directed the Educational Media Center for Special Education Materials, established and directed the Diagnostic and Preschool Program for Handicapped Children, established and chaired the Special Education Teacher Education Program, and served as director of public relations and development.

"Dr. Marion McKee was the director of Child Development at the time, and we pooled our resources; the years between 1967 and 1974 were full of intense activity. We worked out a teacher's education program, got a preschool started, and the whole thing mushroomed. It led me to examine state laws regarding treatment of persons with mental retardation."

As a result of work done by Sister Janice and other concerned people, the legislature passed a law guaranteeing that every child and youth in the state would have access to free public education.

"My best teachers were always the children, the adults and the families I worked with. They taught me that anyone can learn if we keep working on an environment in which learning is possible and that what the environment can call forth from us is truly remarkable."

In 1974 Sister Janice asked for a leave from the faculty to become a legislative lobbyist for the Vermont Association for Retarded Citizens. She was also executive director of the Champlain Association for Retarded Citizens while she worked full time on the legislature.

"My main emphasis was to go to all the fourteen counties, giving training sessions, making these citizens come alive to others, making sure that the legislature knew they were there and understood the importance of their education.

"The real story is *power to the people.* This association doesn't have money to give out, but they do have dedicated, committed people who are willing to work hard."

In May 1979, Sister Janice was asked by the Trinity College Board of Trustees to come back as acting president of the college.

"I felt I had to do this since Trinity College is sponsored by the Sisters of Mercy. I could have said, 'No, I don't want to leave the Association of Retarded Citizens and would like to stay for at least another year,' but I felt the presidency was an obligation."

The experienced convinced her, however, of the importance of the post in widening the doors of education to more people. In January 1980, she applied to, and was appointed to, the permanent position of president.

Sister Janice Ryan thereupon resigned from all affiliations, national, regional and state, having to do with special education. She was convinced that her complete attention had to be focused on higher education. The time she spent at her new post only intensified her commitment to working for increased student and scholarship aid and Trinity College is now one of the state's leaders in providing a more universal educational delivery system.

Sister Janice pointed out that while the number of students attending college has increased, the amount of money going to the Vermont Student Assistance Corporation has not kept pace. The pool of funds for grants is also below that of ten years ago.

"If we looked at a graph from ten years ago, or even eight, grants, loans or work would balance out. But today, loans are now sixty percent of college costs, which means that when they walk across the stage to get their diploma, this debt dictates the kind of occupation graduates can choose."

She explained that if students graduate in May, the following April they're required to start on their loan repayment. This will be about $126 a month, and is added to other necessary expenses: car payment, rent, food and clothes.

"Why can't there be more creative ways for these loans to be paid back? Why can't there be a sliding scale, for instance, whereby what you're earning provides the base for what you pay back?"

"I'm an advocate at heart," she continued, "and during my eight years at Trinity College my advocacy has been to procure for students greater institutional accessibility and affordability. I firmly believe that if students are studying because they want to and going to the place they want to be, they will not drop out."

With no hesitation, Sister Janice summed up the substance of her belief and her work: "An educated citizenry is vital to maintaining our democracy. We need to examine our national priorities, and I believe that access to education is one of the most important."

ESTHER MUNROE SWIFT

"God wanted this house to live," Esther Munroe Swift said firmly, talking about the General Elias Stevens house in Royalton that she purchased in 1973. She spent several years on its restoration and, while a great deal of the work was done by her hands, she had help from family and friends.

"The original house was built in 1771," she continued. "It was burned in the Royalton Raid of 1780 and General Stevens, the owner, spent the winters of '80 and '81 cutting timbers to build the new house.

"We gutted the house after I bought it. It hadn't been lived in for thirty-seven years, with no care taken of it for long before that. It was also open season on the house: if anybody needed a building part—windows, siding or most anything else—they'd just come over and cart it away."

As a historian, as well as a librarian, Esther feels strongly about the importance of respecting and maintaining the evidence of our past as a means of ensuring the quality of our future.

Many things inside the old building had to be replaced, but other features had retained their integrity over the years. The east side of the house still has its original clapboard. There are also "tons" of slate on the roof purchased from a company in Fair Haven, and Esther has the original bill of sale. On the first floor is the small room that was part of the earliest house, the only segment left standing after the eighteenth-century fire.

"This was one of the important farms in this valley," she said, adding that Frederick Billings' parents had owned the adjoining farm.

"There were eleven other buildings on the place at one time, but they were gone when I bought it.

"God loved this house," she repeated. "It managed to hang on. That's why I wanted to see it live again, a reminder of the people who settled this valley."

An aspect of history in which Esther has both a personal as well as a professional interest is awareness of continuity.

"In 1771 my family came to Vermont," she said, explaining that ever since that time, the family lived in Berlin and Montpelier. Her youngest son is in Berlin on land that was part of the family's original homesite, and he has his own house restoration business. Her oldest son is operations chief for the Arabian American Oil Company and lives in Saudi Arabia with his wife and four children. He plans to retire before too many years to the General Stevens home and make this his family headquarters.

Esther observed that it was a family tradition to consider service within their community to be not only a privilege, but an obligation. The state, as well as the nation, are included in the Swift purview.

"To make a place for ourselves and to make a contribution has always been viewed as essential in our family. Using your own skills and caring about making things better," she added, "trying to keep this planet going."

Toward this end, she has developed and used varied talents of her own, both professionally and avocationally.

Presently the librarian of the Billings Farm and Museum, a project of the Woodstock Foundation, her charge is to focus primarily on the nineteenth-century agricultural and socio-economic history of Vermont. She is also Vermont chairperson of the United States Place-Name Commission, executive director of the University of Vermont Center for Vermont Studies, and for the past three years, she has served as one of the judges of the Vermont Historical Society's annual Edmunds Essay Contest.

Previously held positions included regional librarian of the Vermont Free Public Library Commission, vice-president and publications editor of the H.R. Hunting Company in Chicopee, Massachusetts, vice-president of the BroDart Company of Williamsport, Pennsylvania, and consultant to the United Nations Library, the U.S. Bureau of Library Services and the U.S. Information Service.

She is the author of: *The Brattleboro Retreat, 150 Years of Caring; The New Vermont Guide; West Springfield, Massachusetts, A Town History;* and *Vermont Place Names, Footprints in History.* Reflecting a different interest is her book, *Sprouts,* a comprehensive manual on growing organic sprouts, first published in 1974 and reprinted in English as well as in other languages.

Avocations include, but are not limited to, gardening, watercolor painting, rug braiding, computer programming, target practice, quilting, sewing, wood carving, sheep raising, and house restoration.

"I've always been in a hurry," she said, acknowledging the appropriateness of her married name.

As her service to the town, she is chairperson of the Board of Listers in Royalton; she is also their computer consultant and has written a program that does the calculations for reappraisals.

She was born in Montpelier, and her parents died before she was old enough to remember them. "I was raised by a bunch of Victorian aunts and uncles, the only child in sight—and I expect it shows."

Brought up in comfortable circumstances, and by people with high expectations for her future, she was never without good examples to follow, and failure at anything was not an acceptable option. In addition, she was the only youthful representative of this old Vermont family.

Sent to Northfield Academy in Massachusetts when she was eleven, Esther was the third generation of women in her family to attend. Later, she was the third generation of women in her family to matriculate at the University of Vermont, her great-grandmother having been one of the first women to graduate from the college. There could never have been a doubt in her mind about a tradition to uphold, and built into her training was the perception of independence as being—without question—a measure of character.

"All the people who were responsible for who I am lived long enough to see my development," she said, with a characteristically straightforward grin. A widow, with two small children to raise and old family friends—Pearl Buck, Robert Frost and Ralph Nading Hill—were strongly supportive.

One of the greatest influences on her life she attributes to her mother's youngest sister. "She was one of the first women executives of National Life. She worked for them for forty-eight years. Started as a secretary for just one summer and never got around to leaving the company until she was ready to retire."

If there's a vestige of indecision about anything in Esther Munroe Swift's makeup, it is kept well out of sight.

"I was brought up to see things as either black or white," she said, in her direct style, "to know exactly where the lines are drawn. Things are all right—or all wrong; there are no maybes.

"That's the way I brought my sons up, too. But there was also another thing I wanted them to understand, that no one is ever completely right in an argument. Sounds contradictory, but it isn't—think about it. World wars start at home; we have to learn to get along right where we are. My sons knew I would never negotiate between them in an argument, so they learned to settle disagreements between themselves."

Working at a full-time job as a state consultant, Esther had no hesitation about sending her boys off to a prep school when they were small.

"I was not going to raise latchkey kids; I thought they deserved better. We lived for our vacations together, and they came home weekends and holidays.

"We're all inveterate readers, so we talked books when we were together and traveled a lot during vacations. It must have worked; I observe them raising their own children in the same way."

After a serious injury in a riding accident when the children were young, Esther was told that a crucial operation, even if optimally successful, would permanently curtail most of her activities.

"They were literally trying to put the middle part of my body together again. It was an incredible reconstruction but now I'm able to do most of the things they said it would be impossible for me to ever do again."

She credits her eldest son with having started her rehabilitation. One of her hands was completely unusable, the other, while not quite as bad, had little maneuverability. "Alex was eight when he came in one day and asked for three dollars. I didn't ask why because I knew that boy; I knew there had to be a good reason.

"He came back with a tool that could be hooked on to my table and was used for putting fabric pieces together into strips for rug braiding. He figured this was something I could do that would develop strength and control in my hands, and it worked. I've been braiding rugs ever since and gradually learned to do almost everything else that was part of my life.

"There's no substitute for patience. You need it to learn how to do anything. It may take thousands of hours, but I don't care. The level of excellence you want to achieve takes time."

She remembers the way an uncle taught her to drive. "I've been driving since I was twelve, and I'm good," she said matter-of-factly. "Have never had a moving violation—or a standing one either—never put a mark on a car. When I was twelve my uncle took me out to the old Saratoga race track and made me back the car around the entire track four times without a mistake before he would let me drive it forward. It made me a darned good driver and a conscientious one."

This kind of patience and determination to learn well whatever it was she put her hand to seems to have been passed along.

She recalled an incident when one of her sons was in basic training. Asked if he knew how to shoot, he replied, "A little."

"Who taught you?" they asked.

"My mother," he answered.

"He was given one hundred rounds of ammunition," Swift said proudly. "He got one hundred bull's eyes.

"The uncle and aunts who raised me, the older generation, knew that what they made of me would be carried on to the next generation. They insisted on perseverance; they knew that's what makes us good at anything, and they wanted to see that carried on in the family."

Tradition, family, and the importance of continuity have much to do with who Esther Munroe Swift is. She wants her children and grandchildren to be part of a continuum, with no beginning and no end, and she sees this as more than individual pride in a family line; it is something that could anchor our society more realistically and make it less inclined to blow itself apart for trivial motives.

"This house is a restoration project," she said. "General Stevens outlived his children. His granddaughter, the only family member left, is elderly. We persuaded her that this would be our home and that we would keep the general's memory alive, always put flowers on his grave and a flag on Memorial Day. He represented our town in the legislature. He helped design what we have around us now, and we have an obligation to his memory."

EVANS
MODARAI

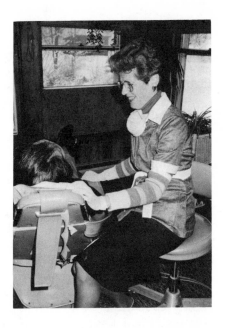

There are more and more female dentists," Evans Modarai said. "In Europe it's a common occupation for women, but I was the only girl in my dentistry class at Columbia, and it was lonesome."

A resident of Springfield since 1971, Evans was appointed to the board of trustees of the New England Dental Society a few years later, the first woman to serve on that board. She became its president after serving eight years as a board member.

"I was told that I was the only woman in the country to have had that position at the time," she said.

When the Modarais moved to Vermont, Evans was the only woman dentist practicing here. There are more now, but she wasn't certain about the exact figures: "Maybe twelve out of a total of one hundred or more practicing dentists."

She received her training at the Columbia University School of Dental and Oral Hygiene in New York and had a full scholarship for her work there, graduating in 1968. During the following year she completed work necessary for a master's degree in public health, also at Columbia.

"My son was the first child born in my class at dental school, and he became a sort of class mascot." A second child was born while Evans was in public health school. After finishing her studies, both she and her husband, Iraj, were anxious to move away from the city.

Evans explained that Iraj has relatives in Canada, where they settled when they left their home in Iran shortly before the Shah fell. Her father's family was Pennsylvania Dutch, and she was attracted to that area. "So we compromised on Vermont. I think it was the birch trees that did it."

They moved to Springfield because the machine tool industry was vigorous then and drew engineers and their families from all over the world. "Having come from New York, we liked the idea of an international community," she said.

Directions given over the phone for reaching her office were explicit: "It's a big brown house among five family houses on the old Chester Road. If you pass Baker's Fabrics, you've gone too far."

Following instructions to the letter, I passed Baker's Fabrics, and went too far, but redirected myself easily and found the house.

The entrance was through an enclosed porch to a reception room that undoubtedly had served as the former tenant's living room. The usual dental reception room furnishings were enhanced by a large white teddy bear waiting astride a hobby horse, and an old-fashioned child's school desk with papers and crayons invitingly placed.

Evans Modarai appeared soon after I arrived. Of medium height, slender, and very erect, she swims, plays tennis and walks the 1½ miles to work every day. She combined a cordial smile with a brisk, no-nonsense manner.

I was invited to wait briefly while she finished work in progress and was then joined by her husband, who suggested we have coffee while we waited for her. This turned out to be the only interview that included a spouse for the entire time, and I began with misgivings. My reservations were soon dispelled as I realized that Iraj Modarai, a practicing pediatrician, did not diffuse the focus of attention from his wife, and I sensed a purely supportive interest as his reason for being there.

Iraj poured coffee, and when Evans joined us she pulled up a chair and sat across the table next to him. Facing us was a bay window overlooking a pleasant backyard bounded by a small, swift river. Evans' two dental offices were just beyond, also looking out over the yard.

"Iraj is very sympathetic," she said. "He's a marvelous cook, and also enjoys sewing. What's more, he was all trained before I married him."

"When she was president of the New England Dental Society," he added, "I was like the wife at the conventions we attended."

"I was raised in the Bahai religion," he said. "Our religion emphasizes that women are the first teachers of our children and that it's of the greatest consequence that they be well-educated. The women in my family were always indpendent and well-educated."

During the interview, both Modarais referred often to the importance of a good education for all children. Both feel this could solve many problems confronting us today; despair, violence, and the inability of many young people to feel a part of anything, even of their own community.

"There are many talented children who can't afford to go on to college," Evans said vehemently. "It should be free to anyone with the ability and the desire, and it would certainly be a good investment in developing better values in this country."

She was born in Brooklyn, New York. Her father was a physician and her brother also became one. Her own vocation came about as a natural flow of circumstances, but "not necessarily in a straight line."

"I started as a chemistry major at Connecticut College, and since their chemistry department wasn't very good I switched to history."

After graduation, however, she worked in several hospitals as a lab technician and was later employed at the Rockefeller Institute.

"I kept taking courses because my father really pushed them. He always said, 'You either regress or progress, so you must keep going to school.' "

And to this day, Evans and her husband continue going to school, generally at night. "Currently, I teach a fitness program, and I also take one. We've taken all kinds of courses, that's our recreation. Iraj and I just finished studying computer. He needs it for his medical practice and I studied it just for fun. We're not super-achievers, but we both believe in education."

After receiving her college degree, Evans attended both Brooklyn and Hunter Colleges at night. "I took biology, chemistry and physics courses," she said, "and worked at my job during the day."

She met and married Iraj Modarai, who urged her to make up her mind about her career. "Either go into medicine, or into dentistry," he said.

Evans explained why she didn't want to go into medicine: "There were too many medicine men around me—my father, my brother and my husband. Both my father and my husband made house calls and I saw what a drain that was. My husband still makes them, and my father made them up until the day he died."

Her decision was to go into dentistry, and after an initial interview she was offered a full scholarship at Columbia's Dental College.

"My teachers were all gentlemen to the core," she continued. "Couldn't have been nicer. I tried to fit in and I did."

"I loved Columbia," she added. "I also loved working at the Rockefeller Institute. And if there's a problem with being female I haven't seen it."

Evans' circumstances were unquestionably privileged, not only financially but educationally. She had the additional bonus of a father who believed strongly, not only in the value of a general education for his daughter but also in her capability for excelling in the sciences. She seems to have been raised with unquestioned confidence in her own proficiency as well as in her ability to use it in competition with primarily male peers.

Her mother had the luxury of free time and chose to fill it with extensive volunteer work. This was a commitment that she passed along to her daughter.

"I was brought up to believe that this was part of everyone's responsibility to their community," Evans said, and described her mother as a Vassar graduate who volunteered to go to Europe during the First World War. "Since then she's been a 'gray lady' in hospital auxiliaries for years. She's now ninety-seven and still going strong."

Evans has an identical twin sister, but their educational paths as well as their lives have been different. They attended Connecticut College together but her twin's strongest interest was tennis. "She's now teaching tennis; that's her major interest. I did it with science because it came naturally to me."

When the Modarais moved to Springfield and Evans started her practice, she always had someone at home to help with the children even though she ended her working day at three o'clock. Her son was then four, and her daughter one. Both children are now in college.

"We were working in Chester at first, and it was twenty minutes away from where we lived. If an emergency came up we couldn't be there immediately, but as the kids were growing up we always had a mature adult in the house."

Helping other women go out and make better lives for themselves is important to Evans. She belongs to the Business and Professional Women's Club in Springfield, and is enthusiastic about projects undertaken by the club that have as their goal helping other women gain more independence. She's interested in discovering ways to give moral support to women with talents so they're not afraid to use them.

"I'd like to see more social concern shown within the community. Helping hands not free handouts. Helping with groups like New Beginnings, and Battered Women. Better provisions for child care are also important."

About Springfield, the town they chose to spend their lives in, she said: "It used to have music and theaters, but when jobs were lost in the machine industry, the higher echelon people left, the culture and the vitality of the place went down, and no one knew how to fight it.

"In Springfield now there's a lack of education, lack of jobs, and not enough regard for the environment. There's also a lot of waste, but then, these things are true all over the world. Still, we can do more to improve ourselves here than in a big city; you get heard more."

"Yes, I'm satisified that we came here, and I'm satisfied to stay."

About her own profession, she's confident that everything considered, dentistry is a good vocation for women.

"There are certain beliefs about women in this practice, whether they're true or not. There's the perception that women have smaller hands and are gentler than men. Also, that they're more understanding with people who're afraid. But I know a lot of male dentists who are gentle and also understanding. It's hard to make generalizations about these things."

And while Evans recalled no hardships in the pursuit of her education based solely on gender she did express dissatisfaction with the relatively small number of women who have elected this profession.

"It's a lonely world for a woman; we perceive things differently from men. At meetings and things like that I'd like to have more women to talk with about our practice. Camaraderie is missing because there aren't enough of us—but that's changing."

ARTS

MICHELLE HOLZAPFEL

*T*he realm of woodturning has been dominated by a specific group of people. White, middle-class males have written its history, and all that's been said, it would seem, has been said by them. But I think there's a vast amount more to be said!"

Michelle Holzapfel is a woodturner. She's now thirty-six and in a position to spend less time worrying about "getting by" and more time to concentrate on her work. Her reputation is growing and her pieces are represented in many corporate and private collections, and in galleries.

She explained that in woodturning the dominant mystique has been centered on the technical skill required to turn a thin-walled, hollow vessel: "For years this has seemed to be the essense of what wood-turning is all about, the peak of its virtuousity, but to me this went against the grain. It leaves no room for heft, or weight, or substance.

"My pieces are not hollow, they're heavy; they also have surface carving which takes a lot of effort, but to me the surface has meaning.

"I also push domestic images, and they've not been considered as valuable, not as worthy to be made into art; but I think there are all kinds of things that can be said in art. I believe there's another kind of reality that deserves exposure."

She smiled as she continued: "The problem ten years ago was making a living; it was hand to mouth in the beginning, but both David and I are definitely established now. People come to us and want work, they talk about investment and resale value. It's all part

of the game. It does give me pleasure, though, when people understand and admire my work."

Michelle and David Holzapfel live in Marlboro. They have two sons,
Simon, sixteen, and Forrest, fourteen. Their home and the shop where
they both work in wood is on Route 9, not far from the entrance to
Marlboro College, the school they attended some years ago. They call
their shop "Applewoods," a translation of their German name. While
they occasionally collaborate on a wood piece, their personal styles
are distinct.

Michelle works with a metalworker's lathe that her father adapted
for her use, which makes the work less stressful than would be the
case with a regular wood-turning lathe. After the pieces have been
more or less worked out with the lathe, the finishing process is done
with gouges, sanding drums and burrs. Endless experimentation has
marked her progress from basic wooden vessels to still lifes, with
fruit, vegetables, dishes, trays, pastries and breads; to her more recent
work that departs from the strictly realistic; to pieces involving fantasy
and whimsicality.

"Woodturning and woodworking are male-dominated professions," Michelle continued. "There's kind of a locker room attitude,
at craft fairs or at exhibits; when the men were talking shop, they
often made me feel left out. But my husband and friends didn't have
this kind of attitude.

"There are always some people who'll accept you, whoever you
are, but for a woman it takes more work, and there continues to
be a certain amount of self-promotion one has to do. There's also
the tendency for a woman's work not to be taken as seriously as a
man's.

"Another thing that's important to me is being able to work at
home. I have a work existence and a home existence together; they're
not two separate lives, and I think that's wonderful. Sometimes it
seems a little chopped up, between the kids, their school, our home
and our economic realities. But this is what my life is, it's what I've
chosen and it's what I want.

"My basic feeling is that the home is supremely important: it's
where everyone comes from and everyone goes to, but it's been triv-
ialized by television and the other media. The hearth used to be
worshipped, and it stood for a great deal. From earliest times the first
altars were hearths; the economy was centered in the home, and it's
still an important part of where people are."

She spoke of the industrial revolution and the impact it had: taking
women out of their homes and putting them into different living
situations where they lost their support system.

"We're clearly moving into a post-industrial society now, and the ones that lost most then—women, older people and children—all want to have a role in saying what's going to happen now."

"The community is also important to me," she continued. "It's a way of sustaining an environment that one can work in. Every time there's a growth spurt here in Marlboro, everyone is concerned about the changes it will make in our lives."

She attributes the several years she spent on the school board in Marlboro with teaching her about politics in microcosm: dealing with groups of different people, and with other people's money and children. It also concerns her that often it's a case of two worlds meeting in conflict: the old, rural Vermonters and their values, against the young couples with "two kids who've just moved up," and want lots of different things for their children.

"I realize that I've been a part of the change. But I sometimes marvel at the way we've displaced a whole way of living that is perfectly valid."

About the place she was raised in northern Rhode Island she said: "It's built up now, but it used to be lovely." Her own parents grew up during the depression in Winsockett, a Connecticut mill town. Because of a predominantly French-Canadian population it was called "Little Quebec." After they were married, her parents bought an old house with no water or electricity in a nearby rural area, and they made improvements as they were able. It was what they could afford at the time, and they wanted their children to grow up in better surroundings than were provided by the mill town.

"They wanted us to have a different chance," Michelle said. "They were constantly drilling us to study hard and to read. There were always lots of books and magazines around; they gave us good tools for living. They were like early hippies in a way."

She maintains that drawing was always important to her, and from her earliest years she's been interested in making art. Her situation in school was unusual: a first grade teacher was also her second and eighth-grade teacher, and in high school her art teacher. "Mrs. Blake was a mentor for me. She was always interested in my work and I'm still in touch with her."

Doing woodblocks for a printmaking class in high school was her introduction to carving wood. "In retrospect it was like carving in low relief, and I'm glad I experienced hand carving; it gave me a feel for the wood. You have to understand the grain, feel it in order to work with it. I also made some money carving signs."

"My father was a tool and die maker," she recalled. "It's a demanding craft, but he was definitely a blue-collar worker.

"I was the third of six kids, five girls and one boy; and he was one of the youngest."

"My father had a workshop in the basement with all his tools, and he also did plumbing, electrical work and carpentry. I helped a lot and I also learned a lot. Trying to be like a boy for him developed the male part of my personality. That's been the motif in many women's lives—the work of pleasing one's father; we have instant acceptance from our mother, but with a father it's different."

She laughed, without too much irony, as she continued: "Father tells me now to come to him if I need any help with a project, but he passed along the sense of stewardship to my younger brother. Tells me that if anything happens to him I can always go to my brother for help. He doesn't realize, or accept, the mastery I have over the tools I use."

There was a pause before she added softly: "Still, working with him empowered me."

"Also, having kids of my own has taught me what a good mother mine was," she continued. "She was more of an artist than my father, but with six kids she was always busy. There's a story in my family about the time I was two, and drawing on a wall with my crayons; but when my mother found me she didn't get mad, she gave me some paper to use instead."

A scholarship to Marlboro College was Michelle's first exposure to a different world. Many of her classmates were from wealthy families, and their outlook on life was far more relaxed than hers. Formerly a serious student and valedictorian of her high school class, she eased up a bit on herself in college and developed a different perspective.

During her two years at Marlboro she took art classes as well as science. "I was also interested in biology and math, but it's hard to combine them, especially for women; hard to find a vehicle. The teachers and the guidance counselor were steering me to become an art teacher instead of a biologist."

She also did the cooking for the Grazers (a student vegetarian group), and there was something about this that appealed to her. But she didn't get her bachelor's degree, and that was hard on her parents.

"College was a dream for them, but to their credit they didn't make it hard on me. Now I understand how they must have felt."

Michelle met David during her second year at college and they started traveling together. Six months were spent in Rome, and Michelle made lots of drawings, visited many museums and became pregnant.

"At the time it was kind of a shock. I was twenty when Simon was born. I really didn't know what I wanted to do, and all my friends were going on to graduate school. But there's nothing like four or five years of changing diapers to teach discipline.

"Now I'm about to begin doing my best work. It's been an apprenticeship up to now, refining my skills, finding out what I really wanted. When I first started turning I did just vases and bowls for four or five years. This is what woodturners do before making a personal statement. Now I'm ready to express stronger personal feelings in my work.

"I can't have the wisdom of a sixty-year-old when I'm only a thirty-six-year-old. I see young artists achieving instant fame, and I don't understand where society places its values. I don't know what to think of the current art scene, it's very confusing.

"A ceramist once asked me, 'Does it ever bother you that people consider your work decorative?' This irritates me, although it's part of the times we live in. Crafts are seen as sort of an illegitimate style. People want handmade things because there are so many disposables around. Surely art has something to do with craft as well as with expression."

A small woman with tight curly hair framing her face and an impish expression, she consistently spoke with humor and deliberation about her life and her work.

"Success is such a relative thing. I used to think how nice it would be to have an article about what I was doing in *Fine Woodworking*, and then it happened. My work also started selling well; there were other articles about it, and all of a sudden it began to seem that I was successful at it, but there was really no change in the way I felt.

"I always try to define things, get to the bottom of the reason for doing things, and I realized that success doesn't mean that much. So I've just stopped thinking about it."

CLAIRE VAN VLIET

*T*here's no doubt about the difficulty for women in art; everybody has their own list of slights, and opportunities missed. You can dwell on them, or move on past," said Claire Van Vliet.

Claire is an artist, the owner and operator of Janus Press. As a limited-edition bookmaker, she is one of those small, dedicated publishers who are phenomena in a world where the printed word is as ubiquitous as dust in a gypsum plant. She lives and works in a remote section of Vermont's Northeast Kingdom. Her reputation, however, extends far beyond the borders of the state.

"I make my living from selling my work," she said. "My house was built from the sale of my books and my prints. Over the years I've slowly developed a number of collectors who pretty much buy everything I do. They're standing-order patrons, and they've given me a base of security that's grown steadily."

The Janus Press has traveled with her around the country since its beginning in Monterey, California, in 1955, when it was only a couple of portable boxes of type. A Vandercook letterpress was added when she moved to Vermont and gave it a permanent home. She has since added two other presses.

A mischievous smile accompanied her statement that: "Janus Press is now thirty-three years old, I am fifty-five, and the year is 1988. Giving significance to those numbers is totally frivolous, but it's kind of fun to point it out."

"Once I was in charge of my own life, I've pretty much stayed in one place," she added, and offered her rationale for moving to this out-of-the-way corner of Vermont in 1966, with her second husband, Michael Boylen, a glass blower and ceramist. "I'm a very conservative type of person, and I can't deal with fast change. We didn't have much money to spend on a home and and we weren't looking for Nirvana or the perfect social community. We wanted a quiet place where we could work and one that we could afford.

"Another reason was the clouds; I wanted to feel that I was in essence touching the sky. I wanted a rising landscape and a full day of sun—sunrise as well as sunset. When we decided to settle in Vermont that was one reason not to settle in the southern part where the valleys are steeper, the clouds low to the hills, and the days cut off earlier."

Claire explained that Janus, for whom the press was named, was an ancient Roman god of the rising and the setting sun. During the Renaissance he stood for balance, because of his ability to look both forward and backward. The name had particular meaning for her because of her belief in a necessary balance between the many aspects involved in the books she prints; not only the text and the illustrations, but the paper, the binding, the typography, even the weight and feel of a book.

The back of her 2½-story house is oriented towards the south, the direction one looks from the windows of her studio, or from the downstairs living-kitchen area, across a twenty acre field sloping upward to meet the sky. The horizon lies on a diagonal across the view.

Sun, clouds, and colorful sky changes have furnished inspiration for many of her drawings and watercolor paintings. More recent are the pulp paintings, a process that involves placing the colors for creating the image directly into the pulp as the paper is being made.

One of the results of this process is *Aura*, with text by Hayden Carruth and folded pulp paperwork landscapes by Claire, published in an edition of fifty, with grant assistance from the National Endowment for the Arts.

"I'm mainly interested in books that can't be printed in the usual way," she said. "The books are really hand held art, which is an art form in itself."

Claire has always worked, and continues to work, in other media, but the art of fine-book making forms the core of her professional life. Some of the texts have been illustrated with her own lithography, etchings, or paintings, and others are collaborations with different artists and writers. Editions range from about five to five hundred, some of which are out of print today and highly prized as collector's items. Roughly one third of her patrons are book dealers, one third museums and other institutions, and one third private collectors. Her paintings are handled by galleries in New York and Philadelphia.

She speaks positively about the technical constraints of printing.

"I like a medium that limits you, things that maximize the limitations like wood cuts or lithography. This presents a certain kind of challenge. I also like the medium to have a strong voice of its own."

She is clear about her reasons for working on her own: "If I work for somebody else, I have to work on things that are not my decision. My mind moves slowly in developing ideas, and ideas need time to grow. I must have time for the book to make itself clear to me. I may start with an idea, but it has to be developed with my hands as well as my eye."

Claire's attitude towards making books is characteristically straightforward. "I like printmaking, and I like reading. Books are magical: so much in such a small space; but they don't overwhelm you, you're always in charge. You can hold them in your hands while you're reading or looking at them, and you can put them away when you're finished."

Her route to Vermont was indirect. Born in Ottawa in 1933, her father was a flier with the Royal Canadian Air Force until his death when she was nine, and she lost her mother when she was thirteen. The children, two girls and a boy, were separated. Claire was sent to an aunt in California.

"As a child we had moved every year," she recalled. "I went to a variety of schools in many different countries."

San Diego high school was her first experience in spending more than one year at the same school. She was there for two years, graduated at fifteen, and followed up by graduating from San Diego College at eighteen. She received her master of fine arts degree from Claremont Graduate School when she was twenty.

"I've basically been self-supporting since I was fifteen," she said. She started after high school as a live-in mother's helper, working for many families, and learning different ways of doing things. To this experience she attributes some of the ease with which she combines the details of bookmaking, printing, painting, housekeeping, cooking and gardening, all of which she does well.

During college Claire never worked less than forty hours a week in addition to her school work. "I was probably better off working hard," she said. "I didn't have to be a paper tiger, just a tiger. It gave me a strong sense of knowing that if I was going to rely on anyone, it had to be me."

There was poignancy in her next observation that she loved to dance, but hadn't had much of an opportunity. "I went to my first dance when I was twenty-nine."

Soon after graduate school she married her first husband, an expert on Russian intelligence with the U.S. Army. Joining him in Germany, she was there for three years, long enough to be convinced that the marriage wasn't working. During this period she also started an apprenticeship as a hand compositor with a German printer.

"It was pretty disciplined and boring," she said. "You start at the bottom: clean the shop, distribute the type, and put it away after they've used it, but you learn."

She came back to the United States in December 1957 and tried to get a job in a distinguished printing house in New York City, but the international Typographer's Union was opposed to women compositors.

"Women were not allowed to be hand compositors," she said, "we were only allowed to proofread."

Discovering that the union was also strong in San Francisco, another place she had been considering, she contacted John Anderson, head of the Pickering Press in Philadelphia, a non-union shop, and "He hired me," she said, "but then he was a maverick."

She learned more about letterpress printing and typography and worked under Anderson for two years until he moved from the city. After teaching at the Philadelphia School of Art, Claire spent a year at the University of Wisconsin and then moved to Vermont.

Between 1962 and 1973, Claire made several trips to Denmark and Norway to work in the lithographic workshops of two publishers, one in Copenhagen and the other in Oslo, and made a series of illustrations for the work of Franz Kafka, the Austrian novelist.

As an artist working at home and devising her own hours, she explained that her day is generally divided into three parts; one third on work related to the books, one third with her art, and one third on records and housekeeping projects.

"I like housework," she said, "that's why I made a house that's easy to keep; otherwise, a lot of times you're working against yourself and that's not conducive to the flow of work. I'm not poison clean but I do need visual serenity."

And even though there's a great deal going on inside it, the house projects a sense of tranquility. White plaster walls, honey colored wood floors, dark beams, with colors used primarily as accents; the clear blue cover of a cushion, a translucent piece of violet glass, or a gray green afghan she has knitted.

This house was planned specifically around her work. There is ample studio space, as well as room for her three presses and the many cases of type she has managed to find over the years. There's space for deskwork, with file cabinets and book shelves containing most of her printed editions, as well as a room where she makes paper, and also an area upstairs for book binding.

Since she lives in a relatively isolated area, Claire combines the solitude necessary for creative work with the stimulation provided by the people who seek her out. Two spare bedrooms are frequently used by artist collaborators, friends and apprentices.

Claire creates an impression of control and self-containment, but one senses an undercurrent of excitement. In a superficial encounter, she might seem stern, somewhat wary of revealing herself, but a more than casual aquaintance belies this impression. An infectious, spontaneous laugh also indicated an unguarded generosity, a glimpse through the armor that protects a sensitivity laced with intensity and compassion.

"My view of what will affect social change is the work each of us does by ourselves," Claire said. "The only one you're in charge of is yourself, and that's your first responsibility.

"As a woman you have to concentrate on the fact that it's the work itself that's interesting to you. And you have to be realistic in your expectations.

"There were many women artists throughout history, but their names were deleted long ago—the history books weren't written by women and may never be. We live in a patriarchal society shored up by moral law, but I believe we have to accept this reality and not waste our energies."

But goals are never achieved without payment of some kind. The very independence Claire has struggled to sustain creates difficulties in sharing her life with another person. She regrets this, but has accepted those aspects of her life and her work that are the most necessary.

Wrapping up her attitude towards living, combining all the contradictory and potentially exhausting details that are part of putting a productive life together, she said: "I've long since stopped worrying about what I'm going to do each day. I've decided instead that if I put in my hours it doesn't make any difference. My work is my life and my work is always involved with self-realization."

DOTTIE BROWN

Dottie Brown's gift for fiddling is matched by a gift for living; there's always been interaction between the two. Ideally, it may be the way talent develops best, with the strength, humor, and patience gained through living translated back again into a form of expression.

"A fiddle and a violin are the same but the music is different. I like classical music, but we were poor and that takes training," Dottie said.

"I came up third at the National Fiddler's Contest in Montpelier a year or so ago, won fifty dollars, and wanted to go again this year but I couldn't make it. I've played a lot for squares and bar dances for thirty years."

"My grandfather was a fiddler too. He lived here in Bristol on North Street and I'd go up to his house after school and he'd teach me. He always told me if I learned to play better on the fiddle he'd leave me his fiddle—he did too."

She described her grandfather as having one leg four inches shorter than the other. He figured a way of raising the short one by building a platform fitted onto the bottom of his shoe.

"My grandfather was Nelson Santaw," she said with pride. "He used to say, 'We're lean and we're poor—but we're good.'

" 'Wake up and learn to play,' he'd say. Started me out on *Go Tell Aunt Lucy—The Old Gray Goose Is Dead*. I scratched away at that, played and played until I learned it, and then he started me on *Red Wing*.

"When I was eleven, almost twelve, I earned my first two dollars playin' a fiddle at a kitchen tonk," she recalled, explaining that this was a gathering held at some neighbor's house for dancing.

"The rugs would be rolled back and a fiddler would set in the doorway between the kitchen and the dining room, everybody else would dance. There was lots of dancin'—lots of hard cider too.

"The old gentleman that was supposed to fiddle passed out from too much cider, so they put me in his place. I can't play but three songs, I told 'em, but the dancers said, 'That don't matter, just keep playin' 'em, so I did."

Many years later, and with a greatly expanded repertoire, Dottie Brown is still fiddling. She was third at the National Old Time Fiddler's Contest in Montpelier, and at the Vermont Bicentennial she carried off a silver cup and a pewter emblem, as well as a first at the Fort Ticonderoga Bicentennial. Since then there have been three trophies at the Addison County Field Days. She also stays in touch with other musicians around the state and is included in many performances and contests.

She's active in the Champlain Valley Fiddle Club, and also plays for dancing, Christmas parties and other programs. She plays regularly at the Porter Nursing Home's Project Independence.

"We go up once a month, play in the hospital in the forenoon and in the nursing home after. Then they give us a nice lunch.

"It's very rewarding when you go to nursing homes. People hear us play the old songs and before long the tears are comin'. Before long, you've got some comin' too.

"I was born on March 31, 1911, and I always spend that day in Richmond," she said. "Mother had two birth certificates for me, one from Jericho and one from Richmond because the building with the records was burned out. But I always thought the Richmond one was right.

"Mother was born in New Haven; we were all born in Vermont but we've got quite a lot of Indian blood—Blackfoot tribe from somewhere in Canada. She and my father moved here to Bristol so he could work on the farms. He worked as a foreman for the Bartlett tree service some of the time and I always went to school right here.

"I've lived in Bristol all my life, all but eight or nine years of it. I have twenty-one great grandchildren, thirty-one grandchildren and ten children—and it's kept me out of mischief," Dottie said with an expression on her face that appeared stern until it reached her eyes.

Her store of memories is vivid and chronicles a way of living in Vermont that is disappearing. Her eyes sparkled as she described a particularly fond recollection, playing with the singer Cecile Le Joy.

"She was brunette, very beautiful and had a lovely voice. She weighed five hundred pounds, and it took fourteen yards of cloth to make her a dress. Her favorite was a soft pink one, with ruffles."

Dottie described the way a place was made for Le Joy to sit securely when she sang for a dance. The men would lay heavy planks across two strong saw horses and test it carefully to be sure it could hold up.

"Everybody loved her, they used to haul her onto the back of a truck just to take her swimming in the summertime," she added, shaking her head and repeating, almost in disbelief, "She was so beautiful—and died when she was only forty of heart failure."

For years Dottie played with two groups: The Warmovers, and the Roadrunners. "These were the two bands we had," she said, explaining that the name for the Warmovers came from their guarantee that "if the audience don't like somethin' we play, they can throw it back in the pot and we'll warm it up again."

"I'll get my scrapbook and show you some of my things," she said, hastening into the bedroom and returning with an album bulging with newspaper clippings, photographs, programs, awards and citations all connected with her performances over the years.

I visited Dottie Brown in the trailer park where she and her husband lived for fifteen years, until his death two months before.

"We sold our old house and bought a trailer. The old house needed too much work and we couldn't afford it. We sold it and bought a trailer—put the extra money into a burial fund." After her husband's heart attack they moved to the smaller trailer, comfortable and compact, where she lives now.

"Carl Lathrop owns this trailer and he's puttin' a new rug and a new sink in here. The rent's only $105. We couldn't afford $310 after Social Security for the other one."

We sat talking in the living room, Dottie opposite me on a chair next to the television set. She wore a cream-colored pants suit with a lacy top and sensible brown shoes with a good sole. She explained that the shoes were necessary since a freak accident she had a while back. "I broke both my wrists pickin' dandelions. Passed right out when I got to my neighbor's door. I had on my sneakers and slipped on the wet grass."

Leaning over her scrapbook she carefully pulled out a sheet of paper and read aloud the poem written on it. Composed by a friend, it was dedicated to her late husband. Nearing the end, as she brushed some tears from her cheeks, she said simply: "Livin' with somebody for sixty years—I haven't got over it yet."

But Dottie Brown is not one to linger long with sadness. As music is to be played, so life is to be lived, the flow of it sustained, so she went on to other things.

Dottie's hair is short and wavy around her weathered face, and her strong hands rested quietly in her lap until needed to emphasize a point. Her manner and gestures are vigorous, and she's accustomed to being with people. She enjoys an exchange of stories.

"Most of life was good—but it was hard," she said. "Had seven children before I got a washer. Had one where the kids spelled each other turning the crank, and the next one ran off a tractor.

"We raised our children up on the old Neil Farm, and those were the best days. Nine children around the table, eleven in all counting the two adults. We raised carrots and potatoes and had meat once a week. Lots of vegetables—that's how we lived. We always had a good garden. We'd buy fifty chickens to raise, can half and have the other for fresh meat.

"I used to smoke a pipe when I was pregnant, and I always stopped after they were born." Dottie chuckled before she added, "I guess that was instead of pickles and ice cream. I used to smoke and play my fiddle."

There wasn't much money for clothes and Dottie remembers going barefoot in summer. "I liked it better that way and it'd save money for the children's clothes later," she added, explaining that each child would have a new pair of forty-cent sneakers every year. Snow suits, another highly important item, were made from old sweaters.

"We'd put their feet through the sleeves and tie them around the waist. They were like overshoes, with socks and shoes underneath. They picked up ice balls on the feet, but their toes inside stayed warm.

"We used to take cigar boxes and put screws in, put wires across and tune 'em up so the kids would have their own instruments," she said.

Raised at a time remote from today's consumer society, Dottie doesn't put much emphasis on what more things add to life.

"We didn't have running water, but we lived. Had a radio, the old organ, and the kids would sing," she continued. "We'd go fishin'— we had good times. Them was fun days! Today kids have to have computers for Christmas, and sixty-dollar jeans."

"One Christmas, we had three kids and only one dollar to spend", she added. "Got a little tea set for the girl, fifteen cents for the set, with tiny little cups and saucers. We got caterpillar tractors for the boys, they was little and cheap. We made popcorn, and I made 'em each a bean bag, and they had a good Christmas."

She remembered that her husband was firm with the children. "He was harsh with them, just one whack with the razor strop, or mostly a shingle with a handle—and they understood. He was harsh but a good man," she said.

Dottie's own father died young. "He was one of the five men who died, out of the twenty-seven who used to meet in the back room of the drug store to play cards. They'd all chip in to buy a bottle of pure alcohol, but this time it turned out to be wood alcohol.

"They put the druggist who sold them the alcohol into prison for a year, but it was a mistake, not intentional on his part."

Dottie lived in the druggist's house with his wife while he was in prison because her own mother worked out during the week. "Mother had a place upstairs over the harness shop. She had to get out real early because she worked in the box mill until it burned. Mostly women worked there, and she'd bring home ten dollars a week."

"I was with my mother on the weekends, and with Mamie Bisbee during the week," she said, adding, "I used to brush her beautiful gray hair every night. She was an evangelist."

Dottie stayed at the Bisbee house from the time she was five until she was twelve years old and her memories of Mamie Bisbee are graphic. "She had toast, an apple and strong black tea every morning. She made a pot of black tea early, heated it up and drank it all the rest of the day.

"Mamie Bisbee had a retarded son and made a special kind of bird soup for her boy to eat. She gave me and my brother five cents a head for every bird we brought her. There were always lots of little birds on the manure pile and we'd use a bent pin with a little bread on it to catch them. They'd eat it, swallow the pin and then we'd stomp them. She never knew how we caught 'em."

"It sounds awful now, but we'd get a nickel every time," she said with a hearty grimace. "In those days that was quite a lot of money."

Dottie described the time she and her family lived back in Hillsboro, "Ole Ireland they called it." Her stepfather did logging there for a lumber company in Bristol.

"It was beautiful back in there, big beech trees and a great big rock. I remember sittin' on it while I was waitin' for the school bus. It was three miles from where we lived, and in winter I'd get home in the dark—slide down on my sled in the mornin' but I had to drag it all the way back up in the afternoon."

The school bus was a horse and wagon: "It took two horses to pull, and we kids sat in the back on two planks set up on each side. Lordy, was it cold!"

Another time, they lived in a hollow down by the river and her mother had to leave the house by five every morning to go to work.

"She did laundry for the barber shop, and the drug store, and she washed the heavy underwear for the farm workers on the Browley farm. It was waffle-wear underwear she washed for them, and boy were they dirty! She'd get three dollars a basket. She'd sponge her bread in the morning before she went to work and bake at night with a woodstove. But she was healthy and strong! The doctor took a tumor off the back of her neck right on the kitchen table. Fern Chadwick give her ether. Mother married three times and was eighty-six when she died."

Music was part of her lineage. "There were four in my family, one boy and three girls, and they all made some kind of music. My mother's grandpa had twelve kids, six boys and six girls, and they all played instruments. My mother used to dance, and play the harmonica."

Like her mother, Dottie is healthy and strong. A hernia keeps her from driving the car these days, but doesn't keep her from getting around on a three-wheeled bike that had a motor on it before the troopers made her take it off.

" 'Hot Rod Dot' they called me. I'm never unhappy and I like to go. I'm seventy-seven but who wants to act like seventy-seven? As long as I can crawl, I'm goin' to keep doin' things!"

GLADYS OGDEN (PEN) DIMOCK

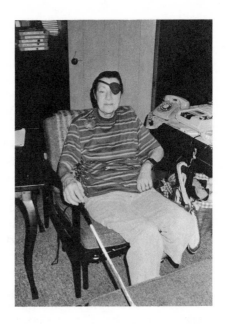

*I*t was a comfortable kitchen that Pen Dimock and I walked through after she responded to my knock on the door around back. A large old wood range, fired up and working, dominated one end of the room with mellowed, dark wooden cupboards at the other. This was a kitchen suggesting respect and appreciation for food, with no sense of the casual and quick.

One side of the room was open, with three steps leading down from the kitchen to an inviting study that had high bookshelves lined with books along one wall and plant-filled sunny windows facing out onto the garden. Pen led me past the study into the living room so we could talk "where we won't be interrupted."

"I've done more reading since going blind than in my whole life. I'm getting an education now," she said, settling into her chair, knitting and tape player within easy reach. Pen Dimock spoke about herself and some of the insights she's gained since the "closing down" of her vision some eleven years ago.

"Sixty-eight years of good sight gave me a rich store of visual experiences to draw from," she said. "I don't have anything to complain about now. I'll be eighty in about three weeks."

Her reading is part of the talking book program, originated by the Library of Congress and distributed in Vermont by the Division of Special Services of the Vermont State Library. Both flexible records and tapes are available as well as the machines for playing them, and they can all be obtained without cost by the blind and visually handicapped.

"New books may be ordered every two months," she said, "and I lay in a good supply. I always have something on hand."

"That's one thing about going blind," she continued. "You don't have quite as many demands on your time, and while professional reading has always been part of my work, I haven't had the chance before to simply read what interests me.

"There are insights I've developed that I would never have experienced otherwise. But then this applies to all personal disasters, I guess.

"First I began to figure out what I couldn't do, and one thing was plain. I couldn't drive a car! But in general I've found that if something comes up I really want to do—and I think I can't—I give it a try.

"Tending a stove for one thing. At first I thought I could never do that again, but now I take care of the stoves." (Pen and her husband Marshall cook their food and heat their house with wood.)

Pen, like other people with a disability, has worked out several tactics to make her life simpler. One such is a slender, flexible rod attached to a loop hanging from her shoulder: "Gives me a chance to wear a brooch," she said of the attractive pin securing it. This wand is lighter than her cane and she uses it as a sensor, or "feeler," to help her move freely around the house.

"Those steps leading down from the kitchen to the study are not very good for a blind person's house," she said, "but with my device I can immediately tell where I am. I can also touch things lightly without knocking them over the way I used to do with my cane."

She uses her white cane whenever she leaves the house but finds that her own invention is better inside.

"Also my memory is very good," she continued, "not only for the past, but the short-term memory, which often gets fuzzy as folks get older. Things flash into my head in very vivid form."

She chuckled as she continued, "I sometimes tell people that the best thing for the aging mind is loss of sight. Then your memory gets put into use because it's such an important tool.

"I have to remember the way things are placed, and I never bother with a grocery list anymore."

Pen's life has been full and adventuresome. As a juvenile diabetic, she claims to have far outlived any expected life span.

"I grew up on a farm in Connecticut," she began. "A *gentleman's farm* is what they called it then. My father was a lawyer in Stamford, and I was the eldest of six children, five girls and one boy. I attended a one-room school until my mother decided to bundle the children off to Switzerland. At that time, she had an idea that to give the girls a good education would be cheaper and better in Switzerland."

They were there for three years, and when they returned Pen was sent to the Kathryn Gibbs Secretarial School in New York; it seemed the proper thing for a bright young woman to do at that time. When she finished at Gibbs in 1926, the family went back to Europe and spent a year in southern France. Since Pen had developed a strong interest in international relations while she was at the Gibbs school, her family decided, when she was nineteen, that she should go to Geneva and find a job. The League of Nations was in full swing, and she found a job in three days. She spent the next five years there and remembers, "The old town was beautiful then, and there were people from all over the world, working and visiting."

Back in the United States she was accepted at Bennington College in its first freshman class. She was twenty-four and finished in three years, the college's first graduate. She went from there to Washington, D.C., to take a job as a research assistant.

Washington was an exciting and hopeful place to be in 1935. When she finished her job with the Federal Work Relief Program, she was asked to write the final document from which the public report was prepared. Someone then suggested that she should be working for Marshall Dimock, assistant undersecretary of labor to Frances Perkins, who was the first woman cabinet member in U.S. history.

In Pen's words: "I had an interview with Marshall at two P.M. on a Friday and at five P.M. he called back and asked if I could report for work on the following Monday morning."

"We worked pretty well together for a couple of years, and in June 1940, we were married. It was a second marriage for both of us."

A month before their marriage, Pen and Marshall bought a farm in Vermont, just outside the town of Bethel, and they spent their summers there in the old farm house, "more or less camping out." In 1947 they moved to Vermont permanently.

"Marshall and I have written a great deal together," she said. "He has about forty-five books to his credit, almost all political science in one form or another, some animal stories and an autobiography. I've been in on forty of those.

"Marshall writes fast, he can do as many as eighteen pages a day, but he can't revise. That's where I came in; I would edit, and came to regard myself as a kind of translator of his ideas."

Pen now does her editing by ear; someone reads the script to her and she indicates what needs to be done. "We've done six or eight books this way."

Over the years, even though Marshall occasionally accepted a temporary university professorship here or abroad, the farm remained their permanent residence. There was only one period that lasted for several years, when he was "seduced" back into teaching at New York University, and they lived in Brooklyn Heights.

Pen's time was not spent solely in editing Marshall's work; she also did her own writing. *A Home of Their Own*, a book chronicling their life and adventures in moving to Vermont, was published in 1963.

In the past thirteen years she has completed four manuscripts. "I practiced by talking into the tape machine," she said. "It took three years to write my first one, about Geneva in the days of the League of Nations. I've also written one titled *No Pride of Authorship*, which is the story of our writing and my part as editor."

Her most recently published book is about how to live in the country, a "philosophical and practical round-up," called *Home Ground*, published in 1985.

"It took me a year to get used to speaking into a tape. It's a different process; instead of thoughts moving from my head to my hands to the typewriter, they move from my head through my mouth to the tape, and there's a difference."

"Another thing about losing your sight that I realized some time ago—I'll never see myself growing old," she said, smiling at this curious bonus. "Seven years ago I suddenly said to myself, 'By golly, I'm now elderly,' and I was seventy-three. I still don't regard myself as old, and I stay very busy."

Pen works actively with the Vermont Association for the Blind. She was on their board of trustees for several years, but has more recently been on a committee concerned with their Rural Independent Living Project. She prefers the latter because it means she has a direct involvement in implementing policy. The new director of VAB (Vermont Association for the Blind), Jules Cote, is himself blind, she said. Pen believes this makes a basic difference in understanding the real needs and problems of people he is working with.

"We're reaching out to the rural blind," she explained, "people who could otherwise be very isolated. We've started a system of peer counseling.

"Other blind people who've been trained to cope for themselves are now helping others to cope. They're furnished with a car and a driver and go into other people's homes, talk to them there, gain an understanding of their actual problems, and help them confront and solve them."

She spoke with pride about the newly restored building that VAB has recently completed in Burlington to better meet the needs of its constituents.

The work being done by the VAB is very much on Pen's mind; and while meetings in Burlington are not necessary except once or twice a year, there are frequent, and full, telephone conferences between working committee members and the director. For these regular consultations, Pen, and all the others involved, allow a three-hour phone period.

"I feel unhappy about blind people who are afraid and suspicious. They could have a whole new life opened up for them."

"Learning to use a cane was a whole new thing for me," she recalled. "At first I resisted it and had several bad falls. But a cane is very helpful, and white canes can prevent accidents."

"I remember seeing a young man striding down the street in San Bernardino, California. It must have been fifteen years ago because I could still see," she said, flashing an easy smile with no trace of irony as she continued. "He looked confident and free—and he was using a white cane. I suppose he was familiar with the area, but even so, I'll never forget him. I've always enjoyed walking, too, although I don't do much of it anymore."

"Sight can be such a distraction," Pen added, almost as an afterthought as I was preparing to leave. "When I ride to Burlington now, the time seems much shorter than before. There's always so much to think about."

GRACE PALEY

I just was always a poet," Grace Paley said. "Just kept writing, that's all there is to it. My own idea was that somehow, that was what I wanted to do."

Her Vermont life, however, has not distanced her from the activities she views as important. She finds the world too small, and the issues too large, to hide from; only the faces change. Her life and her art seem inseparable, and she fuses them in the unique fire of her creativity.

Her short stories have been collected in books in several slender volumes, *Enormous Changes at the Last Minute*, 1974; *The Little Disturbances of Man*, 1973; and *Later the Same Day*, 1985; as well as published in periodicals: *Atlantic*, *Esquire*, *Ikor*, *Genesis West*, *Accent*, and others. There's also a collection of her poems: *Leaning Forward*, 1985.

In 1970 she received the Literary Award for Short Story Writing from the National Institute for Arts and Letters, was elected in 1980 to the American Academy of Arts and Letters, and has been a Guggenheim Fellow. She started teaching some years ago at Columbia University, spent two years teaching at City College in New York City, and from there went to Sarah Lawrence College, as a member of the literary faculty, where she has been ever since.

Her most recent publication, with paintings by Vera Williams, is *Peace Calendar 1989, 365 Reasons Not To Have Another War* and is published by The War Resister's League (WRL). The poems, short stories and personal statements she has included in this work exemplify the exquisitely simple connection she makes between her life and her art. In her introduction Grace said, "We hoped that the WRL Calendar would by its happiness and sadness demonstrate against militarists, racists, earth-poisoners, women-haters, all those destroyers of Days."

Grace Paley stands for many things. As a writer, a teacher and a human being, she understands much about the connections among us, and she appears to have no fear about using her person and her pen to further what she believes in. Although it was contradictory to the feeling for people she expresses in her writing, I was afraid that her broad reputation might make her somewhat unapproachable, guarded. I had a lot to learn about Grace.

Her characters are primarily women. The children, men, friends, parents, lovers and casual acquaintances that circle their lives are drawn with sympathy, humor and a recognition of the common humanity tying their, and their reader's, world together.

Explaining her route to Vermont, Grace said matter-of-factly, "I'm a New Yorker, but Bob Nichols, my husband, is really a Vermonter."

"He lived here, in this house, as a boy and until he went to war during World War II. Afterwards he returned and was here off and on until he moved back for good five or six years ago. Bob's father built this house. Bob has three children, and I have two, but of course they're all grown now."

"I began coming with him to Vermont in 1968," she said. "First in summers, then a year's leave from teaching, but as time went on, I've spent more and more time here."

"Since the Seabrook protests in 1976 and 1977, I've been more and more involved with people from around here," she recalled.

"Three drafts of the protest against it came out of this house, and later there was a lot of Central American stuff. There've been various women's activities, and Bob does solar things at fairs; he's interested in what goes on in agriculture and is part of a conservation group in Thetford."

Her own recipe for fitness seems to lie in vigorous and involved opposition to things she doesn't believe in: war and militarism, unfair treatment of women, environmental destroyers and racists.

"I also helped with the Conference on Women and Life on Earth, The Northeast Regional Conference in Massachusetts. That was in nineteen eighty. We organized that—planned for three hundred and had six hundred.

"Lots of us from here also went to the Women's Pentagon Action. There are several women's groups up here, and they work on different things. Many women are not doing professionally what they started out of their idealism when they were younger. Some of these things have since been funded—help for battered women, for instance. And that's good; that's the way it should be. When they started there was no funding, it was also quite dangerous."

Grace does readings every year at the Bread and Puppet Resurrection Circus in Glover. She believes in the group's strong message for peace and cooperation and the way their art is incorporated into their lives.

Directions given over the phone for finding her house were clear. "On Thetford Hill, it's at the end of a long driveway off the main road, just before the firehouse." It turned out to be a country driveway, with tracks creating as little disturbance as possible over the land they crossed; it was indeed long, coming to an end without flourish or fanfare, just a few yards from the house.

Grace greeted me at the door; she's a smallish woman, with soft curly hair, a quizzical smile and remarkably intense eyes. They seemed to embrace, inspect, register and communicate in one brief glance. I had the distinct impression they could penetrate whatever armor a visitor might be wearing.

There was a simplicity about the house. Comfortable, but not fussed over, my impression was that its most essential function is providing shelter for people and for ideas.

Equipped with tea, we made our way into Grace's study to talk without interruption; there were other things going on in the living/kitchen area.

It was an informal room with her typewriter set up at a desk, some comfortable chairs, a bed and one notable big brown couch pillow on the floor, also lots of pictures, photographs, papers and books.

Grace laughed as she explained the history of the big pillow. "That was from one of my mother's overstuffed chairs. I had four of them at one time, and I've carried them with me all over the place."

She moved directly into a brief accounting of her past. "I started in the Bronx, was born there in 1922. My father was a doctor, and we lived among some pretty poor people. My parents were Russian Jews, photographers before they came to this country. When they arrived here they started working for an Italian photographer and learned to speak Italian before they learned English.

"My father was twenty-one, he later studied to become a doctor.

"We were a large family; I had lots of older brothers and sisters, a grandmother and aunts, uncles, cousins—the lot.

"I never finished school, and my parents were very disappointed, thought I was going to be a deadbeat, thought that if I didn't get a good profession I'd amount to nothing. They were immigrants, and education for a profession was very important to them."

"All the other children got into professions," she added with a grin, "my own idea was that I needed to work by myself. I was reading all the time. I went to school for awhile, and then I just quit.

"I left home when I was a kid—married when I was nineteen and left home."

This happened during the Second World War, and since her husband was in the army, they moved to many different army bases. It was the first time Grace had lived in other places, and she was interested in everything she saw, and the people she met.

"I loved it, and he hated it," she said, explaining that he had to go overseas. "I didn't have to do that."

Later, they were separated for good, and while raising two children as a single parent, she took different jobs to keep things going including typing as a temporary office worker at Columbia University as well as other places.

"I did a lot of that. But I was writing all the time. I always liked language. I liked to hear it, and I love dialogue. I wrote poetry most of the time, but never got any of my poems published though so I began to write stories when I was well into my thirties. Before that I'd had no luck."

"I also took care of someone else's kids to earn money, and I wrote the stories, mostly about women, from my own experiences."

She was living in Greenwich Village during these years, before the Vietnam War. During the 1950's she got interested in the peace movement, the anti-civil defense and anti-nuclear causes, with a growing consciousness of the arms race and what it meant for the future.

"I'm in the FBI files, too; they have me in the criminal division because I signed a petition for rent control, back in 1948. There were twenty names on it, and mine was among them. I've applied to get my file back. All of this because I was interested in rent control! You can imagine what happens when people do any more than that.

"Back then the Quakers established centers and invited people in the different neighborhoods to join. They invited people working in the PTA, which I was, and there were all kinds of other people. We were given an introduction to the philosophies and strategies of non-violence. 'Thinking globally but acting locally' was stressed as an attitude towards the world. This was my principle education at that time."

Grace is also a teacher. "I began to teach in 1966, and I liked it," she recalled. And, as the kind of person whose concern for people as well as ideas could never be casual, the interest she takes in her students is not confined to the arbitrary bounds of a classroom. Even while I visited, a student whom she hadn't seen for several years called. The student was in a crisis and needed to talk. Grace was there.

Accessibility appears to be an extension of her convictions, and as a working principle, she makes herself available—possibly too much so in terms of her own work. "Bob is disciplined, he works every morning," she added, with a kind of little girl smile, "but I never have been." Bob Nichols is also a poet.

Regardless of where she happens to be physically, Grace is, in her own reality, a deeply conscious member of the world.

Many of the situations she writes about might seem hopeless on the surface but there is a basic affirmation: a belief in life that is celebrative and projected through the small things and relationships that provide substance to living. Nothing is beneath her notice if it serves the purpose of her story, and I believe this applies to her life. Nothing is really insignificant, no shade too soft, no color too gaudy, no word too crass if it fits. Her words weave relationships, make visible the feelings we can recognize but don't always note.

She's an individual who combines innocence with wisdom. As a mother she's known the messy world of infants and their curiously poignant early years; as an individual, she's overcome the need for an alert and protective ego with well-defined boundaries to shield it; and as an artist, she's developed the gift for returning, to an increasingly abstract and inanimate world, a sense of its own humanity.

Some of her stories, poems and statements are fables for our times. Many deal with city life or ethnic characteristics, with which we are not necessarily familiar, and yet we are all there. The feelings she evokes are recognizable as our own, and reading some of her work breaks the spell of isolation that has been laid upon us. We accept with more understanding and comfort the transient nature and significance of phenomena and people's place within it.

When I read Grace Paley's work, I'm struck by the notion that the story couldn't have been told another way. And when I met her, I was struck by the notion that there was no other way she could be.

"I'm interested in how people live on this earth, politically with my body and intellectually with my typewriter," she said reflectively, as I prepared to leave.

And then she added firmly, "But we all need to think a lot before we stop being thoughtless."

SABRA FIELD

*C*ome over today or tomorrow," Sabra Field told me over the phone. "I'll be printing on both days. We can talk while I'm working."

Later, sitting on a stool at one end of her large press, I watched as she worked steadily at the other end. There were ink blocks on a work-bench to one side, and she used a well-inked brayer to roll a cerulean blue sky onto the woodblock she was printing. The sky color ranged from pale blue to almost white where it met the textured gray of the hills. Against these were three dark, intricate tree shapes throwing their deeper blue shadows onto a foreground of white snow.

Sabra Field is a renowned printmaker living in East Barnard, where she has her printshop, studio and gallery adjoining her home. A small sign outside identifies it as Tontine Press. It's located in the old building that functioned as an inn many years ago in the early history of the town.

The primary subject of her work is Vermont. Simplicity of form and a direct point of view mark her approach, and her images are reverent and dignified. Evening or early morning heavens, the dramatic shapes of tree skeletons in winter or their lush volume in spring and summer, mountains and the changing skies around them that determine their character and color, farm buildings and the dignified old houses in a Vermont town are all part of the subject matter she draws upon.

Over the years, she has developed a following for her work and collectors eagerly await the catalogues of colored reproductions that are mailed out each year. Three of her prints have been chosen for the UNICEF greeting card collection; one of these, *Apple Tree, Winter,* is one of their best-selling designs. UNICEF card designs are chosen from the work of outstanding artists around the world.

"In a way I'm lucky," Sabra said. "The printmaker has an advantage over the painter. Our work is far more accessible to the public—easier to show and to sell. A print costs far less than a painting, and once the woodblock is cut, the impressions can go on and on unless it's a numbered edition.

"I've started working larger recently. I can use the full capacity of my press now, and I've just decided to take advantage of it. It started with a commission from Dartmouth. Frank Smallwood has always been a collector of my work, and he was instrumental in getting this commission."

The completed work is a collage, about twelve feet wide, and was installed several years ago in the lobby of the auditorium in the Rockefeller Building. The colors were printed on full sheets of paper, and while the final effect is similiar to one of her prints, it is one-of-a-kind.

Asked how she got her prints before the public and developed such a loyal following, Sabra explained that when she started, she took her work on the exhibit circuit, to arts and craft fairs, retail shows— wherever she could display it. She has also been with Ellison Lieberman's Gallery 2 in Woodstock since 1967, as well as the Frog Hollow Arts Center in Middlebury.

"I've also built up a mailing list, name by name, all people who have bought my work or requested specifically that their names go on my list," she added. Her color brochures are mailed to people all over this country and abroad, and there are people on her mailing list to whom a visit to Vermont would not be complete without a visit to her studio.

"Each print is different," she continued. "Some people like to come here to buy them so they can compare the different impressions; others don't want to be faced with that kind of choice.

"I reproduce myself over and over and constantly make minor adjustments," she explained.

By this time the block she was inking when I started to observe the process had moved easily through the big press, and the sky was intact on the paper.

Sabra spoke of the restrictions imposed by working on wood blocks for printing and the degree of craft involved in cutting them.

"Thank God I started as a printmaker," she said, explaining that when she began making pictures, abstract expressionism in art was the only style recognized as acceptably presenting a valid twentieth-century image. This thinking negated much of the former emphasis on the craft of painting and the validity of representation. She pointed out that, for many years, the recently rediscovered and acclaimed work of the painters Fairfield Porter and Milton Avery were "out of style."

"But among real printmakers there was always a tradition of craftsmanship and of representation that remained valid, even during this period."

She emphasized that professional standards for her work are maintained by submitting pieces to important juried shows.

"For me a high spot is reached when I have a print accepted in a national juried exhibition," she said. "In these a print is accepted or rejected completely on its own merits. Artists and printmakers of stature make the selection, and today there are thousands of entries per show."

Recent prints in this kind of exhibit were her *Autumn Pool, 1 and 2,* which were part of the Eastern U.S. Print and Drawing National Exhibition, in Charlotte, North Carolina.

"I was once advised by a well-known printmaker to have two names for signing my work, one for the strictly commercial things and one for the things I'm proud of," she added, heatedly. "This really made me angry. I think it's the obligation of the artist to do the best job she can on everything she does."

Sabra came to Vermont to live permanently in 1969. She was a 1957 Middlebury College graduate and went on to Wesleyan University in Connecticut. She received her M.A. in teaching there in 1959, and also started printmaking in earnest.

"In those days, teaching was about the only profession considered available to women, other than nursing," she said. "I remember there was one woman in the architecture department there."

"What I've done took a lot of pig-headed determination. I recall the days when only one or two people knew where I was, or cared," she added.

She spoke about the imposed necessity, for women, of "external validation." "It's a sorry fact that unless someone tells you, preferably a man, that a picture by a woman is good, you're not prepared to believe it."

"It's horrifying," she continued. "I didn't realize this for a long time. Also, when someone asks me, 'How did you do it?' meaning making a career in this field, it's usually a man. There's a hidden message to subtly let me know they didn't expect it of a woman.

"But there's no difference now in the people who collect my work, male or female, young or old," she continued. "If they like it, they want to buy it."

About the part-time printmaker's assistant in the studio, she said: "This is the first year I've had job applicants who were men."

She takes exception to the romantic association built up about "the starving artist." "This has affected the way an artist feels about herself. If she's successful, then it seems to mean that she's probably not a good artist. This myth has been fostered since sometime during the nineteenth century. People buying the work liked the romantic image of the starving artist. But I feel no shame at making a living from selling my work."

Asked about some of the artists who have most influenced her work, she mentioned the contemporary printmaker, Leonard Baskin.

She also credited the influence of two great Japanese artists, Utamaro and Hiroshige. "There were lesser-quality Japanese prints in my house while I was growing up," she said, "prints my parents picked up in the thirties. This kind of approach has probably been in my subconscious ever since."

She went on to explain: "I don't consciously ape their style but I am influenced by the clarity and brilliance of the oriental technique. Western printmakers never achieved this—even Durer was all black and white."

"When the great calligrapher, Ogawa, was visiting UVM [University of Vermont] from Japan, I was honored to be invited to one of his courses in calligraphy," she continued.

Asked about her own progress as a printmaker and the success she has achieved, Sabra laughed, "Success is always what's up ahead, isn't it? We're never content with the past, with other people's ideas of making it. I've never achieved what I want, and I think my goals keep stretching. Success is only in the eye of the beholder."

Sabra and her second husband, Spencer Field, are partners. She explained that he is also an artist, a painter, but in a much more private way, and that his specialty is wildlife.

Explaining the practical ways in which their partnership works out in real life she said, "Every day is for me a long working day, and every week is a work week, and that's the way I like it.

"I don't fuss much with housekeeping. I have a part-time helper in my workshop, but I believe it's important to stay small. Staying small ensures my freedom to continue to make new images. If I were just printing constantly I wouldn't have time to cut blocks. I'd become an administrator.

"Spencer does the mounting of my work, framing, packing, shipping, plus keeping the books. He can't go to the dentist for me, but he shops, even buys clothes. We're way beyond even noticing role distinctions.

"He doesn't get involved in my imagery, though. I need positive reinforcement, but I don't want to discuss the imagery. I'll ask him, 'Is it understandable?' but I don't want anyone to tell me how to do it, and he understands that."

They occasionally collaborate on the work itself; he did the original painting of the bird in the UNICEF print. Any drawing or print of Sabra's with an animal or bird has originated from a drawing or painting of Spencer's.

Sabra was standing at the door of her printshop as I drove away. The setting seemed perfect both for her and for her work.

"There is great peace and quiet in this tiny community," she had said, "and it's a comfortable place for an artist to live. Everyone is busy with their own concerns, but they're always willing to pitch in if any of their neighbors need help."

JANE BECK

I learned more in the last ten years then I ever learned in school," Jane Beck said about her position as a Vermont folklorist and director of the Vermont Folklife Center in Middlebury. Working against the sweeping tide of change taking place within the state, she and her staff are intent on recording and presenting characteristic aspects of rural Vermont life that are rapidly disappearing.

"We also want to become an archive for the spoken word," she added, explaining that while the center has the capacity for mounting exhibits of folk ways, it is also in the process of using computer technology in developing a data base to allow public access to the tape interviews.

"One of the great things about this place is that people come in here who have never been in a museum before. They come to see something on display that one of their grandparents or someone else in their family made many years ago. This adds to the real meaning of the place."

The Folklife Center recently opened in the old Gamaliel Painter House in Middlebury. Initially Jane was hired by the Vermont Council on the Arts for the position of Vermont folklorist; in 1978 there were only eight such positions around the country. Today there are forty-five. This indicates a keen hunger for preserving connections with our past in the face of a rapidly changing world.

Jane spoke lovingly about surviving crafts. "As a rule now it's the older people who are involved in traditional crafts. They're the ones with time to create after they retire from everyday work.

"I'm interested in the way these things have been passed down," she added. "There's a lingering attitude that work and play are two sides to the same coin. Quilting, for instance, was a way for women to be creative, but it was still functional, a way to keep warm and of using up scraps of material.

"A number of things are still being made traditionally; many of today's quilters learned from their mothers or grandmothers. There are hooked and braided rugs, carved decoys, brown ash baskets. These skills have been passed down informally from members of the older generation."

When Jane first accepted the folklorist position, no serious thought had been given to a Vermont Folklife Center. Formerly a student at Middlebury College, she explained the way her interest in folk culture developed. It happened largely because of a lecture given by Reginald (Doc) Cook, a distinguished professor.

"I was majoring in American literature, and Doc Cook spoke one day in class, just off-the-cuff, about Willa Cather's book, *Death Comes to the Archbishop*. He loved the Navahos, and the story was about the Navaho Cliff, the enchanted bluff. I was inspired by it, and I can point to that moment as crystallizing everything I've done since. That lecture really directed the rest of my life."

Her enthusiasm prompted her to go to the Bureau of Indian Affairs in Washington looking for work.

She had already applied for a summer job with a camp in New Hampshire near where her family lives. When she didn't hear from the Bureau, she accepted the first job. An hour later she got a telegram saying she had a job with the Indian Bureau. But it was too late. Nonetheless, her interest in origins and folk culture continued to grow, and when she heard about a folklore program at the University of Pennsylvania, she decided to attend.

"My parents went along with the idea, mainly because they could see that it captured my whole being. The first year was so successful that I stayed for a second. I also married a folklorist. I continued my work at the University of Pennsylvania to get my Ph.D., and about the time my first child was born, I was taking my Ph.D. exams. My dissertation was finished shortly before my second child was born."

Jane's husband, a professor at Middlebury, had a leave of absence and was doing research in the West Indies for his book, *Folklore and the Sea*. Jane and their children spent a year with him there in 1971, and Jane did research of her own. She had the opportunity of working with an obeah man who "first began teaching me protective magic. I soon realized he had a deep knowledge of obeah, a kind of West Indian sorcery."

She was able to persuade him to let her write a book. Initially this was to be based on his life as a fisherman, but as time went on, it also became a discussion of his teaching her magic.

"I became his 'unprotected daughter,' and he taught me magic to make me a 'protected woman.' As his 'white daughter,' my heritage was to be half of everything he knew. If he taught me more than half, it was believed that the student would become more powerful than the teacher.

The result of their work together was *To Windward of the Land: The Occult World of Alexander Charles*, his account of protective magic.

In 1978 the job at the Vermont Arts Council became available. "Their charge to me was to do field work, to discover what was left of traditional Vermonter ways of doing things," she recalled.

The potential material was so vast that she decided to concentrate on two things as a start. She chose apples as her first motif because she felt it would give her the range of lore—tales, songs, beliefs, weatherlore and folk cures—with new traditions being introduced by the more recent practice of bringing Jamaicans in for picking.

The next topic was the general store in Vermont, and she produced a slide tape and a book, *The General Store in Vermont: An Oral History*, about the role of these stores as the cultural center of many communities.

"These two topics were the key to getting my feet under me, in knowing what to expect in establishing a network and what I might find to work with. I was driving three thousand miles a month, and was learning more than I ever could have imagined."

From the experience she was gathering by moving around the state, Jane formed the idea of putting a folk art exhibit together.

"Ellen Lovell, the director of the Vermont Council on the Arts, was supportive, but the trustees were shaking their heads on that one— they didn't think there was enough material. But when the five members of the selection committee met to review 750 slides of possible objects, they unanimously selected 175 things to be included."

The ensuing exhibit opened at the Vermont Historical Society Museum in 1982 and was planned to travel to three other locations in the state: the Bennington Museum, the Shelburne Museum and the Christian Johnson Gallery at Middlebury College. It was still on view in Montpelier during the Governor's Conference on the Future of Vermont's Heritage, and its viewing helped stimulate a resolution by the conference that something like a Folklife Center should be established in the state. A steering committee was pulled together, a board of trustees formed and a non-profit organization incorporated in the winter of 1984. The Vermont Council on the Arts served as host to the fledgling organization and partially funded it during the period of early growth.

In the fall of 1986, Jane and Townie Anderson went to the Board of Trustees of Middlebury College with a proposal for putting a Vermont Folklife Center into the old Painter house; owned by the college and built in 1801, it was the original home of the founder of the college as well as of the town. On the basis of that proposal, although they had initially planned on selling the building, the trustees decided to restore it for rent to non-profit organizations and became actively concerned with its restoration and continued use.

By this time, Sonja Olsen had joined the staff of the Folklife Center. Working together, Jane, Sonja and the Vermont Folklife Center Board conducted a feasibility study concerning the Folklife Center and its possible location in the old Painter home. "It came out positive, with some very nice pledges made to ensure its financial feasibility. The Arts Countil also donated ten thousand dollars as a bridge to carry us over," Jane said.

The Vermont Folklife Center opened officially on January 1, 1988, with its first exhibit, "Lure of the Lake: Traditional Arts of Lake Champlain." "We had a lecture/performance series in conjunction with the exhibit and had no idea if we would attract any kind of an audience. To our surprise, the first event attracted over one hundred people, and for the second talk we had to move to another location!" she added almost in disbelief.

Since beginning her work in Vermont just a little over ten years ago, Jane has been part of many exciting things. One of her particular favorites is a videotape she was able to make of the life of Daisy Turner, the daughter of an ex-slave. The oral history of her family spans two centuries, taking it from Africa into slavery and eventually to freedom on a hill farm in Vermont.

"How fragile is the spoken word. Listening to Daisy Turner, hearing her anecdotes and watching her expression as she told them was an unforgettable experience. But even though Daisy is gone now, we at least have her life story on video."

She is currently working on a video, *As the Twig is Bent*, that shows how heritage affects family traditions in Vermont. It starts with a recent Cambodian immigrant, includes an early Jewish peddlar and members of other immigrant groups which have played a role in the life of the state. The center's staff has been enlarged; there is now a full-time archivist, and the data base is being developed. Both Jane and her staff give talks to organizations around the state. "I give about twenty a year," she said.

A recent exhibit of the quilts and other handiwork of Amber Densmore brought a National Endowment for the Arts Heritage Fellowship award to this eighty six-year-old Vermont woman.

With the help of her staff, Jane has also put together a series of curricula packages that go to Vermont schools. These include video-tapes, with booklets to explain them, along with an exhibit of photographs and artifacts that can be displayed on lightweight panels.

For a Bicentennial project, the center hopes to work with teachers to conduct oral history projects with their students and shape what they learn from these interviews into some kind of artistic product—perhaps a miniature village showing how these towns looked fifty years ago and a ballad of an important town event. At the end of the school year, there would be a Bicentennial Fair for the students to show off their work and to celebrate their local history and traditions.

"In the time since all this started, my own children have grown up," Jane said with a disarming smile. "The youngest is a freshman at UVM [the University of Vermont], and the oldest a junior at the University of Pennsylvania.

"I think I've known all along that this is what I wanted to do. I love the work and every part of it. I believe in this place so much, I even like fund-raising.

"If I ever had time, I would really like to do a book on Daisy Turner. Talking with her was a major experience, and those hours spent with her were like little isinglass windows on the Civil War. Her story was incredible," she said, leaning forward, eyes almost closed as she allowed a moment for the vividness of that encounter to live again in her mind. We sat in her small office just off the main exhibit space at the center.

"It's curious," she mused, "the farther removed we are from our roots, the more interested we become in looking back."

"My great grandmother lived to be ninety-nine—and I never taped her," she said with obvious regret. "Just think what she would have had to say about things she had seen."

BUSINESS

VIRGINIA BLACKERT

I'm really the sole owner of three magazines," Virginia Blackert began. She was talking about *Woodstock Common*, *Rutland Seasons*, and *Stowe Country*. Virginia started Prosper Publishing, Inc., the publishing company responsible for them.

Getting a small publishing empire underway has been demanding, but she displays a natural exuberance which can be brought into formidable focus. She spoke freely about the process of getting her magazines started, and the fact that their success demanded the better part of her life during the five years it has taken. It is only recently that she's been able to envision a life with room for anything else.

"Current circulation is twenty thousand per issue, per magazine," she acknowledged. "They're all free, because they're supported by the advertisers. But I've always tried to keep them looking good enough so people don't throw them away. There's more design and more thought in these, and we're doing a better job than anyone else."

The three handsome publications are abundantly illustrated with color as well as black and white photographs and well-designed graphics. The format is similiar in all three, and the articles included are lively and readable. Because the magazines are seasonal—winter, spring, summer and fall for *Woodstock Common*; winter and summer for the other two—any one of the three groups, or all of them, could be collected, to be reread or used for Vermont reference without putting undue strain on anyone's shelf space.

"I have a half-time secretary and a full-time graphic designer. There are also freelance photographers and writers. Production costs run around $22,000, not including salaries," she volunteered.

"One person gets to be in charge, and I'm that person. I just have women on my staff because they don't have ingrained the old saw, 'I don't take orders from women.'

"Women also take a concept and carry it further. A lot comes from femininity, an outlook on the world that keeps them in touch. Men are out of touch as a species. If a man gets mad at the dinner table and smashes things, it's the woman who cleans it up. Women see the larger picture."

She believes that in Vermont the traditional male-female roles are well-defined, but she had expected it to be more sexist. She claims to have only experienced two or three instances of this.

"In Vermont they tend to judge by actions; they're less likely to prejudge."

But she believes that there are more problems here with women against the Equal Rights Amendment. "And if you need ERA, it certainly says something about society."

Like many others of her sex, Virginia was not pointed in a particular vocational direction as she was growing up. When she had to assume responsibility for herself and her small child, financially and otherwise, she had few specific tools to work with. Developing her own diverse skills and interests, she has managed to put them together into an enterprise that is now a complex and successful business. This ability to create a whole out of seemingly discrepant parts has been matched by many other women as a way of combining the variety within their experience into an effective means for achieving personal independence.

"When I came to Vermont in 1972, I had no saleable skills whatsoever, but I always read a lot, and I liked to write. I worked for some of the time as a waitress for sixty dollars a week to support myself and my kid," she said.

But while Virginia was short on commercial expertise, she was long on energy, drive and an ability to work with ideas. Confidence too never seemed to be lacking. After marriage, when she lived in Boston, she did some campaigning for Mayor Kevin White and was also active on a rent control project, which stood her in good stead later after her marriage had broken up and she was looking for work.

Moving to Vermont became a goal when she and her small child visited the state with a friend on a four-day trip. They were on the Appalachian Trail in the Brandon area, and she remembers thinking she'd never seen such beautiful country. The visit was right after Labor Day and by December 1, Virginia and Hilary had returned for good.

Her choice of a place to live was serendipitous. Without calculation she put her finger near the center of a Vermont map, and Rutland was the spot it covered. Virginia was there for eight years, where she honed the skills which she later combined as a basis for magazine publishing.

She couldn't type well, but well enough to work as a temporary typist. She organized a candidate's congressional campaign and did some publicity for Jerome Diamond when he was running for Vermont attorney general. Then she saw an ad in the *Rutland Herald* for someone to do layouts and advertising.

"I went in every day to talk to them about the job until they got tired of it and hired me," she said, maintaining what seems to be a characteristic attitude of looking for humor in an otherwise grim reality.

Her experience at the *Herald* led to work a little later from Phil Camp, who had a publicity and public relations agency in Woodstock, where she moved in 1980. Several highly successful accounts were developed, among them the Mt. Mansfield Corporation, for which she put together the *Essence of Stowe* magazine. That gave her direct magazine experience. She was able to save ten thousand dollars for living expenses and during the next year, she started her own first magazine.

Woodstock Common was launched in the summer of 1983. Virginia's partner in the venture was a neighbor and friend, Alan Schroeder.

"Our first issue had thirty-two pages, with eight pages in color. Alan's in Chicago with his family now, a highly paid insurance man, but at the time, we had no capital. We sold ads on a cash basis and put out our first issue.

"We made $250 from it and were ecstatic—we'd expected to lose money. With that money, we bought twelve shares of Ben and Jerry's stock at ten or twelve dollars a share. I bought Alan out three years later and retained the stock. It has split three times since and is now at fifteen dollars.

"*Woodstock Common* is in its sixth year now. After the third year, it really clicked. I loved the creative challenge of it, and it's still my pet. I learn new things all the time.

"Woodstock is a charming town, that's part of the draw of the magazine. People in the town also pull together as a community, and they've adopted the magazine as their own."

Virginia is proud of the fact that her magazines do not back away from controversy affecting the areas they serve. One issue of *Woodstock Common* questioned the development of too many condos, and supported preservation of the Ottauquechee River.

"We try to be fair, we presented both sides of the argument, and it didn't bother our advertisers," she said.

Another feature that has been highly successful, but which some of her mentors questioned at the start, is the section describing "People Who Make a Difference."

"Some of them said, 'These people are already known; there won't be enough interest.' It's turned out to be the most popular thing I've ever done. I have even more advertisers now.

"There are also several advertisers from out of town: they plug into the Woodstock mystique. Thirty percent of Vermont's tourist population passes through there. There's a lot of money around, and a lot is invested in Woodstock."

When the opportunity arose to buy the Stowe magazine, Virginia took it. The title was changed to *Stowe Country*, and it is published twice yearly. She maintains that Stowe is more of a community than most people realize, and she wants to reflect some of that "togetherness," working with a photographer who lives there.

The third endeavor is *Rutland Seasons*. "I try to present the area," she said. "Not just the Pico ski area, but really Rutland. It's hard to do because the big excitement is on the mountain, but I've discovered that if you make material interesting to local people, it will also interest the others who are just passing through."

Virginia's background furnished some clues about the factors that nourished her confidence and momentum.

"My drive came from my mother, we were a matriarchal family. She came from Italian immigrants, my grandfather was working on a ship and got off in this country.

"My mother worked from the time I was thirteen. She was self-taught, with no formal education—only went through eighth grade. She started with a large company and worked her way up to become the manager of a large number of bookkeepers and tax preparers. She was always good with numbers.

"She worked in the office where my grandmother worked; that's how she met my father. They had a four-year courtship while he was in the army during World War II.

"She's a real strong person, a go-getter, non-stop achiever. My father is a quiet person, a sweet man with a steel backbone, but with really strong opinions. Most of the time he's very quiet, but when he makes up his mind about something—look out! I fought violently with my mother, but he was easy to get along with.

"We were a typical middle-class family with a mom, a dad and three kids."

The family lived near Teaneck, New Jersey. They summered in an area of New York where her father's people had settled in the early eighteen hundreds. Virginia has discovered in the old family home thousands of old postcards, photographs and letters and has reconstructed a family history.

Her father was a musician, a clarinetist, but after he and his brother bought first one gas station and then a series of them, he had less time for his music. He played swing and Dixieland on weekends until Virginia was about thirteen and then gave it up.

"My own child was born before I was twenty-one, and it was the smartest thing I ever did," she said resolutely.

"I was in school at New York University. My husband was a draft resister during the Vietnam War, and after we were married, I didn't want to live in Philadelphia, where he was living—and he didn't want to live in New York—so we moved to Boston where we had friends.

"I had Hilary in Boston. Her name comes from a Greek work meaning *joy*. Her middle name is Berrigan, after Daniel Berrigan, the peace activist. I came to Vermont with Hilary after my husband and I split up.

"One of the best things about coming to Vermont is that I didn't finish my education. But if I had stayed in New York, the editors there would have wanted to see my degree. I think I would have been considerably more hemmed in, creatively speaking."

And while she doesn't question her success, there are aspects she hopes to alter. She mentioned some of the pitfalls.

"My publications take an inordinate amount of time, and since I'm less apprehensive about money now, I'm working towards having more time for my own life and relaxation. I put in an enormous amount of work: the other staff can do several things, but I do everything.

"I plan to build more structure into the business so my personal life doesn't suffer. I'd rather dictate how I spend my time rather than have the magazines dictate to me. I've had sixty- or seventy-hour work weeks long enough. It's too much when I have to ask myself whether I go swimming or get four hours sleep."

As if to prove her point, we met for breakfast at a restaurant a few miles from where she and her publishing business share living quarters.

"The phone is always ringing, and there'd be constant interruptions if we tried to talk there," she said.

"I want to make it more like a business and less like a personal extension of myself. The people who work for me, and with me, are the people I want in my life, but if I talk about business all the time I start feeling I have nothing to offer but the magazines."

And then, almost in contradiction to the very real sense of accomplishment she feels from her magazines, she added, "But acting was what I always wanted to do."

However, she hastened to draw a parallel between the creative demands involved in publishing and the process of developing a part for the stage. "There it is—a production for all the world to see; that's what it comes down to."

PATRICIA C. HEFFERNAN

I'm fortunate in that I need little sleep, five hours will do me and six hours is plenty. I wake up naturally at five every morning." And looking over a partial list of Pat Heffernan's accomplishments, one wonders how she can dawdle in bed so long.

She is presently a partner in charge of marketing and management consulting for Sandage, Inc., in Burlington, one of Vermont's largest marketing and consulting firms. She was a Vermont delegate to the White House Conference on Small Business, a member of the Governor's Commission on Women, on the board of directors of the Rutland division of the Chittenden Bank, a trustee of the Killington Mountain School, and member and president of the Killington Planning Commission for twelve years. Pat has also been associate dean of the Vermont Law School, and one of the founders of the Women Business Owners of Vermont. This list is only partial but gives a sense of the way she's spent her time since deciding to settle permanently in Vermont, shortly after completing college.

Pat chuckled as she described her own departure from the conventional profile of successful small business owners.

"I was the first born, but not male," she said, as she reviewed a list that revealed her deviation from the norm. "Parents who were self-employed is a classic pattern but there was none of that in my house while I was growing up."

"My mother was a traditional, non-working mother, but a strong-willed woman, and my father worked on the management level for a large corporation. As a matter of fact, my parents were shocked later when I left my position at the Vermont Law School and went into business for myself. But I was very, very fortunate to come from a happy family—a secure and loving family," she said.

She described her route, from summers spent at her family's summer home near Lake Bomoseen as she was growing up to her final decision to settle permanently in Vermont.

Graduating from the University of Virginia as a major in English and comparative literature, she entered a three-year Ph.D. program, but decided not to finish. There were school debts to pay off, and she worried about an ivory-tower syndrome from lack of contact with the real world.

Pat taught school in New Hampshire and waitressed in Killington on weekends but stopped teaching after one semester. Not only did waitressing pay better but she was discouraged with the inability of her students, many older than she was, to write a coherent sentence.

About the same time, from her experience in running a dining room during college, she realized that many young Vermont girls applying for jobs at Killington lacked the necessary training. As manager of a Killington restaurant, The Wobbly Barn, she made their training part of her job.

Killington, at that time, she described as like a large international family, with a very cosmopolitan feeling. The ski instructors were from other countries, as were many visitors, and it had the kind of atmosphere "you'd find near a college—or a resort."

After two years, Pat Conner married John (Joe) Heffernan, who was also in the hospitality business. On their vacations, every spring and fall, they traveled to many places, including the Virgin Islands, Costa Rica, and North Carolina, looking for a place to live that equalled Vermont in beauty. They loved the state but were dubious about the prospects of finding work here that would upgrade their pay in relation to their increasing skills.

"For myself, I was looking for three things: a way to feed my family adequately, work that I love in a place that I love. My father was with a large oil company, and the family had always traveled a lot. But we had a summer home in Vermont, and I decided at an early age that I would probably end up living here. Nonetheless, my husband and I wanted to be sure before we settled in."

But settle in they did and spent the next twenty years living in Killington. During this time, Pat was on the planning commission, serving as its president for twelve of those years. She was also a member of the zoning board.

"It was hot, heavy and bloody with a lot going on. A lot was played out there in advance of a state program dealing with growth. Zoning and town planning were a sour note; but as the ski area grew, so did the town, and we understood the pressure of tourists sooner. We also developed a better appreciation of them—and what they think of us."

After five years, though, Pat was no longer enjoying her work; the challenge had disappeared, and she was ready for new pursuits. She had been increasing her skills by taking correspondence courses in accounting and felt ready for another business.

"At the Wobbly Barn I'd been office manager as well as dining room manager, and doing free lance accounting for several other small business. But education was always a love for me, so when I was invited to go the Woodstock Country School as business manger, I went."

"I've never had to job hunt," she added with pride. "People have always approached me about work."

After two years in Woodstock, one of the school's board members invited her to another institution that was being formed, and she accepted.

"I went to the Vermont Law School and was there for nine years, first as business manager and then as associate dean, and it was a great challenge. I was part of the team brought in to get things rolling, and during this period, it went from an unaccredited to an accredited school, from fifty to four hundred students, and grew from one to nine buildings, all historic. It's now an accredited professional school."

Nonetheless, Pat continued to plan. She received her master's degree in business administration from Suffolk University during her years at the law school. Every weekend for three years had been spent on this project.

A realistic look at the ceiling on financial reward in too many Vermont jobs convinced her that further credentials were needed in case she had to look outside the state. She was increasing her business and management skills, but she wasn't sure that her earnings here could continue to match them.

"Nobody else in Vermont was paying what I was accustomed to earning," she added. "So there was no choice but to start my own business. It was a management consulting business in fields that I knew: finance, administration and computerization. I worked with the professional schools and nonprofit organizations like the Woodstock Foundation, also lawyers, doctors and a lot of smaller hospitality businesses both in and out of state."

"I was still living in Killington," she continued, "and commuted to Woodstock for the next five years. I put on a thousand miles a week and ended up with driver's elbow. The doctor compared it to tennis elbow," she said with a grin, "sounds funny now but it wasn't then."

"But I made my own hours, and I enjoyed the work. Still, I felt the need for networking with other women on their own," she added. Out of this need Women's Business Owners of Vermont (WBOV) was born. Pat recognized that there were few business women in other high-level positions within the state, and she wanted to find ways to help them.

"Burlington has colleges, but throughout much of Vermont, there's little chance for women to have an exchange with their peers. Isolation was a major problem, and from my own experience, I'd seen how useful networking and contacts with other business women could be. So in 1984, a group of us started Women Business Owners of Vermont."

She reminisced about their kickoff meeting that had Madeleine Kunin as their main speaker, shortly before her first primary. Over two hundred women showed up from around the state, a board of directors was formed, and Pat Heffernan was elected as the organization's first president. She has served on their board of directors ever since.

There are now seven local chapters that meet monthly to share business information, and a bi-monthly newsletter is distributed to all the members. To bring them all together from around the state, there are occasional round tables and an annual conference. WBOV works on issues such as getting more women involved in local affairs, means of securing appointments on state boards and commissions and general practices like discrimination against women in obtaining commercial credit.

WBOV also took a stand against recent legislation to mandate maternity leave for female employees. They were opposed to the concept of mandated employee benefits in general and to certain provisions of this bill in particular. Among their concerns were the costs to small businesses, as well as the possibility of subtle hiring discrimination that could result from its passage.

"We are a business-oriented group, and one of our purposes is to improve the visibility, the voice and power of women entrepreneurs," Pat said, pointing out that she is an active member of the Governor's Commission on Women and that seven WBOV members were delegates to the last White House Conference on Small Businesses.

Pat met her current business partner, Barbara Sandage, through WBOV. "We had shared the experience of being delegates to the

White House Conference on Small Business, so we had a lot to talk about.

"I was considering the expansion of my own consulting business and had already begun to weigh the advantages of the Hanover/ Norwich area against those of Burlington.

"Barbara said, 'Take another look at Burlington,' so I did, and we merged our businesses."

"To be a management consultant," Pat explained, "is to consult with management about improving the performance of their organization. In our office we have about five different specialties, and I tend to focus on general management research and marketing systems, using technology as a tool. My strength is in service industries, any non-manufacturing concern—but our company handles any business."

As an example of the scope of her own work, she mentioned the Billings Farm and Museum in Woodstock. "It was a start-up and they needed everything: hiring procedures, posters, catalogue, gift shop inventory, curator. Our firm was the consultant on this and made it happen."

Pat explained that there are both positive and negative attitudes associated with Vermont consulting firms and that national certification is important to counteract the negative response. "The positive attitude assumes that you're honest, down-to-earth and practical; but the negative can also assume that you're not up-to-date or as professional as your urban competitor.

"A process of peer certification is handled by the Institute of Management Consultants, and this gives credibility to your professionalism," she said, pointing out that she started this five-year process as soon as she opened her own business. She is now a Certified Management Consultant (CMC), and it has advantages in obtaining work outside the state.

The rest of the staff had long since left before we finished talking. Pat Hefferenan was generous with her time and interested in the project.

Her office was filled with books and manuals, and there were paintings, posters and photographs on the walls. She wore a bright red suit and a black blouse with a small ruffle at the neck. Corresponding ruffles at her wrists showed off her hands, which she used frequently in making a point. She's a little shorter than average, with a tendency towards plumpness. She has straight dark brown hair and alert eyes that twinkle enthusiastically, even at the end of a long working day.

Pat Heffernan's admission to being a compulsive planner did not come as a complete surprise. Responsibility for harnessing her kind of energy and natural ebullience is not to be taken lightly; misdirected, it could be as riotous as a munitions plant gone out of control.

"I always have a five-year plan that I update each year, and I've always been well organized," she said. "Also I've always had an optimism about life—but then I was a happy kid."

As might be expected, the scope of her interests is formidable. "I'm a golfer and a skier. I'm also an avid reader. I read just about anything, and I always have a list of other things I want to read, my house is mainly a library in disarray. When I'm traveling it's trashy stuff that I read, but there's also philosophy, trade mags, technology publications, business stuff and things about women and women's issues."

As an instance of the latter she described a national report on the correlation between the drop-out rate, teenage pregnancy, and self-esteem. "It ties the teenage pregnancy rate to their level of self-esteem and self-confidence," she said.

"But being a housekeeper is not one of the hats I wear," she continued with a smile. "I'm married, have no children, still like to travel, and I like to play bridge. My husband has always been supportive, and he's still in the hospitality industry. He loves to cook, and one of our hobbies is cooking together."

"I'm also an epileptic," she continued, adding that this was never a condition she wanted to be identified by or used for hiding behind. "I was very ill as a teenager and entered college from the hospital. I also graduated from high school while I was there."

"I'm very, very glad to be alive," she said convincingly. "And I've always believed in positive thinking. I'm also happy with what's going on in Vermont; it's a special place and it continues to be. It struck me twenty years ago that many of us took its beauty for granted— but now we just have to work a little harder at keeping it that way."

GERTRUDE HORRIDGE

I was born in Dorset, Vermont and delivered by the doctor there in my parents's home. My mother went to Bennington (to the hospital) to have my sister.

"Dr. Little delivered me; he was well-known in Dorset, a real horse and buggy doctor. Later, he always treated me free, but he charged for my sister."

Gertrude Horridge, proprietor and owner, with her husband Bill, of the Eagle Tavern in East Poultney, sat back in an easy chair, one leg propped on a foot stool, crutches resting on the table nearby. She was recovering from a fall taken the week before, but while it interfered with her maneuverability, it had little effect on her spirits. She is affable, interested in people, has a hearty laugh and a well-exercised sense of humor.

Late on a hot summer afternoon we talked about the bed and breakfast business she and Bill started. They've been told that the Eagle Tavern is one of the ten oldest buildings in the state.

"This is the new Tavern, and it was built in 1785," she said, explaining that unlike most old buildings in Vermont, long since gone, the original had not burned but was torn down and a new one built in its place, back in the eighteenth century.

The Horridges are part of the revival of a business once commonplace in Vermont, taking summer guests into one's home, in small towns or on farms, a pleasant way for city people to enjoy country life and cuisine. It also made a modest contribution to rural family incomes during the late nineteenth and early twentieth centuries. Bed and breakfast today is extended to visitors year round and offers travelers a pleasant option to the impersonal and overtly commercial motel chains that replaced the earlier custom.

Many, within the past few years, who have opened their homes to visitors are themselves relative newcomers to the state. From urban backgrounds of their own they understood the lure of old places and the attraction of more personal hospitality.

But Gertrude Horridge has returned to her birthplace after an absence of almost forty years. The bed and breakfast that she and her husband started is in the area where she spent her first eighteen years.

"Even though we'd never done this before, my husband and I have always wanted to own a big old house, an early house, and take in guests.

"I can remember the very day in August 1984, while we were still in New Jersey, when I said, 'It's getting too crowded here and it's time to move.'

"Father and Mother were well-known in this area when I was growing up," she recalled. "Father was caretaker of an estate that was familiar to everyone in Dorset. My mother was German and came here as a governess. After they married, they bought what had been the post office in the town—and the home next door—started an antique shop and a small restaurant, and my father did paintings and sold them."

Her father's people, the Parks of the famous Parks-McCullough house in Bennington, had originally come to Vermont from Mystic, Connecticut.

Gertude's father was still young when he developed a crippling bone disease, and she remembers that he was on crutches from 1940 until he died in 1975. "Daddy being on crutches didn't make a big difference to us; he didn't let it. He took us to the pond to ice skate, both my sister and I, but he wouldn't go with us for swimming. Used to say that he'd never forgive himself if one of us started to drown and he couldn't do anything about it."

He was also in the legislature as town representative from Dorset. "My sister and I used to go and visit him there. I remember hearing him speak about wheat for India and in favor of coloring oleomargarine.

"We were proud when we heard him speak at great length in the legislature. The people in town loved him, but he was known as a quiet man; he thought about things, and in the legislature, he had plenty to say."

Gertrude remembers that while he was in Montpelier, he had a special permit during hunting season to hunt from his car.

"Mother and Daddy worked very hard. They were also very frugal because they owed a lot of money to doctors and to hospitals, and they all got paid."

During World War II, Gertrude worked in the Barrows House as a waitress during the summers. "They couldn't get more experienced waitresses, and I made spending money that way," she said, pointing out that in those days, all the kids in Dorset, visitor or resident, rich or poor, worked during summer vacations.

"After high school, I either had to go to college or go to work. There weren't many vocational choices for women then. It was either nursing, and I got sick at the sight of blood, or teaching. UVM [the University of Vermont] had a wonderful, cheap teaching course, but you had to sign a pledge that you would teach for four years in your state in order to be accepted."

But she yearned for something a little more adventuresome. She had grandparents in New York City, had often spent holidays there while she was growing up, and she was drawn to the city.

"I can still see the look on my parents' faces when I said I wanted to go to New York City to work. I was eighteen, and they were very courageous; they let me go. I got a job as a switchboard operator for an ad agency, since I'd already done that during my senior year at high school, on nights and Saturdays."

In 1949 she was both switchboard operator and receptionist at the advertising agency; she also studied typing, learned bookkeeping, got to do some copywriting as well and enjoyed all of it. Her salary was twenty-eight dollars a week to start, and by the time she left in 1952, it had climbed to thirty dollars.

Her living arrangements were made through the librarian in Dorset, who had a friend working at the Webster Apartments for Women. Built by R.H. Macy in the late 1800s, its purpose was to make certain that the women who worked in his store were of good character and clean habits, with a decent place to live. It was also well-guarded, and well-chaperoned. While working at Macy's was no longer requisite, it continued over the years to function along the same lines.

Rent was based on salary, and Gertrude paid thirteen dollars a week to live there. This included a "nice room with a sink," maid service, and two meals a day, with three on Sunday.

She was sixteen when she first met Bill, and he was twenty-two. "We dated a few times then, but he was too old for me. I met him again when he came to Bromley one year on the ski patrol, and the second time he had changed," she added, eyes sparkling. Age was no longer a barrier, and the relationship became serious. Gertrude had been skiing since she was eight, and this was an additional bond.

"When Bill and I were married it ended all thought of my going to college. But my mother was disappointed. She'd wanted us, my sister and me, to have something to fall back on. She'd always worked in the store and knew what it was like to have to work that way."

An ex-G.I., Bill had gone to the University of Pennsylvania first, and quit; his father wanted him to become a dentist, and he hated it. Then he went to Marlboro College in Vermont, where he majored in social studies and labor relations.

"After we married, Bill wanted to stay in Vermont, so we lived in Chester. He worked for the National Survey, I worked for a bank, and between us we made about fifty dollars a week."

Later, Bill's former commanding officer convinced him to take a better job working in intelligence and security in the Pickatinny Arsenal, the largest research and development center of conventional ammunition in the world, located in Dover, New Jersey.

"When we were in New Jersey, I had an antique shop for eleven years. I also managed antique shows, did publicity writing, and felt honored when newspapers accepted my work verbatim.

"I had fun doing all these things. In those years you could make good money in antiques. Today they're hard to find, expensive, and the margin of profit is small. It also meant I could be home while my children were small. We even built an addition to our house for the business.

"In 1965 we bought our first tent trailer and have been all over the U.S. and Canada since then. We wanted our kids to know there were things beyond the state of New Jersey. We lived there for thirty-two years.

"We're good innkeepers now, because we saw the way a lot of people managed this kind of thing."

Her voice dropped as she explained that the family has one son living now; they lost one of their sons when he was nineteen. He was attending the Colorado School of Mines and was killed in an avalanche at Arapaho Basin in November 1974. She spoke thoughtfully of the displacement felt when a child dies before its parents, as though a natural order has been violated.

But with the ebullient spirit that seems characteristic, she moved on to the happy subject of her new grandson, who lives with his parents in New Jersey and whom they see frequently.

"We left something good behind in New Jersey," she said with a pleased smile.

"We've been here three years; started our fourth year on June seventh. Bill took an early retirement from his job in '79. He was fifty-three, but at the time, I didn't feel ready to move. We did several things, we also bought a small house in Dorset and spent several winters there. We'd rent it in the summers, but were never quite ready to move up."

Finally, on a visit to Gertrude's mother in 1984, they ran into a real estate agent who told them about the Eagle Tavern. They saw it, and decided it was what they had always dreamed of.

"We've renovated the building, and everything else went quickly, everything, that is, but our own bedroom, and that has to wait. We stripped the wall paper and repainted, and Bill is like George, the handyman on the *Bob Newhart Show*. He's repairing the pillars now; tried to get someone to do it but nobody wants to tackle jobs like that now."

While modern conveniences have been added, the Horridges have carefully kept the spirit of the old place in its furnishing and decoration. On a tour of the building, Bill showed off the small bedroom where Horace Greeley lived for two years while he was apprenticing at the Northern Star Printing Company.

"He paid forty dollars a year, including room and board," Gertrude said later.

"Ethan Allen and his boys also used the Eagle Tavern, and it was mentioned in several accounts of the Revolutionary War. The Allen family owned a lot of Poultney at one time, and Ethan Allen's brother is buried up there in our little local cemetary. There are also three former owners of the Tavern buried up there.

"In some ways it's been like an ongoing house party you don't have to make dinner for. You'd be surprised at the people who come to stay here. In this business a lot depends on personal recommendations, and word travels fast."

They have six rooms to rent, including the stunning ballroom, and can house eleven people. Gertrude described the young English woman who stayed for several days and was so enthusiastic that her parents also paid them a visit a short time later. Robert Trent Jones, a well-known golf course designer, came to receive an honorary degree from Green Mountain College, stayed at the Eagle Tavern, and they became friends. "We would never have met him otherwise," she said.

History buffs also make a point of stopping over, as have people related to Horace Greeley. Over the weekend following my visit, they were expecting a descendant of one of the earliest owners of the tavern.

"The fun part is the thank you letters, and even gifts, that come from many people. We've made many friends," she added.

Gertrude and Bill had always wanted something they could manage themselves, not a big inn requiring a staff. But she also pointed out that most bed and breakfast establishments can only account for a part of anyone's income.

"Don't even try it if you're going to have to scramble. These inns are too small to give anyone their entire living. But if you like people, they're just right for supplementing income."

"There's a tremendous history in this town, and the Inn is paying for itself faster than we thought. East Poultney is a gem," she concluded.

"All our married life we wanted to own a inn. It was always a dream that someday we'd have the money to buy a big old place and make it into an inn, and here we are."

GINNY CALLAN

*A*n abundant crop of vegetarian restaurants, established during the 1960s and 1970s, has come and gone without leaving so much as a carrot behind, but The Horn of the Moon Cafe in Montpelier, started by Ginny Callan in 1977, has continued to flourish. Several reasons account for its success, not least of which is the food. *A Horn of the Moon Cookbook: Recipes from Vermont's Renowned Vegetarian Restaurant*, was published by Harper and Row in 1987 and is now in its third printing.

"I've been a vegetarian since 1971, and the restaurant was a way of sharing vegetarianism with other people," Ginny said.

She has a talent for basics. The reverence she holds for food is apparent in the way it is handled, prepared, and served at her restaurant.

Ginny Callan is a gratifying example of how unexpected qualities, working successfully together, create an unstereotypical whole. She doesn't conform to the concept of a rotund cook, an ebullient, hard-edged business woman, or uncompromising idealist; yet she combines aspects of all three.

Exceedingly slender and tall, she has long, straight hair that frames a face from which round dark eyes view the world in apparent wide-eyed wonder. Behind this expression, however, one finds an idealistic, as well as discerning, businesswoman who has discovered an appetizing and practical method of combining her principles with her work.

"The original Horn of the Moon Cafe started in 1977," she said.

"There was no place in town for a vegetarian to eat then; all you could get was salad, french fries, or baked potatoes, if you were lucky."

Ginny was twenty-five, a Goddard college graduate whose interest was Vermont history, but whose prospects for work in the field were slight. "I didn't have a chance, there were people with M.A. degrees out there looking for jobs."

She found employment managing a clothing store, but because of her interest in an alternative way of eating, she was drawn to a friend's wholesale sandwich and vegetarian food business with outlets in natural food stores.

"If you get tired I'd like to pick up your business," she told him.

"Why don't we just become partners and expand it?" he replied.

So they did, and together made and sold Mother's Best sandwiches in Burlington, Stowe, Warren, and other towns.

"I continued to work full-time at the store, but I was up at five in the morning and working late at night making sandwiches, all summer long. I liked what I was doing, but I knew it would slow down in the fall. I also like to cook, so I looked for a spot in town where I could open a little restaurant. I found a store on Main Street that had been a small grocery, and it seemed like just the place. I figured I could seat thirteen people there."

With a little over three thousand dollars she had managed to save, the business was started. A friend helped with the renovation and carpentry, which included building the tables and the counter; only secondhand equipment was used in the kitchen.

"I hired a plumber to hook up the sink," she admitted with a grin, "but we did everything else."

Ginny approached the Small Business Administration for help, but they laughed. "Come back when you have ten thousand dollars, and then we'll talk," they said, considering even that amount to be trifling. They could have learned a lesson about judging character, as well as understanding the potential of small business in the hands of a dedicated entrepreneur.

"The Horn of the Moon took off from the start," she continued. "First the alternative people, then state workers, then professional people, lawyers, and others." People were not as health-conscious then as they are now, but they came. The restaurant now offers nondairy choices as well as those including cheese, and during the last two years, there has been even more growth.

"Ninety percent of new restaurants go under in the first five years, but I was really committed to making a go of this. During the first year, at the old place, I worked eighty to a hundred hours a week.

In the beginning, it was just surviving, but before long, people were standing in line out in the street, waiting to get in.

"At first I was idealistic; I'd never worked in a restaurant before, and I've learned a lot. The food business can slip away pretty easily if you're not careful."

The labor costs of natural food are tremendous, she explained, and a profit is hard to realize. She now buys organic food when it's available locally, but found she couldn't keep her prices reasonable and pay the increased costs of importing it from California, as she tried to do in the beginning.

After making a decision to move into larger quarters in 1979, Ginny went from one employee to twenty. She started with lunch and dinner only three nights a week, but soon expanded the service to include breakfast, lunch and dinner, Tuesday through Saturday. On Monday the restaurant is open only for breakfast and lunch, and on Sunday just for brunch.

Her interest in the present Langdon Street quarters, next to the old iron bridge over the north branch of the Winooski River, is derived from its location. She pointed out to the potential landlord that a restaurant there would be good for the street, with a craft shop just across the way and a good bookstore at the corner. She also liked the idea of being near the river, and hopes someday to build a deck out over the water. But she approaches large debts cautiously.

"I tend to be a conservative in fiscal matters," she continued. "The stockmarket crash really scared me. I've borrowed as much as $2,000 or even $3,000 at a time, but never large amounts, only what I can handle reasonably.

"In the last two years, I've bought some new equipment, two new stoves and a dishwasher. It's a nicer place to work now."

She is able to offer health insurance to her employees, paying half after one year and full after two, and she gives bonuses twice a year. "Sort of a profit sharing," she said, explaining that she now has ten full-time and ten part-time employees.

"Some people have been here ten years, one person was here nine years and left town a year ago. But people leave and then come back, and I'm glad to have them return. I like to be flexible."

After completing the manuscript of her cookbook, which customers had repeatedly urged her to do, she completed a package that was sent to about forty publishers.

"I read about how to be your own publisher later, and found that I'd done everything the wrong way. But then someone gave me the names of a couple of senior editors at two good publishing houses, and that helped a lot. I never got a response from the others.

"My friends at Laughing Bear Associates designed the package, and Ed Koren did a drawing. It was published last May and is in its third printing now. Local people look through the book, get hungry and say, 'I don't want to make this—I'll just go over there and get it.'

"I've also had lots of nice letters, and people traveling to Vermont who have seen it make a point of stopping by."

Ginny's conservatism towards fiscal matters also carries over into a concern for protecting the resources and rights of everyone to have good food, pure water and clean air. The restaurant is one outgrowth, and as a political activist, she deals with the other two, as well as related issues.

"I've been arrested a number of times, by way of making a strong personal statement, and I met my husband, Cort Richardson, through our involvement in the Seabrook antinuclear movement."

Ginny was born and raised in Queens, New York. Her father died when she was twelve and she and her mother were left alone. She pointed out with pride that several years later they had started dating at about the same time and have been close ever since.

"We would come home and talk together about our evening," she recalled with obvious pleasure.

"My mother later married a man she'd met an an anti-Vietnam demonstration and had been with for about fifteen years."

Ginny went to Goddard College because she was looking for a less regimented situation than she had in New York.

"I always went to public schools. But I had time off for catechism every Wednesday afternoon, and I had some resentment to overcome about being brought up as a Catholic, and a lot of guilt. I consider myself now a recovered Catholic."

She only lived on campus for one semester because she wanted to put roots down in Vermont and felt too alienated from the rest of the community.

One summer she raised a big organic garden. "I was a city girl, and I wanted to pull some carrots right out of the ground. We were part of the back to the land movement and got support from each other. A lot of us ended up opening our own businesses; we couldn't find jobs, so we had to figure something out for ourselves. Goddard was kind of a seedbed.

"Everybody was so idealistic during those years, and nobody imagined going back into the system. The idea was to do what *you* wanted to do and not what the system forced you into. I feel very fortunate in the way I've found to make my living.

"My husband is the director of VPIRG [Vermont Public Research

Group]. We were married in 1981, and we're in the process of adopting a child. We found a piece of land, ten acres with some amazing old apple trees, and we built a passive solar house on it."

Ginny and her restaurant are something of a legend around the state, and in a kind of business with one of the highest potentials for failure, she has succeeded beyond expectations. As for the future she defies the conventional wisdom of expansion or franchise.

"I made a conscious decision to keep the restaurant small, and not open a second or a third branch. People have wanted to back it, but I'm not interested. That would add extra stress and dominate my whole life.

"I've had a lot of support from the community, and the restaurant is a real center. People seem drawn to the place."

The Horn of the Moon provides a genuine coming home atmosphere, and even though at regular meal times it becomes busy and the noise level heightens, its air of cordiality remains. Casual dress, good food, reasonable prices, and waitresses and waiters who appear to enjoy their work help account for its success. But to Ginny Callan goes the credit for maintaining a successful business that has never lost contact with the purpose fueling its start. And one of its constants is the quality of its food.

"I really enjoy people, and I enjoy food; that's why I've always had an open kitchen. People are important to me. I have regular customers who have been coming for eleven years. Every now and again someone will say, 'Why don't you close off that kitchen?' but I just tell them that I haven't got anything to hide."

MARCY
HARDING

*P*eople should be made comfortable talking about their finances—
feel uninhibited," Marcy Harding said pleasantly.

By nature, as well as by demeanor and dress, she was well-suited
to make this happen—relaxed manner, blue eyes, wheat-colored hair,
no makeup—combined to create a convincingly friendly style. She is
the Central Vermont regional manager for the Howard Bank and out
of eight senior vice presidents, she is the only woman.

We spoke in her large, comfortable office at the bank building in
Montpelier, just off the first floor, where the routine business of
banking is carried on. And while an air almost of serenity dignifies
her space, the tall corner windows facing out on State and Langdon
Streets are a reminder of the world outside.

When I expressed interest in the responsibility of her position, as
a woman, within a traditionally male structure, she pointed out that
banking has made some significant changes regarding gender bias in
the last few years and that it is becoming a rewarding career for
women. She views her particular achievement as not that unusual.

"The Equal Employment Opportunity Act of the late seventies
heightened awareness in the banking and other industries of the
necessity of giving women a chance for career development within
their organizations."

"I benefitted by the times," she continued earnestly. "The bank
was looking for qualified women, and in December 1976, I was promoted to commercial loan officer in Burlington. It all started there."

Up to that point, she had followed an uncertain vocational direction,
not unusual for women even in 1971. Graduating from the University

of Vermont, she was primarily looking for "a nine-to-five job with regular hours." Although she'd majored in math at college, her courses were not directed towards a particular goal, and no thought had been given to a long-term career in finance for her. And while skilled performance by women in the management of finances is not new, recognition and expanded use of this skill within male financial structures is.

"I was hired in the Howard Bank under the man who's now my boss," she began. "On the day I applied, seven of their young women tellers were taking a vacation together in New Mexico. The man interviewing me said, almost in desperation, 'Yes, we'll hire you. You may be just stuffing statements, but can you start this afternoon?'

"I was a teller for a little less than a year, and I got to know the banking business. I also got to know customers, and I was ready for more challenge."

Marcy explained that this took place around the time the bank formalized its credit department, the section that does background work for commercial loan officers; her work included preparing spread sheets and financial statement analyses. She started working with the business and commercial lending officers.

"In December 1976, the fellow who is my boss now transferred to the Rutland office, and I was promoted to the position of commercial lending officer in Burlington. I stayed there as a specialist and dealt exclusively with commercial accounts.

"This was about the first step the Howard Bank took to move a woman into an area traditionally dominated by men," she added, explaining that only one other woman had a job of this importance and it was in advertising.

On the domestic front, as well on the business level, Marcy represents some departure from custom. "My husband is the primary caregiver in our family," she stated with pride. "Our children are three and five years old, and we have a special daycare provider for up to three days a week. I really feel that because of this arrangement—the even sharing between me, my husband and our wonderful daycare provider—neither my husband nor I get burned out.

"I also feel fortunate to have a husband who doesn't have other responsibilities, who can be there when a child gets sick or any other emergency arises, and who enjoys it."

Dan Martin, Marcy's husband, is a woodworker and designer, and before their daughter was born in 1983, the couple had planned on full-time childcare. But her husband's firm went out of business at the same time that the childcare arrangements fell through.

"My husband decided that he could take care of our daughter,

Chelsea, full-time and with where I was in my career, it made more sense. We started building our own home in 1980, but it was still unfinished. He planned to work on the house while she was in day-care part-time.

"It's an ideal arrangement, and there's still plenty else for him to do: woodlot management, gardening, all the necessary work connected with heating our house with wood, volunteering with the Solid Waste Board and the after-school ski program. He still does woodworking and has just completed a woodshop and studio."

This domestic arrangement differs from her own background.

"My mom was a stay-at-home mom, and my dad was definitely the breadwinner. Both of them had traditional roles and ideas. I was raised in very comfortable circumstances, with one younger sister."

Marcy was born in Schenectady, New York, but her family moved to Shelburne when she was six months old. She believes that since she's spent every winter of her life in Vermont, this gives her some claim to calling herself a native.

"In my own family the roles are quite different. My mom was the primary caretaker, seven days a week. She was also an active volunteer and founded the kindergarten, worked with Girl Scouts, took us to piano lessons and dance lessons, and she always seemed very happy.

"Still, I've noticed that when she sees how much my husband and I enjoy our children, she's a little surprised. She never felt she could just step back and enjoy hers in the same way."

Speaking of her immediate family Marcy said, "We enjoy being together as a family. My husband and I don't have as much time for each other as we might like, but that will change. I also feel strongly that I'm in a position now where the time I have to spend with my children is very precious, and I enjoy all of it."

Citing her recent attendance at a twenty-year high school reunion she said, "The oldest looking women there had their children when they were the youngest. I believe that having children later has kept me young."

About the combination of children and serious interest in a career, she made another point. "Career women can fall easily into a pattern of putting off having children until it gets too late. I did this until I was thirty-four, and I'm forty now," she continued with a broad smile.

"I made the decision to be careless, just once. Five minutes and that was it; I was pregnant. It's harder to combine a family and a career, but I never realized how much joy there is to having children.

"I went through one marriage in the seventies. My first husband and I were divorced, but we remained friends and I feel good about that. We had no children. I never thought of having children with him."

Marcy remembers enjoying some of the rebellion of the 1960s. "I marched down Church Street with placards. It was during the early years when the baby boomers were becoming activists, and we were part of the Vietnam and Kent State protests, and there was also Woodstock."

In the spring of 1987, she was offered the opportunity to move from Burlington to the Montpelier office, with the idea that she would be in training for the regional management position expected to open up soon. The bank had changed to a regionalized structure only a year or two before, and within the five regions, Montpelier is the third largest. When she made her move, she worked with the central Vermont manager until his retirement in June.

"Curious the way things work," she continued, eyes widening as she savored the vicissitudes of fate. "I now report to the man who originally hired me, many years ago. Today he's the senior loan officer of the entire bank."

She finds her work challenging, as well as demanding. "I've been dealing with a lot of responsibilities in these last six months, administrative responsibilities. But I get my head above water often enough. I don't dread going to work in the mornings anymore, afraid I'll never get caught up.

"I've not been able to take two consecutive weeks off for a vacation—only managed to get days off—but I'm going to do that next summer. We're planning on going camping as a family."

Marcy is optimistic about her work and some of the changes that are being made within the state. She is enthusiastic about Act 200, passed by the legislature in 1988 to encourage local and regional communities in their plans for growth management in their areas. She believes this legislation will have a salutary effect on growth.

"Another issue I'm interested in is the captive insurance industry. I'm one of three people in the Howard bank involved in this."

She explained that a captive is an insurance company owned by, and providing insurance for, its parent organization and the subsidiaries belonging to it. Before Vermont passed a law in 1981 permitting captives to operate here, most were located offshore. Since that time, the industry has mushroomed, and the future influence of major corporations on Vermont life could be significant. Some of the largest corporations in the world have located an important part of their business in Vermont, and its supporters consider it to be one of the state's biggest growth industries. Multi-nationals like Alcoa, Mobil, Hallmark, and Toyota have set up their own captives here.

Marcy is among those who believe that this new development has benefitted Vermont, but there are others who question the influence of multi-national corporations on the future of this small state.

There's an ambivalence about Marcy Harding. While she works in the area of high finance her style is less that of hard-edged business woman than of small-townsperson, dressed nicely for work and eager to hear what a neighbor, dropping in to her office has to say.

Speaking about her success within the banking structure she continued, "I was with the Howard Bank credit department in Burlington, and when the opportunity arose to advance, I clearly had the right background. I just happened to be in the right place, at the right time."

JANE NEWTON

*I*t was March 9, 1985, when we sawed our first log in our own mill," she said, "and we've done nothing but grow ever since. Sales pretty near doubled in three years, and our employees number about thirteen. We're beginning to settle in now, know what works and what doesn't."

Jane Newton is a trim-looking woman, with clear blue eyes, straight, short brown hair, and an even-tempered manner. On the day I visited her, she wore jeans, workboots, and a dark green work shirt with a pocket emblem reading *Calendar Brook Lumber*. She is one of three equal share owners of a sawmill in Lyndonville.

We sat on a graduated pile of honey-colored planks in the covered shed where the sawn wood is stored, and she talked about her business. She also recounted some of the unexpected turns in her life that led her to the position of successful saw mill owner and skilled sawyer.

In this self-service lumber mill, customers go to the office, get a slip, then go to the large storage shed where the different boards are kept to pick out what they want. The stacked wood in varying widths and lengths made dramatic patterns in the large structure.

"All the logs come from around here. We don't buy any finished lumber, only what we can do: pine, spruce, balsam, fir, hemlock, some popple, tamarack. Getting logs hasn't been a problem." She pointed out that they air-dry most of the pine cut during the winter and send the rest to the Caledonia Kiln in South Lyndonville.

"We saw lots of logs for post and beam construction, eighteen inch by twenty inch by twenty-two foot timbers," she continued. "Sometimes we have trouble getting these, but we work closely with the Department of Forest and Parks, which is involved and helpful.

"My job now is supervising the mill, tending to production, and maintaining the connection between orders and operators, but I did all the sawing for most of our first three years," she said, explaining that she sawed something like two and a half million board feet a year.

"I decided I needed to get out of the mill and learn more about the business. That had been inaccessible to me when I was in there running the saw, so I trained a sawyer, but I still go in and saw once in a while. We made John (the current sawyer) foreman of the mill, and I'm still looking for another sawyer, someone who wants to work in the mill. This takes a special kind of person. It's intense, meticulous work."

A lot has happened in Jane's life since February 1974, when she loaded her things into a VW micro bus and set out from her home in southern Vermont for the Northeast Kingdom.

"I wanted work that would keep me outdoors," she explained. "I'd been involved in trying to be a homemaker, but I really wasn't ready to settle down.

"When I first came up here, the fellow that I worked for later had a little sawmill down in his pasture. He'd been a school teacher but had just retired from teaching so he could operate his mill year-round. When I got here and let it be known I was looking for work, a couple of people said, 'Warren might need some help; you ought to go over and see him.' "

Sawmills were new to Jane, but she knew something about machinery.

"Growing up on a farm, I was always expected to do my chores, I enjoyed driving the trucks, and I knew how to keep them going. I have a feel for mechanics that I was born with.

"The day I went to see Warren, he was fussing over a little tractor that needed repairing, but he would have had to shut his mill down to take care of it. Since I knew something about mechanics, I offered to fix the tractor. I took off the leaky hose, took it to town, had a new one made up, took it back, replaced it, and had a job.

"From then on, it was a learning experience, and it fascinated me to see logs turned into lumber. The mill itself was pretty rinky-dink, which meant that we were always tinkering with the old machine to keep it operating."

Working for Warren Fox was valuable to Jane in many ways. For one thing, he never assumed there was anything she couldn't do, so she did things she'd never dreamed of doing. He taught her about handling logs as well as about scaling them, the crucial skill of estimating the number of board feet in an uncut log. Since his own dad was a sawyer, Warren had been around this work all his life.

"He was raised in the woods—went from the woods into the classroom, and he had many skills. My partner, Jim Norris, says that Warren always had a big following. He knew all kinds of things, and he enjoyed teaching people.

"From 1974 'til 1980 I worked for him pretty regularly. But one year I did a firewood business on my own and spent the winter in the woods. Then I bought my own piece of land from him, up on a hill behind the mill building. I cut the trees, skidded them down and built my own house, with help from friends."

During the next few years, she also remodeled the old mill building, sawed out all the lumber, and the rest of the crew put it together.

Later, to become more independent, she bought a small, portable mill. She spent a year and a half traveling within a radius of fifty miles, sawing other people's logs on their sites.

"I didn't have to do any trucking that way. It was pretty interesting work, and I met all kinds of people—farmers and others who needed lumber for different kinds of construction. I learned a lot more about building."

But one night coming home from work, she saw billows of smoke rising from the mill's location. Warren's place was in flames.

"It was ten below zero on March 9, and the mill burned flat," she said, a pained expression crossing her face at the thought. "All the machinery twisted out of shape. Warren was away at the time."

Later, when Warren asked Jane and Jim Norris if they would like to buy what was left of the business, they got two other friends together and worked out a plan. A financial package was assembled; they got their loans approved and went to work rebuilding the mill in the fall of 1984.

"There were four of us who were interested," Jane said. "Jim's background was logging and machinery. I knew the business pretty well by that time. A third partner, Doris Riley, taught school and could manage the books, and the fourth partner was a contractor who knew the market. He went back to contracting, and the three of us have been running it for the last two years," she added.

The new building was constructed with materials that wouldn't burn: concrete walls and steel rafters—otherwise, insurance would have been prohibitive. (Today, as further fire protection, it is routine procedure at the mill for the employees to stop fifteen minutes before quitting time to clean up their stations.)

The owners bought second-hand equipment for the mill, adapted the machinery, and, in the course of the winter, moved it in. On March 9, 1985, exactly one year after the fire, they sawed their first log, and Jane was their sawyer.

"At first I stood up with a manual set and sawed for two years— just me. The mill we originally put in was semi-automatic, but then I heard that computers were getting into sawmills. 'Oh no,' I said at first, and then I visited a small mill that had one and I thought, 'What a good idea.'

"So I adapted a computer for our business, built a room, glass enclosed, away from the saw. It was warm in winter and there was the additional advantage of the sawyer being able to sit down and saw."

She showed me where the sawyer had stood before, for the manual operation, and described an incident illustrating the danger inherent in the work when the sawyer had no protection.

A log kicked back one day and was driven through two concrete blocks in a wall behind it. It slammed into a bank several yards on the outside of the building after being propelled at least ten feet inside before exiting through the cement block wall. Luckily, it missed the sawyer on its way.

Recalling her early years, from growing up on a farm in Westminster to the highly independent career she now has, Jane explained that as she grew up, she took college preparatory courses, assuming she would complete four years of college. She felt this was expected of her and had spent two years at a boarding prep school.

"Then I started thinking, 'Who am I and what do I really want to do?' I really wasn't into what I was doing at the time, and my mother said, 'You don't have to go to college, you know.' This started me thinking.

"Mom had gone to UVM [the University of Vermont], and Dad to business school, but he's really a dairy farmer at heart," she added.

For the last twenty years, her mother has been head of Vocational Rehabilitation in Windham County, but on the farm, as her children were growing up, she was a mother. There were three children in the family, and it was not until they were older that she started working for the social service department. Jane's sister is now a writer, and her younger brother a dairy farmer.

Before Jane moved north, she was married and living in Windham. She avers that at the time she was simply not ready to stay at home and settle into being a homemaker.

"I have a child, a son who is now sixteen. He spends the summers with me and the winters with his father." She lives in North Danville now, and the house she built is rented. In addition to the sawmill, she has had an interest in building ever since the construction of her own house.

Later, Jane took me into the mill so I might get some idea of the transition from log to plank. The noise was fearsome, and everyone wore ear guards. The carrier, shuttling back and forth with the logs to be sawed, operates and sounds like a locomotive engine in constant motion. Then there is the whine of the saw and the clunking of the machine stripping off the bark.

"Debarking logs is like rolling a drunk," Jane said. "The log is dead weight and it's juggled around so the debarker on top can scrape off the bark. Wheels on the bottom carry it along."

Outside the building, a forklift moved the logs into position for their entrance, and another at the other end picked up and stacked the cut lumber as it emerged. A large trailer waited to truck lumber to the planing mill.

Standing outside after leaving the din of the mill, Jane said, "Without Warren I couldn't have done it. I struggled with the idea of learning that skill, learning to be a sawyer, and it took me a while to know that it was indeed something I could do—me, a woman.

"The lumbermen were males, and my own idea that it is a male role was the only reason I had any trouble with it. Still, I got nothing but support from the men around me.

"That decision was a major stepping stone in my life," she continued softly. "It was one of the hurdles I overcame. And when I get into tough places now, I think back on what I did then—and how much harder that was to do."

Suzanne Gillis

*E*very woman has a story to tell," Suzanne Gillis began. "Every time a woman becomes more evolved there is some process that happened along the way, a click, or maybe a series of clicks, that brought her to a new realization about herself and what's possible for her."

Publisher and founder of *Vermont Woman*, a monthly newspaper produced in Burlington and offered without charge from distribution centers around the state, she speaks from experience.

"The first issue was printed in November 1985, and I still have a sense of mission."

To this end the newspaper includes articles, calendars, reviews, newsbriefs, pertinent political and business news, and other features related to events and ideas perceived as being of particular interest to women. With no feigned modesty, Suzanne pointed out that of the twenty-eight other regional newspapers devoted to women's issues currently being published anywhere in this country, *Vermont Woman* is one of the best.

Research of similiar projects before she started publishing indicated that most women's newspapers were targeted just towards the business woman and that at least twenty thousand printed copies needed to be distributed in order to attract advertisers. Suzanne was convinced, however, that there would also be other interested women readers and that part of the publication's significance would lie in the information it contained about women and the occupations and values they pursued.

"The other publications are targeted primarily to business and professional women, and their editorial thrust is narrower. I think the editorial mix we have makes ours far more interesting," she said.

"There were two largely introspective questions I had to resolve within myself before I could make a start. 'Who am I to start a newspaper—do I know enough?' and 'Who cares?' "

She explained that these spawned a series of related questions, about her own values, her willingness to take the risk, financially and every other way, as well as the responsibilities and the commitment entailed in starting a new business. She felt it also had something to do with facing the eternal question of "what I'm all about as a woman."

Although she continued to do other work, Suzanne rented an office for herself in preparation for this venture; but she was immobilized before the enormity of the risk ahead of her. In her spare time she sat around in her new office, did research, temporized.

She recounts with amusement the experience that triggered her decision to start, one year and a half later. "I kept saying to myself, 'No, I don't know enough.' " But in January 1985, she was accepted for a part-time job at St. Michael's College, a position putting her in charge of raising funds from corporations.

"I went to the development office on my first day of work, had on my career clothes, and everybody else had on theirs. The men all wore gray suits, and the head of the office was a man. The women were all dressed up, but most of them were typing."

Hired as the director of corporate giving, Suzanne was shown to her office but found two desks there: a big one, with a man behind it, his feet resting on its surface, and a little one that was hers, off to the side. "I remember saying to myself, 'I want my own office or I'll get sick.'

"I stayed until noon and then came up to this office. I sat alone here for about two hours, and that's when I finally decided to start publishing. I made the commitment that same day, and I said to myself 'I'm going to take a risk—do something I really believe in.' And I've never stopped since."

After this decision, her next step was to find an editor. "After an extensive search I found an excellent editor, Rickey Gard Diamond, and together we created *Vermont Woman*. The way we did it was to come up with an answer to the question, 'Who is that Vermont woman we are going to target our newspaper to?' "

They developed a Vermont woman profile and a formula for the *Vermont Woman* format. On the cover of their first edition, a composite of ten photographs illustrated women from a variety of fields; and its title, *Women: Redefining Achievement*, established their goal. This redefinition has been the principle followed ever since. Their intent was to show, at the beginning, the kind of variety that would be included: women in farming, social work, business, trades, the arts, education, medicine; the list was open-ended, and the voyage of discovery begun.

Since then, however, their original idea of one woman on the cover has usually but not necessarily always been followed. There are also concept issues which are published two or three times a year, and they frequently have a montage of several women.

"In these issues, we tackle controversial topics of concern to women," Suzanne said. Editions have been devoted to women in non-traditional trades, women and aging, AIDS, incest, equal rights, battering, and other topics. "Our next issue will be about women in poverty. We feel that there's a principle involved in the information we carry and that part of our mission is to explore subjects of concern to all of us."

Returning to the subject of women's evolution, she made a comparison between her own progress and that of Rickey.

"There are different ways women arrive at the realization of their own possibilities. Rickey started out by doing everything she was supposed to. Married at eighteen, she had three kids and lived through a period of quiet desperation, unaware of her choices. Her evolvement was slower.

"I became angry at a young age because I was denied certain activities on the basis of my sex. My anger was fueled by coming up against traditions that didn't work for me as a woman. My marriage was one of them. It didn't work, and I was divorced. Still, our experiences are what add up to making us who we are."

Suzanne and Rickey established basic values and principles that the newspaper would follow, its mission being to promote the equality of women—economically, socially, and politically."

"We want to make it a more equitable world for men and women—we're in it together. But we didn't want to just tell pretty stories about successes. We try to mesh our editorial content with the struggles women have had and continue to have today."

"We also planned an anniversary celebration, an annual event presenting a widely known woman as its featured keynote speaker. This was intended also to honor the women who had appeared on the newspaper's covers during the previous year by seating them on the stage with the speaker."

This event, held at the end of their first year, featured Gloria Steinem as its speaker. The following year Jehan Sadat, widow of Egypt's assasinated prime minister and author of *A Woman of Egypt*, played that role. This year, Helen Thomas, dean of the White House press corps, spoke to a packed auditorium.

Confident, vivid, and enthusiastic, Suzanne Gillis illustrates the image of *Vermont Women of Achievement* that her newspaper espouses. Her personality is direct and the impression she gives is of a woman who uses hurdles as an opportunity for becoming airborne.

"Men are reading it too, and that's great. I know that the paper is effecting change—subtly, without women or men feeling threatened," she said.

Publishing a newspaper had no place in Suzanne's plan when she moved to Vermont. Her reason for coming here was possibly not too different from the Connecticut ancestors of many contemporary Vermonters. "I moved from Connecticut to Vermont to start a new life," she said.

But the date and means of travel were at some variance: "In 1974 I packed up my station wagon and headed north."

She remembers well her first view of Burlington, the town where she chose to settle. "It was the first time I crossed Lake Champlain. The sun was setting, and my heart was racing. I used my sunglasses as a filter over my camera for a picture.

"The next day I walked down Church Street, and the people all seemed bright-eyed and full of bounce. I felt these people had something very special, had an energy that I wanted to be part of; so I chose it as a place to live.

"I wanted to be in a place I cared about, around people who care about their town. I was tired of living in a place where people race up and down thruways to get to work, people who don't really feel connected to their own town or environment."

Her move to the state was precipitated by divorce.

"I was married at twenty-seven and divorced at twenty-eight, and at that it was much too long. We plan on spending our lives with someone without really knowing who we are or what we're looking for. Too often our parents never said anything about what the experience of being married actually means.

"Mother passed away a year before my marriage, and I hadn't even completed my bachelor's degree. I was in Colorado for a while after the divorce, but my family was all in the East, and it seemed very far away. I also had a grandmother who was eighty and I didn't want that kind of distance between us.

"I chose Vermont because there's something special about it, it's a state small enough for individuals to make a difference. I had a strong background in marketing, promotion and sales. I sold radio and magazine advertising, worked for several daily and weekly newspapers. Even so I floundered and had many jobs. In 1980 I went back to UVM [the University of Vermont] and got a B.A. in political science."

She became interested in the idea of starting her own publication while she was buying national advertising for Gardenway, Inc. She picked up a copy of *Connecticut Woman* on a trip to Connecticut and stopped in at the newspaper's office in the town where it was published. "It was a spontaneous move on my part but things were pretty informal there, and I was lucky enough to meet with the publisher, the editor, and the advertising director. We talked for three hours, and I left with an armload of their newspapers and a lot of information. Still, it was another year and a half before I published the first issue of *Vermont Woman*."

"Of course I've had to recommit to the idea many times since. It's not just starting a new thing, but there's also the necessity of maintaining growth and development.

While Suzanne has been successful in eminently measurable ways, life is not always easy for pioneers. For an independently owned newspaper to exist in competition with corporately owned publications is to assume the position of a mouse that roared at an elephant. Yet the independence of the alternative press is our only guarantee of news we can obtain in no other way.

The yearly cost to publish *Vermont Woman*, a quarter of a million dollars, while inconsequential to a large corporate structure, is staggering to an individual, especially one committed to incisive advocacy for women. In the case of *Vermont Woman*, committed as it is to exploring topics of importance to women, Suzanne pointed out that there's always a significant drop in advertising after the publication of a controversial subject.

"It takes us a couple of issues to get back up again, and we're constantly trying to balance our editorial content with what our advertisers will support. Our newspaper is free, so we can't very well ask for subscriptions," she said.

Another problem in advertising she pointed out is that many advertisers only use the paper when that particular issue has a theme relating to what the advertiser is selling. Herbs for an herb issue, services related to health in an issue on fitness, and so on. This makes developing a predictable financial base difficult. There is also the curious irony that most of their advertising comes from male-owned businesses in the area; there is a lack of support from women-owned businesses.

But while there are still problems, there are successes. "We've expanded regionally, and we've added staff. We now have a production manager and we're leveraging the business. At this point, we are marginally successful, and we even showed a small profit in 1988. The print run is the same but the entire paper is now produced in-house. We have desktop publishing so after it's finished, we put the boards on the bus and sent them to Bennington to be printed."

On the morning I visited Suzanne, she was the only person in the office. "We have a staff retreat every six months. We close the office and take the day just to talk and eat," she said, and explained that she was joining them later.

"Six full-time people create this paper every month. Because *Vermont Woman* has a mission, the staff has to have a higher type of commitment. With my style of management, the entire staff has input. And with this type of paper, I have to have commitment and involvement by the staff."

With pride she showed me the February issue of *Vermont Woman*, which featured the smiling face of Dr. Athur Kunin on its cover. The accompanying caption read, *Dr. Arthur Kunin: The Man Behind the Governor*, and the inside article detailed some of the many ways Arthur Kunin has supported his wife in essential ways, assuming much responsibility for their children as the demands of her political career increased. This has been in addition to his function as a specialist in kidney disease and a professor of medicine at the University of Vermont.

"This was a first for us, running a man's picture on the cover, but I think it was a valuable contribution. We might even do it again sometime with another man who has been outstandingly supportive of his wife's career."

In a more reflective vein, she added, "I've often wondered what it would have meant to me back in 1962 when I was a teenager, if my mother had come home with a copy of *Vermont Woman* under her arm. She would have had a different perspective, and so would I."

The large room where we spoke displayed examples of three years of publishing, framed front pages of *Vermont Woman* in several tiers around the walls. It was an impressive display. Suzanne leaned forward, her voice rising in excitement. "I understand what it's like to be scared and take risks, what it's like to do something you've never done before—to leave before lunch and never go back—but I wouldn't have missed this for the world."

LISA LINDAHL AND
HINDA SCHREIBER MILLER

In the beginning it was known as Jogbra. The corporation's name is now JBI, and Jogbra is just one of its products, but it is still the perfect business for these two New Age entrepreneurs. The product Lisa Lindahl and Hinda Schreiber Miller chose to build their business upon is intrinsically worthwile; meeting a need that both personally and in the marketplace was waiting to be met. As a result, Lisa and Hinda's canny mix of business acumen and marketing skill has catapulted them to a highly successful place in the world of business.

I visited the creators of the first Jogbra, designed and marketed specifically for joggers, in their conference room at the JBI/JOGBRA headquarters in Williston. The nature of their business, and the way they merged contrasting talents to make a successful whole, seemed to dictate that they be interviewed together.

"I'm more task oriented," Hinda explained.

"And I'm more relationship oriented," Lisa said. "Joining those two qualities provided a good base. We are uniquely New Age females.

"We didn't choose each other as partners, except perhaps on a cosmic level. It was a blind date that turned into a marriage."

She retold the story of their meeting and subsequent partnership in the business they founded on the better mousetrap theory. The vehicle for their success—bras with a difference: a bra for women runners, a previously unexplored innovation with its potential future unrealized. Also, sports stores, initially targeted for sales, were new markets to open up within the intensely competitive field of women's lingerie. Sporting goods shops had not heretofore stocked women's intimate apparel, relying more on the jockstrap connection.

"Hinda was doing costumes for the Lake Champlain Shakespeare Festival in Burlington," Lisa explained. "A mutual friend, also a costume designer, had a room in my house and the three of us began working together on the jogbra project."

Lisa was a serious runner at the time and plaintively asked her sister, another runner, "Why isn't there a jockstrap for women?"

"Why," she asked, "do active women have to endure random movement in a situation that men have had under control for years?"

As often happens in successful enterprises, one thing led to another, and the working model for the first jogbra was created when two jockstraps were joined and adapted for breasts. The result of this first union worked, but not well enough, and the quest was on for translating initial inspiration into practicality.

A visit to New York City on a search for fabric led the two women to a DuPont product, new at the time, a blend of cotton, polyester, and Lycra that proved suitable. A prototype was created, and a struggling South Carolina firm was hired to manufacture forty dozen bras. What started as a notion developed into a full-fledged industry. Most of the manufacturing is done domestically.

"We had no idea what business was, had forty dozen bras on hand, and we set out to market them in sporting goods stores. This was really a coup," Lisa said.

And Hinda added, "Sporting equipment was right on; it was an open market, and we had a new product. We were learning, and the retailers were learning; it was not yet an established product, so there was a vacuum, and we filled it."

"We moved into our own corporate headquarters last April," she continued, indicating the building they now occupy on Avenue D in the Industrial Park in Williston. The administrative quarters are characterized by the soft gray of the walls, the carpet, and the drapes; the warehousing section, by the yellow tan of corrugated packing boxes, stacked high, ready for shipment; and the combination of colors suggests success. They are neighbored by similiar buildings, all of recent vintage and all representing new and expansive growth.

Lisa explained, "We have double-digit growth every year, and as the volume grows, we need to spend more time managing. Now it's not just Hinda and me; we have five other managers. When we first started, we were small and could afford to make mistakes but not any longer."

Were there clues in their background pointing to this sort of financial success?

Lisa describes her father as a corporate businessman. Her mother didn't work and was a Junior League member in the New Jersey town where they lived. Lisa was the youngest of four children.

"I was upper middle-class, good prep school, summer house and winter house. I never expected to be in business; it was never in anybody's plans for me, or at least if I did anything like that it would have been education, teaching, or the arts."

After college she attended the Kathryn Gibbs secretarial school where she learned the "right" way of doing everything: how to perform in an office, quietly, efficiently and attractively; how to do high-level, executive secretarial work. She also learned some of the technical skills such as typing and filing.

Since she grew up in a family that despised and distrusted organized religion, she remembers slipping out with other children to Sunday School, but to her disappointment she found it boring. Later, as a young adult, she applied for and got a job as secretary at the Princeton Theological Seminary.

"It may have been the need for some sort of spiritual awareness that got me into this, and during my life as secretary there I discovered Christianity. I read the literature, saw how the papers were written, saw the politics in Christian dogma, and finally saw men playing little boy's games.

"I first accepted—and then rejected it—all within a period of twelve months. Then I looked into eastern religions."

Meantime, she had married a seminarian with two more years to go. During the second year she did a lot of work on his papers for him. She became a Buddhist.

"I went back to the Creative Process, Life Force, and Spiritual Energy and ended up with a belief that every self is a manifestation of God's energy. You can choose to use it, or you can block it. This is the challenge, and every day I still ask if I do this for God, for Life, or whatever you want to call it."

By the time the jogbra project started, she was enrolled at the University of Vermont. "I was six weeks into graduate school, with classes in the morning and jogbra work in the afternoon and evening.

I was torn about which direction to take, and spoke to my school adviser and he said 'Why don't you go with the business? You can always go back into education.' "

"By that time, Hinda had moved into my house—and my husband had moved out—and the business was on."

Hinda was brought up in an upper middle-class, Jewish family in Montreal. "My father didn't know the difference between a man and a woman in terms of what either could do. He said, 'If you needed to do it, you did it.' He made no allowance for female ineptitude.

"He was an independent real estate developer, a corporation developer who had no self-imposed limits about what could or couldn't be done if one was contemplating a project."

Hinda said that it never occurred to her father that she wouldn't be working after college, and he talked a lot about what she would do. She went to the Parsons School of Design in New York, where she received an M.A. in fine arts with a major in costume design, and she also took classes at New York University. She was attracted to the technical end of theater because she liked the way projects were viewed, with no right or wrong way of doing things as long as the work was well-done. She also perceived it as the kind of work that rewards creativity.

Becoming interested in Eastern religion, she studied at a Yoga Integral Institute in New York and later spent six years teaching communication between mind, body, and soul.

"This was a result of the drug years and the general turmoil of the sixties. Our generation was the New Age generation, the one that didn't trust anyone over thirty.

"But the sixties were a gift to us. The first generation off the boat had to scramble to live, the second generation worked to improve things, and the third generation was able to look around. It was a prosperous time for the country, but in a way it was a gift to us: we had leisure, and we found false values that were important for us to rebel against."

Lisa continued: "There was a separation between church and business. Males went to business and practiced religion on Sundays. This generation is trying to integrate what they learned about spirituality into everything they do."

After receiving her M.F.A., Hinda taught at a South Carolina university. In the summer of 1977, she came to Burlington to design costumes for the Lake Champlain Shakespeare Festival, met Lisa, and their business partnership began.

Hinda, thirty-eight, has been married for three years to a psychologist who works in New Jersey, and they spend their weekends together. She was expecting her first child within two weeks of our interview. Hinda practices low-impact aerobics.

Lisa, thirty-nine, is divorced. She was forced to stop running as a result of an overworked knee, but she replaced that activity with wind surfing. She is also a serious gardner and enjoys dating "every chance I get." She loves to travel.

The two maintain stoutly that their philosophy does not correspond with what the *Wall Street Journal* might advise, that they are not hard-line.

"More than that, Lisa and I each have a commitment to personal growth. Our world view is similiar. Truth is truth, and you might ask, if we believe in individual growth, how do we manage that in running our business?

"Our management philosophy is to empower our five managers to make as many of the daily decisions as possible."

In the summer their hours are more flexible; employees may work longer hours during the week so that they can leave on Fridays at 12:30 P.M. They also try to be flexible about sick time or kids at home sick. "We try to be understanding and helpful about this." But there is no flex time per se, or parental leave.

Both women agree that more people are needed to work and that one problem Vermont faces in attracting industry is the lack of a labor pool.

"Williston has only two percent unemployment, and this is a problem for industry," Hinda added.

The owners of JBI are not part of the Vermont Women Business Owners (VWBO), belonging instead to a group called "The Mountain Group."

"It's a group of business owners, men and women, who share common concerns. We meet once a month, and they're not all small businesses by any means," Lisa said, pointing out that Ben and Jerry's Ice Cream owners, Ben Cohen and Jerry Greenfield, are part of their group.

She continued, "Men are very interesting creatures, and they're bringing in a lot of good women. I think it's important to stress that VWBO is a good organization, but in our group, it's not so much being in business as owning a business. Also these are all privately held businesses."

They estimated that the most serious problems faced today by Vermont businesses are the specters of a raise in the minimum wage, tax burdens, and high employment.

"We must look out-of-state to stimulate the labor market. And Vermont is either a great drawback to people or a drawing card. Of course most flatlanders want to keep things the way they were when they first came here, but an organism has to grow. That is its nature. It would be nice to have controlled growth, but that isn't always possible," Hinda said.

"In my individual life there is a spiritual side," Lisa continued. "There's got to be a spiritual base, of loving instead of hating. We can't negate the basis of loving. People have a stereotyped image of business people, that all of them see Mammon as God, but that hasn't been my experience.

"It's really a challenge to be in the world of business, very challenging and very exciting. But I don't see a lot of difference between us, as a service product business, and the many religious or meditative organizations that are so successful today.

"We're not really too different in our types of organization or methods—it's just that we're selling jogbras—they're selling meditation or God."

[Hinda is now the mother of a son, Noah, born August 1988.]

LOUISE DOWNEY-BUTLER

I can't emphasize enough—the driving force of my life has been economic security for myself." Louise Downey-Butler spoke frankly about her business, and the "hard-nosed" aspect necessary for survival and growth. "It's a jungle out there, particularly if you're a woman. You've got to speak up in order to get treated right. You have to know your facts, too." Without dissimulation she added: "My motivation has always been to hear a ringing cash register bringing in money."

Behind this open espousal of business success lies a longstanding interest in herbs and growing things. The result of this union is Rathdowney Herbs and Herb Crafts, assembled or manufactured at her workplace in Bethel by twenty-four employees and sold through her own three retail shops as well as to over two thousand other shops nationwide.

The parking area at the old farmhouse beside the White River, where the business started in 1982, has long since been increased to accommodate UPS trucks pulling in regularly to pick up cartons from Rathdowney for delivery around the country. Space is also available for an impressive array of employees' cars parked in the back.

Entering the Bethel retail shop, one is transported visually, and every olfactory nerve is put on full alert. There are numerous and varied herbal mixes, both culinary and medicinal, skillfully packaged and displayed, as well as all kinds of baskets, books and periodicals related to herbs and other growing things, preserves, hand-woven fabrics, soaps and potions, kitchen utensils, ceramic containers, chocolates, coffees and teas, condiments, and a host of other kitchen or home-associated products. Behind the shop is the part of the house that was once its living area but is now where the serious business of putting together packets of herbal mixes from heaps of aromatic dried leaves, blossoms, seeds, and stems takes place. Upstairs is a continuation of assembly and packaging, bookkeeping and other business functions.

"I function now as the chief executive officer of my company, and that's my best skill," Louise explained later. "I still enjoy both the cash register and the herbs, but I've started detaching myself from the mechanics of the business, the things that can run by themselves. I'm still involved with its creative aspects, but I'm more oriented now towards writing.

"It's been a wonderful learning experience," she continued. "I've learned all aspects of the business, and I've achieved success with very little capital: a $1,500 loan to be exact. Here I am now with a growing business, and I'm starting to feel comfortable."

However, for most of us, the subject of herbs triggers an association with wild things and places, somewhat distant and more esoteric than the down-to-earth business of volume—production and delivery, personnel, and cash flow. There would seem to be contradiction between these two concepts, yet in talking with Louise over lunch at her new home, some miles in the country from the business, she fitted things together about herself and her goals that made them less dissonant.

About the serious business aspect of her success she explained, "My math and science background helped with the business end. I know how to hypothesize and how to assemble and work with facts. I'm not a big risk taker, not really so much of an entrepreneur as I'm able to act like an entrepreneur. Also, because of techniques I've developed, I'm able to analyze information."

She believes that her organization, with relatively few employees and an effective computer system, could be compared to a much larger corporation with big teams of personnel: "I enjoy organizing people, and I've more or less invented my methods as I went along."

She's beginning to see clearly what her next wave of activity should be and feels ready for it. Since she's not so locked in physically to the business, she's decided that her next move will be to write a book about the way she organized it.

"This is, in part, preparing me for old age. I can still stand on my feet for fourteen hours, seven days a week, as I've had to do in getting it all started, but how much longer can I do that and not be used up?"

Her interest in herbs is rooted in childhood memories, to time spent outdoors in a rural area of New Jersey once frequented by Indians. "As a child I was forever gathering things, leaves, grasses, plants of all kinds, and I almost felt as though I was replaying an old theme. We found arrowheads left by the Indians; they had also used the different kinds of grasses and weeds growing there. I had a real inclination to gather and find ways of using them. I also wanted to find out what the things were."

She stated with what appeared to be an interested objectivity that she is now forty-two, but she prefers not to focus on the past, only on the possibilities for the future. "In some ways, I've wiped out most of the past forty years, can't recall a lot of it, and I don't believe in dwelling on it.

"My father was definitely my role model, my mother was the more passive one and content to stay home," she recalled.

She was the oldest of five children, with two sisters and two brothers. Her oldest brother was not born until she was twelve.

"My father founded his own business when I was sixteen. He was a tool-and-die-maker up to that point and had dropped out of high school. He was self-taught but he could do what most mechanical engineers can do, and he's been very successful," she added.

"My parents were careful about spending money. If they didn't have it, they didn't spend it. They always had adequate means, but they were frugal—willing to sacrifice as long as their security needs were met."

Her memories of the first seven years of her life, spent in West Orange, New Jersey, were happy ones, but when her family moved to a rural setting in search of a better environment for the children, there were problems for Louise. As a new city kid in a small country school, things didn't go so well.

"My confidence was always there, but I was hated because I was so bright, and the teachers made a show of me. My fourth-grade teacher told my parents that I was definitely 'college material.' None of this helped with the other kids, so I spent a miserable ten years."

"I read a lot, and I didn't just dry up and wither away. The country was rich in fantasy for me, and I was in the woods a lot—but always alone. But this time was valuable to me later."

"When I left high school at seventeen and went to college, I'd been successful in just about every subject. I loved biology and I wanted to become a doctor, but it was 1965 and medical schools felt very comfortable saying, 'We don't take women.' "

She refused to compromise on an all-woman medical college that was, in her opinion, second-rate, and attended instead a women's college with a better scholastic standing. In examinations similar to college boards, she got an almost perfect score in English, and her math scores were close.

"My father thought I was a brilliant student, and I remember him saying, 'God—you really are smart!' "

But his disappointment was intense when, by her sophomore year, she was married and by her junior year had dropped out of school and given birth to her first child.

"Chris was born when I was twenty, and Annie, my second, when I was twenty-three. I stayed home exactly one year with each child, but I went back to college between babies and finished my undergraduate degree in 1969.

"I was reasonably successful at being a housewife and mother, and we bought a house, but my husband was a real mental case, so I lost my confidence again. There was no credit for being good at housework. It became a real down period of my life, but it forced me to do some thinking."

Her failed marriage and her waning confidence prompted her interest in the feminist movement, which she credits with restoring her confidence and her motivation.

"I got back all the youthful spirit I thought I'd lost. And because of my feminist activities, speaking before groups and talking with other women, I regained my confidence. I also realized I needed to find a way to get a decent job."

At first she worked as a waitress to help support herself and her children, but then began a technique of active fantasizing about what she really wanted to do with her life. There were two phases to this self-exploration. The first was picturing her way out of waitressing and into the completion of her education; and the second was visualizing a transition from housewife to successful employee.

Before approaching welfare for assistance while she got the training necessary for a good job, she prepared her presentation well. With graduate records in hand, she presented her plans to welfare in a logical way, pointing out that if she had this kind of assistance, and also procured a student loan, she could enter a master's degree program with a guaranteed job at the end of it. An important aspect of a grant from welfare in all of this was that both she and her children would also be covered by health insurance.

"Going on welfare was not an acceptance of poverty but it gave me the money to live. I knew it was not permanent, and I'd been burned so badly once that I didn't want to be dependent on anyone ever again."

In college she had gained a background in biology, math, and biochemical engineering. Her first job was with a large company in New Jersey, designing cleaning systems. From there she went to work for Allied Chemicals doing water pollution control and was sent to Ohio where she stayed for three years.

"I found myself becoming more and more miserable within the managerial maze and realized I was getting the most satisfaction from the volunteer work I did weekends on an herb farm. So I quit my regular job."

She had met Brendan, her present husband, before she left for Ohio, and they were working out a future together.

"He's a loose type of person, and we're good for each other. He trusts the elements more than I do. I never expected him to keep me afloat, but he has been a part of making it all work.

"We came to Vermont with the idea of opening an herb shop for me and an auto mechanic shop for him. The retail herb shop combined my biology background and my interest in nature. The birth of Maggie, our daughter, precipitated our plan, and when we saw this house," she said, speaking of the Rathdowney building, "we knew this was it."

The original plan was for Brendan to have a shop in the old barn where he would repair foreign cars, and Louise could pursue her interest in herbs by converting part of the house into a shop. The family lived in the rest of the house.

In the beginning, the primary focus of the herb business was retail trade, through both the shop and selling at craft fairs. However, Louise was ready to make the necessary changes when the growing demand for wholesaling her products became apparent. Her gross sales have risen 180 percent in the past four years. Herbs have long since dominated the scene, taking over the entire house and grounds, and consigning the auto repair shop to history.

"I like the idea of a nice home and garden, some travel and being able to fill most of my days with writing, lecturing, and running my home. It's all possible.

"My first book will be about fantasizing—using fantasy exploration to get at what you're trying to do and how to get it to work. I'll put into writing some of the stuff I've used, not just about business but about how to get things done. I've always wanted to be an expert and have people come to me to learn, and now I'm convinced I have something to teach them.

"I want something suitable to my temperament. The herbs are still there, but for five years, I've had no strong urge to study them, nor do I want to go in the direction of the Harvard Business School. I can still absorb change; I still feel I'm on track, and I can still satisfy my basic needs for security, quietness, and recharging. I've just about got it down now, and I can think ahead in terms of keeping this up until I'm ninety.

"I can also see that, in the future, I must split off a bit from the business. I have something to write about now; I've succeeded in what I set out to do.

"And my second book—well I'm thinking about that. Getting focused was my key to the whole thing, and doing a little something everyday towards my goal is a large part of what makes it happen."

Lydia Clemmons

I never expected to do this," Lydia Clemmons said, speaking about the African import business she owns with her daughter, Jocelyn. Except for a discreet sign identifying the house as "Authentica," it could be simply another home along a rural section of Route 7 in Charlotte.

A mail-order catalogue with handsome photographs characterizes their products as "Museum Quality Originals," and the claim is not overstated. On display in the store, as well as on the pages of the catalogue, are objects "handcrafted from natural products and non-endangered species." They include camel hair and cotton wall hangings from Mali; masks from Nigeria; jewelry from Kenya, Nigeria, and Zaire; soapstone carvings from Kenya; hand-blocked prints from Zaire, Ghana, and Kenya; and clay pots by the Zulu women of Swaziland—to mention a few.

"I've always enjoyed business," Lydia volunteered, as she described the route she followed from nursing to the beginning of Authentica, the business she and Jocelyn have been involved with for the past five years.

"In 1984, I was an R.N. at the medical center in Burlington and worked in anesthesia. My husband, Jackson, was a pathologist there," she continued, explaining that they came to Vermont twenty-six years ago from the Midwest after her husband was offered his position.

"We wanted a farm where we could raise all our own food while the children were growing up. We canned and froze everything."

"It was hard work," she said. A smile brightened her face as she continued, "But it was rewarding. During the winter, it was like having our own supermarket, only with better food.

"Now that the kids are mostly gone from the house, I only have a small garden."

The Clemmons live in the original farmhouse next door to the shop, which was the blacksmith shop for the original farm operation. It has been renovated and enlarged. Lydia explained that their goal for Authentica is to have every country in Africa represented there through the crafts they carry.

"We're the only shop in Vermont that carries African things exclusively," she added.

Computerized mail order comprises the most substantial part of their business; their mailing list at present contains over ten thousand names and continues to grow. People have responded to their newspaper advertisements in New York City and other places; many have seen their ads and make a point of looking them up when they visit Vermont.

"It's a very specialized business, and we've never been interested in buying commercial lists. We also had an article about the shop in *Ebony* and plan on doing more magazine advertising," Lydia said.

She described the almost inadvertent way a business of this esoteric nature got started in the countryside around Charlotte. "When my husband was offered a job doing some research in Tanzania, he said that he would only go if his wife could be included. They replied that they'd love it and that I could work, too."

"The medical center allowed me a leave of absence, so I worked on infection control as an anesthesia nurse at the Killamanjaro Christian Medical Center."

All their children were in college except the youngest, who was then a senior in high school. Lydia and her husband felt it was possible to leave for the eight weeks during which the work was scheduled.

In Tanzania, Dr. Clemmons' work was related to the possibility that a sarcoma being studied there might be related to the AIDS virus in this country. To Lydia, the trip marked the beginning of a new venture that now supports many small craft industries in Africa. In turn, she is also making available beautifully crafted objects to people in this country.

"We were there for eight weeks, and I happened to meet someone who wanted to sell her craft. It took a lot of negotiating before all the arrangements could be made, a lot of talking back and forth at first, but they finally sent a shipload to us around Christmas. Now we have more people asking us to buy than we're currently able to handle."

Their contacts with craftspeople have continued to expand in various ways. "Our masks are from West Africa, and there's a person from Liberia who finds them and sends them to us. Jocelyn and I are presently putting together a booklet on masks and have been doing research on them. I'm learning more every day. All African masks ward off evil," she emphasized. "They can't produce evil, they're not like voodoo. Many people have a mistaken idea about this."

She described the way they met a woman in Ghana, who produces marvelous fabrics.

"She had a child with an incurable kidney disease, and some people who knew about it wanted to send her to France for an operation, but it cost too much. A hospital in New York was contacted and offered free medical care, and one of the Burlington churches started trying to sell her fabrics to raise money for the trip. At one point, they brought them to me and the money for whatever I sold was given back to the church.

"She does fabrics, block prints, and tie dye. She's a remarkable craftswoman, and I won't take work from anyone else in Ghana if their work is similar to what she's doing. We handle Kente cloth, also from Africa, but she doesn't do that."

The Clemmons discovered a man in Kenya, living in a shanty town, who made excellent jewelry. Since commencing sales to Authentica, he now has his own business in Nairobi, so Lydia and Jocelyn handle no other jewelry from Kenya.

Lydia led me to a section in one of the display rooms and pointed out the large, beautifully decorated gourds or calabashes that village women use for storing things. "These are from Kenya, and come out of homes," she said, explaining that these hand-incised calabashes, often passed from mother to daughter, are highly valued by the women.

"Jocelyn will go to Africa once a year on a buying trip and my husband and I will go together once a year at another time for six weeks," she continued.

They have also developed an African language correspondence course that is now offered for sale. "People who buy these are generally planning a trip to Africa," Lydia explained.

"We can also tell them ahead about some of the pitfalls they're likely to encounter, things they might not think about on a first trip. When Jocelyn first went to Kenya, I told her to only take skirts, that there are no women in pants there, and since she was traveling alone, people might get the wrong impression.

"When she got back she said she was glad I'd told her about this. There are lots of other helpful little bits of information that are important for people to know, and we're always glad to answer questions and to talk to them about a trip of this kind."

Much of the work at Authentica is displayed throughout several downstairs rooms. One small room, off to the side, is dedicated to wall hangings, some very old, others more recent. Another room contains mainly cloth of different kinds, batiks, Zairian cotton prints, and hand-block printed cottons; this opens onto a larger room with pots, carvings, calabashes, masks, jewelry, and other things.

Lydia pointed out that the calabashes and masks are also both new and old, and that many things they handle can never be duplicated. Nonetheless, while the assortment changes, their standards for all the crafts remain fixed on good craftsmanship.

The Clemmons have sponsored one young woman to come from Africa and finish high school here. "She stayed two and a half years, and had her visa, but she was too far behind the others; she didn't have the educational background. She did have a good business head, however, and when she gets her exporter license from Tanzania, Nakaru will be one of the outstanding women there," Lydia said.

She and her daughter pay all the costs incurred in getting items here. "None of the craftspeople would have the money to ship, and the airlines wouldn't take it without guarenteed payment," she added. "Everything must be shipped by air, which almost equals the cost of the merchandise. But our business is going well, and there's great interest in what we're doing. I stopped working at the hospital last year because we were so busy here," she said.

Lydia's career in nursing began at a nursing school in Chicago. She studied at Loyola University and Provident Hospital.

"I took my first job in Wisconsin and met and married my husband there. We moved to Cleveland for a time so that he could complete medical school," she said. "I was raised just outside of Chicago, and my dad was a welder," she added.

"Both Dad and Mother came from Louisiana, and they weren't wealthy, but they both pushed education. We do this with our own children now. It was always expected that we would have careers and would see that our children had them."

"We have one son and four daughters," she continued. The children all grew up in Charlotte and all went out-of-state to college. Jocelyn had originally planned on going into theater costume design. She has a degree in fine arts from the University of Chicago.

The Clemmons' son, Joshua, was trained as a theoretical physicist and now has his own computer business. Another daughter, Lydia, works for Oxfam in Central Africa. Laura has a degree in special education and has recently returned from doing work in Chile.

Naomi, the youngest, is at American University majoring in anthropology and international studies.

Lydia stressed that when the children were born she stopped working until the youngest started kindergarten, a period of about ten years. But even then, starting to work again was difficult.

"Now the kids say, 'Mom I just hated it when you went back to work,' and they were in high school. I was an anesthesia nurse and I could never take off if a child was sick. Operations are scheduled ahead of time, and you can't very well call in at the last minute and say you aren't going to be there."

Reviewing her career as a nurse, Lydia Clemmons had some forceful things to say. "The structure of nursing has to be changed. For one thing, more men are going into it, and salaries have to be raised. Men usually expect more money, and they'd make a stand.

"They'd point out that they can't live on what they make and say what they think their salary should be. But women too often just say, 'All right, if that's the best you can do,' and take the work. Women are too often willing to keep a low profile.

"And there's an attitude that could bear investigation. Many doctors might say, 'I'm Dr. Smith, and this is Mary, my nurse.' What does this indicate about the way the nursing profession is regarded?

"Hospitals should also allow nurses to have more say in their hours; they need to be more flexible, talk to nurses as one adult to another. Some of the hospitals in cities have started allowing more flexibility in the hours."

But even though she has criticisms of the system, she is proud of the service nursing provides, and her observations are made to raise public estimation and support for her profession.

"Our experience in moving to Charlotte was wonderful," Lydia said, her soft voice almost breaking with the emotion associated with remembered kindness.

"Flowers left at the door, and pies. Any hostility we encountered has not been because of color," she explained, "just the kind of hostility that any differences in personality can cause between people. This is the only truly democratic place we've ever lived.

"Charlotte has been wonderful," she repeated. "It's a good area to raise a family. Of course people make friends more easily if they have children. The responsibility is also on you, the newcomer, to participate in town affairs. My husband is on the school board, and the YWCA has always been a favorite thing of mine.

"I now do some hospice nursing at night, but not more than one night a week, as a backup. And I have a CARE connection through Visiting Nurses.

"We also belong to the Charlotte Congregational Church," she said, adding simply, "I believe in being part of a community church."

Returning to the new business that now occupies most of her time, Lydia spoke about some of the preparations that preceded it, before she had any notions about following such a course.

"I've always felt women should be able to manage, so I took classes in bookkeeping and typing—and even took a course at H & R Block. I felt that if my husband died, I should know how to manage, so over the years I've always taken classes.

"This has all played a part in making this business possible, and to me it has great purpose. I understand what it means to the people who send me their handiwork from Africa."

HUMAN
SERVICES

JAN APPEL

*T*here's an enormous amount of hidden rage out there in society, and children are the ultimate victims," Jan Appel stated.

A poster in the waiting room of the Social Rehabilitation Services (SRS) building in St. Albans read "Half the People Suffering From Unemployment Aren't Old Enough to Work." Illustrating this message was a picture of a small child sitting in front of an empty bowl and an empty glass.

"In working at this job you have to view change in very small degrees, otherwise you burn out; it would seem too hopeless. I came into it with more realistic expectations than some."

Jan, a social worker on a Child Protection Team for over eleven years and recently appointed a supervisor, spoke with me in her small office at the SRS building. Her new job consists of coordinating the work of four child protection social workers and two intake workers; she also supervises a parent educator who works with the families and is under contract to SRS from another agency.

"We work with kids and families," she explained, "kids in the home, if they can stay there; kids who are in danger, principally with those who are abused and neglected, or who are unmanageable or delinquent; kids struggling with problems they have no way of handling."

There was nothing formidable about Jan's office. Small stacks of papers and filing cabinets with more papers, a deflating birthday balloon on a string, a few toys, a plant, and one chair opposite her desk. The effect was something like a general's headquarters in the middle of a battlefield, with crisis a normal part of the day's routine.

The smallish, dark-daired woman at the desk gave the impression of friendly alertness.

"The amount of paperwork required on this job is grueling," she said. "Of course there has to be accountability, and we have to show some success, but I could easily spend forty hours a week just on paperwork."

When litigation is involved, as is the case in the removal of a child from a demonstrably dangerous situation, the social worker must spend time filling out more papers, talking with public defenders, probation workers, police, hospital personnel, and any of the many other public employees that legally must be included. Everything, of course, must also be recorded.

"I hope I don't ever lose my old head-set," she said, talking about her new supervisory position in relation to her former job, one that involved her more directly with clients. "Personal contact is important in working with people. I don't want to substitute flat paper profiles for real human beings.

"Still, I always end up talking with clients. I don't believe I'm a good supervisor if I'm not involved with the people I'm trying to help. That's my philosophy."

She pointed out that in the early 1970s there was a federal push towards a mandatory child abuse reporting law. The Social Rehabilitation Department is the office designated to receive these reports. When it has been alerted to suspicious behavior towards a child, someone is sent to the scene to make assessments.

"If a teacher reports, it often goes through the school nurse or the school principal," she said, explaining that the Social Rehabilitation Office would be called, and one of their workers, sometimes accompanied by a police officer, would go to talk to the child.

"The law allows us to interview a child without her or his parents," she added, "as long as there's a third party present. We try to minimize the number of interviews."

These cases are uncovered in various ways. A next door neighbor, an estranged spouse, a teacher, or a school nurse may notice some revealing behavior or some physical evidence indicating that abuse could be involved.

She gave as one example the teacher who asked her high school class to write an essay about one of the most significant things that happened to them. She received from one of the girls a short, bleak description of how her grandfather forced her to have sex with him.

"Sometimes these things are genuine, sometimes not," Jan said. "But one thing seems certain: abusive parents were probably abused themselves. Our hope is to eventually break this cycle."

While society considers social work a necessity, the rewards for the particular skills, education, and commitment of social workers has never ranked high in either income or approbation. Since their work is generally done with the least articulate groups among us, particularly true in the case of children, their potential in helping solve such increasingly widespread and expensive problems as child abuse, drug abuse, violence, street crime, and homelessness is insufficiently recognized and supported.

I was interested in Jan Appel's commitment, her background, and the motivation that keeps her in this field. She recognizes clearly the problems and the constraints that are part of the work, but her attitude towards it revealed no cynicism.

"I didn't start out to become a social worker," she recalled. "I never even knew what social workers did. My parents were divorced when I was fairly young, and I was raised by my mother and my grandmother. They both felt that women were capable of doing whatever they wanted to do.

"I've always been told, 'You need to go to college so you can take care of yourself. You never know about depending on a man to support you—he's liable to get divorced, disabled, or dead.' Independence in a woman was considered a very big deal."

Her grandmother, the oldest of eight children, had been a nurse during World War I, and Jan remembers that from the time she was small, her grandmother pointed out children with less than she had. "Your lot in life is to help others," was her constant reminder. And it seemed to stick.

Jan was also raised with a strong emphasis on patriotism, on putting service to your country before everything else. Her mother was one of the first WAVES during World War II. This, too, made a lasting impression.

Growing up in the Midwest during the 1950s, Jan remembers that her mother went to work every day, while most of her friends' mothers stayed home.

"My mother was a single parent, and she had to work to support us; but her whole thing was that she didn't go to college, and she wanted to be darned sure I did. Life was not easy for her, and she believed that a college education would have helped."

Jan went to a good college, Smith. It was expensive, but she had a scholarship. "I wanted to go there because it was a women's college," she said. "And I was surrounded by bright women there. Jack Kennedy was our hero, and we were inspired by his idea that it's what you do for your country that counts. And then he was shot."

Jan's mother worked for IBM for thirty years. She wanted her daughter to rise through the corporate ladder and "be successful." But there was a vast difference in the climate that shaped the concept of a successful life for each of these women.

Jan's college years came towards the end of the tumultuous sixties and early seventies. Vietnam was the background against which important questions raised by young people were projected. Many of them were concerned with meaning, purpose and service and had more to do with contribution than accretion. Idealism was high. It was also the period when feminism began to surface.

After college, Jan tried the corporate route to please her mother and worked for a time in a Boston bank's management training program, which included other bright young women from good eastern colleges, as well as their male counterparts. It soon became clear that only the men were being sent on to real management positions. The women were retained for secretarial jobs. Jan quit.

For many of the country's young people, it was an agonizingly unsettled period. Jan and her former husband decided to "go back to the land" looking for roots and meaning in their lives. They moved to Vermont from Boston in 1976 and became teachers and house parents at a state-supported school for troubled children. When the school closed after a year, they helped start another school that was similar in nature. "This one is still operating," Jan said proudly.

They bought an abandoned farmhouse to live in, and when her oldest child was born, she brought him back from the hospital in thirty-eight-degrees-below-zero weather, to a house that was only a few degrees warmer.

"I've always been grateful that I didn't have Gavin at home," she said. "But we learned survival skills with this place, and gradually put it back together into a real house. We also had another child."

But the marriage was not working, and they were divorced in 1980. Meanwhile, Jan had gotten a job with the welfare department.

"I remarried in 1982, and my present marriage is a very good one. I've also had two more children," she said.

An important element in combining her professional work with the responsibility of a family has been an excellent daycare center, run by a mother and daughter. Jan's had children at their center for a total of thirteen years.

"They're unusually fine people who have made a point of taking both at-risk children as well as others, and they've always given incredible support to parents.

"My home life and my work life must mesh, otherwise it would be chaotic. In a job dealing with at-risk kids, you can't just leave work at the regular hour if there's a child in need involved. But then you can't leave your own kids at risk either."

Between a cooperative husband and the reliable daycare women, it's been possible for Jan to maintain her dedication to the work that has importance to her.

Jan spoke of the tendency within any large operation, such as a big business or government, for the system to become impersonal and even, in some cases, detrimental to the people dependent on it. Because of insufficient personnel to maintain connections and keep contacts open, people can become lost and isolated within the very system set up to help them. This may be even truer for children.

She told the story of one young woman. "She's been in the system about ten years and I've had to remove two of her kids," she said. "She's in her late twenties now.

"She's just had her third child, and she only recently revealed that she'd been sexually abused by her father while growing up. The effects of this are still driving her. But she was never helped to get beyond the anger and feeling of helplessness that are part of it, because no one in a position to help her knew about it. She continues to have children, and they continue to suffer, but now maybe we can help her.

"Sex abuse and power rape often happen because mothers fail to protect their daughters, because of a lack of power the mother still feels from having suffered the same situation when she was small.

"Too many girls get pregnant to get out of a home, out of a situation they have no control over. They don't know that women have options and choices. They've never been helped to set goals and make decisions, and they're the ultimate victims. In too many cases, this is perpetuated through their own children.

"Workers in this kind of job often burn out. You do what you can, and hope that as a result the quality of these kids' lives may be improved, so they don't have to keep repeating the pattern after they're grown.

"For at-risk kids, for instance, there's the possibility that daycare services could help alleviate stress at home. If the children can be away from home in a safe place for even short—but regular—periods of time, that could be enough to help a mother get her feet on the ground. And maybe, when that child has children, things will be better for them.

"There also has to be some appreciation of how much effort even small changes demand of the people making them. If you're looking, you can see there's an effect, and I think it's worth it."

"There's no easy answer as to how I ended up in this work," she said. "But the values of helping were always stressed when I was growing up, and giving up easily was not in my family background."

She continued softly: "I was also raised to believe that your expectations for yourself are always higher than what you should expect from other people, and I guess this sort of set me up for this job."

DEBORAH LISI

People are sometimes embarrassed and don't know how to act, whether they should offer to help or look away," Deborah Lisi said, talking about the inability of many people to interact with someone with a noticeable disability or physical handicap.

"If you see someone with an armload of books and they're trying to open a door, what would you do? Would you feel funny about opening the door for them?

"And if, instead of books, that person's encumbrance is crutches, a wheelchair or a white cane, is there really such a difference in what the situation demands?"

My first meeting with Deborah took place while she was still working as deputy executive director of the Vermont Center for Independent Living (VCIL), an organization started in 1979, managed and staffed principally by disabled people. One out of eight people in Vermont is disabled. VCIL provides peer support and allows disabled Vermonters greater control over their lives. Advocating for the civil rights of the disabled is another aspect of VCIL. Like other minorities, disabled people suffer from segregation, discrimination, disenfranchisement, and poverty.

The first time I saw Deborah, standing just inside the entrance to the building where she works, her crutches were barely visible. I was not conscious of any impairment. Of medium height, with curly brown hair, she was wearing a soft lavender knit top and skirt, with a loose, blue cotton sweater. She was lovely.

"From a very early age I had to separate myself from my disability," she said, reflecting on her struggle for independence. As a result of cerebral palsy brain damage, either shortly before, during, or after birth, Deborah uses crutches. She also has a slight balance disturbance.

"Stand on your own two feet" is a venerable axiom. For Deborah, without her crutches, it is out of the question, but her life is, nonetheless, an exemplification of what the metaphor truly means.

She was born in Windsor but spent her childhood both in New Hampshire and Vermont. There were five children in her family, and she was the middle child.

"My mother felt both anger and guilt when I was born. For one thing, the doctors had told her that I would probably not be born alive. This was what she'd prepared herself for.

"But then there I was, born alive, and she was ashamed of the relief she'd felt beforehand. She was also angry. 'Why did this have to happen to me?' was another feeling she had to wrestle with."

Thirty-seven years ago, when Deborah was born, there was little support for families in this situation. It was the kind of thing considered best kept hidden. It was seldom discussed.

From the beginning, her parents insisted that she develop independence. "They made me do things they wouldn't even make the other children do for themselves, and I didn't grow up feeling I had a right to be taken care of."

She remembers her mother making her button all the buttons on her sweater, even though her sisters had help with theirs. She insisted Deborah do it herself, even though it took longer and made it harder for both of them.

A penchant for independence was developed early and has been a motivating factor ever since. "I owe a lot to this reaction of my parents. They refused to let my disability be an excuse to not try things, wouldn't allow me to limit myself unnecessarily. But that was just the kind of people they were; they had a basic respect for individuals and believed in each person's right to his or her own development."

Deborah's mother has worked at a number of different jobs: social worker, legal aid worker and now a position at a large retail store. Her father developed a business selling smoked cheese. She emphasized that he had to have his own business because he never liked the idea of working for someone else; he always wanted to do things his own way. Deborah's parents are now divorced.

"I left home when I was eighteen, lived in different places around Vermont, and married when I was nineteen," she said. The couple had a child, but the marriage broke up before her son was a year old, and Deborah returned with him to Windsor. She ran into a friend she'd known since the fifth grade, and since her friend was also a single parent, they rented a house together, sharing some of the responsibilities. Deborah was then living on her Social Security payments.

Because of this support, she was able to take a creative writing course at Goddard. "I've always loved education, and I love writing," she said, her expression somewhat wistful as she continued, "I've written poetry, but then I've also written speeches and grants in connection with my work.

"I'd be in school for a few days and my friend would take care of the kids. Then I'd come back and she'd be off for a few days."

She planned on working towards a college degree in education so she could eventually support herself and her son by teaching, but she wanted to limit school to part-time while he was small. However, federal regulations decreed that her Social Security payments would only be continued if she was committed to school full-time, so in 1979 she moved to Plainfield, where Goddard College is located, in order to comply.

"For me there was no choice, I knew that the only way I could do the kind of work I wanted to do later was to get the skills I didn't have."

She became a full-time student at Goddard but later transferred to the external degree program at Johnson State College.

"My tuition was paid to Johnson, and they permitted some of that money to be used in payment for outside courses." Deborah graduated with honors from Johnson with a B.S. in education.

"I went to school full-time and also took care of my child. And even though he was good, I must say that working in a library with a four-year-old isn't ideal. He didn't pull the books off the shelves, but he enjoyed racing around the aisles," she said, smiling at the remembered havoc in the stacks.

Several months later, I spoke with Deborah a second time. She was finishing up her work at VCIL in order to pursue research at the University of Vermont (UVM). Her new project relates to her previous work, but there are different challenges.

The Department of Special Education at UVM received a federal grant recently, one of the components of which requires research to be done on causes behind the high rate of school dropout among disabled students and dropout prevention through remedial intervention strategies. Deborah is studying the possibility that some of these strategies might be effective in Vermont.

"I've discovered that even though the dropout rate for the general school population is high, the disabled dropout seems much higher, and there's been no real study of this before."

She had just completed her second week at UVM. So far, her time had been spent reading abstracts and articles based on national studies of the subject.

"I'm trying to determine what similarities there are between regular dropouts and disabled students. One thing seems sure: if these students are to become independent, they have a vital need to learn skills they may only be able to acquire in high school." Surveys relating to this subject have been previously sent to targeted schools around Vermont, and she'll soon be going out to talk to teachers involved in the survey.

Deborah still works for the Center on a consultant basis, helping brief a new executive director.

"My time is now divided between Burlington, Montpelier, and Plainfield, where I live," she said. Since the study is only funded for five months and she has other consultant work in the Montpelier area, she and her son are in Burlington the first part of each week and live in Plainfield the rest of the time.

This arrangement presents no school problems for her son, Gerald, almost fifteen. He has been doing home schooling for the last year and a half.

Deborah explained that this program is supervised by the Vermont Department of Education, and has provided an excellent growing option for the many families electing a more individual educational path for their children. A Home Schooling Association exists with approximately 360 families involved.

"Gerald sees his friends after school and on weekends, and the program seems to work well for him in every way," she added.

In addition to the work at UVM, Deborah also does consulting for Community Action, with low-income families and Head Start. "I'm excited about what's being done and the way the agency goes about it," she said.

"Part of what I will be doing is training outreach workers who do counseling work. Our goal is to help the individual being worked with become an active force in making changes in his or her own life. We want to see these people have more control over their circumstances.

"We also want to help counselors understand that it isn't just the person who is creating a problem for himself or herself, but that the social situation has also contributed. We want counselors to be aware that the problem is partly in the situation, not just in the person."

As an advocate of social service and disability rights, she strongly believes that consumers of a service must take part in planning the services they'll be using, that they should be considered agents of change within its organization and direction.

She also has a deep interest in community education, particularly as it applies to multi-age groups, and has taught adult education classes for Vermont College as well as Woodbury College.

"The largest part of my job at VCIL was advocacy and administration. The grants were important too."

She described one that she wrote for the Center that provided for deaf counselors to work with deaf people. The federal grant for establishing this program covered a three-year period, with funding of $186,000 per year. Out of two hundred applications received by the funding agency, only ten were funded. Hers was one of them.

"There's a whole deaf culture out there," she said, explaining that within the deaf community, deafness has shaped the experience of everyone. For these people to work with someone also shaped by the same experience, with an innate understanding of their particular problems and ways of approaching them, is vitally important.

Some time later, after the program had been put into effect, she recalled her excitement when, at one of the center's functions, a deaf person called her over and introduced her to another deaf person as the person who brought the deaf program to Vermont. He explained that this had changed his life.

"People with different kinds of disabilities need to work together," she said. "We have insights that society needs, but we need the support of each other to change it in ways that could benefit everyone."

For Deborah, the simple need to get from one town to another must be approached carefully. Poor eye-muscle coordination and some hearing loss makes driving impossible.

"I have to plan ahead—can't just jump into the car and go," she said. "It's partly a matter of scheduling, ride sharing with someone to work, or hiring a driver to take me.

"I hire drivers some of the time," she added. "One is a part-time art teacher, and you can imagine living on the salary of a part-time art teacher in Vermont. One is a retired woman who is happy to supplement her income. But it does take some scrounging around."

With a certain glee she added: "I used to call the local transportation association, but they ended up referring people to me who wanted me to find rides for them."

In many ways, Deborah's life is not all that different from other single mothers balancing the requirements of family and work. The activities are much the same, the living patterns determined by individual solutions.

"When he was little Gerald was very protective of me," she said proudly. "Now he keeps the fires up when we're in Plainfield, goes grocery shopping with me to help carry things, does countless other chores that take thought on his part."

She chuckled as she described the difference in their tastes in music. "I'll have my folk music playing downstairs, and he'll be upstairs with his hard rock going. He doesn't like folk music, but he does admit that the words, the message in many of the songs, is the same.

"But still, the jarring music of rock that I find hard to take really fits what the adolescent sees when he or she looks out at the world, doesn't it?" she added, musingly. "I can understand that, even though I don't like the sound of the music."

Within a culture characterized by impatience, the patience required by a disabled person in performing the simplest of tasks offers the rest of us a fuller understanding of the inexhaustible potential of the human spirit.

At the end of our interview Deborah posed a question. "Why," she asked, "is it so difficult getting people to understand that, behind the disability, is a person, just like them. Why is it hard to make them aware that the most important part of that person is not their disability but themselves?"

CONNIE GONZALEZ

Getting off welfare is not easy!" Connie Gonzalez said. A single parent with dependent children living in the low-income section of the Depot apartments in Bethel, she knows what she's talking about.

And while she still needs government help so that she and her children can live, she is presently working forty hours a week as a VISTA (Volunteers in Service to America) volunteer, part of a program to help at-risk children in Barre. Connie is also taking courses to enable her to enter the skilled work force at a salary above minimum wage at the end of her year with VISTA.

"Most displaced homemakers are single women with dependent children. They don't have an education, or as much as they need, to get off welfare, and without education you can only make minimum wage. Between the costs of child care, medical expenses, housing, and food, there's no way these women can make it on minimum wage," she explained.

"It's not that you make more on welfare, but it's there," she said, explaining that with most low paying jobs, if the adult or any of the children gets sick or any other emergency arises, there's nothing to fall back on. "For poor people, one setback is all they need to wipe them out."

My introduction to Connie came at the last Bethel town meeting. It was the time of afternoon when yawns had replaced alertness as a gauge of audience response, and impatience gathered like a cloud over the remaining proceedings. Major budgets had been examined and funded, smaller civic projects requiring additional money had been passed. The citizenry was ready to close the town pocketbook and go home.

Last on the agenda was a request for three hundred dollars for a meagerly-funded federal agency working primarily with poor people in this area, those often caught in emergency situations. It was defended by a chunky, dark-haired woman who strode to the microphone, and in response to an initially negative reception, made a pitch that was intense, straightforward, and impressive.

That her request was subsequently funded was nothing short of a miracle; the round of applause following it even more so. The kind of vitality and commitment she displayed indicated a connection with social concerns that are frequently pushed out of sight by routine town business, which is important in running civic machinery but neglectful of the town's conscience.

I arranged to have an interview with her at the Central Vermont Community Action Center, where she's been working for the last six months as a volunteer in a reach out training program provided by the Department of Welfare for grant recipients who want to work. Her story is one of heroic proportions.

"That was my first time speaking in public. Up until a while ago, I had no idea what town meeting was and wouldn't have been caught dead speaking at one if I had," she said.

In response to my questions, she began: "I was born in Bethel, the youngest of twelve children. I was twelve years old before I met all my brothers and sisters. My oldest sister was twenty-seven when I was born, so I had a lot of nieces and nephews who were lots older than me."

But while the idea of a large family can be accompanied by warm and romantic overtones, the reality, especially when accompanied by extreme financial hardship and instability, can be stressful and devoid of comfort.

Without rancor, Connie observed that, "Mother was forty-two when I was born, and it's taken me 'til now to understand that she was tired by the time I came along—worn out. No hugs, just, 'Get out of my way.' "

Partly to look for work, her father, who had difficulty with jobs, moved the family—the few left together—first to California and then to Texas, where Connie was married at fourteen. She wanted to get out of the house.

"My first marriage was a mistake from the beginning. I didn't know how to do anything, no common sense. Had my first kid, Daniel, when I was seventeen after two miscarriages—one at fifteen—and there were a lot of problems."

"I gave up my education when I first got pregnant at fifteen, miscarried in August when I was four months pregnant, went back to school for two months, quit again, and didn't bother goin' back. I worked as a nurse's aide, eight to twelve hours a day, seven days a week, and my husband allowed me five dollars a month. He did the grocery shopping, told me what to do, how to dress, how to think— I didn't dare question him about anything."

He was ten years older than she, and seemed "nice and considerate" before they were married. "Just wanted to take care of me," she said.

"It was a grand honeymoon!" she continued. "Black eyes and a broken nose, but my mother was from the old school, and when she saw how it was she just said, 'You've made your bed, now lie in it.' "

"Things didn't get better, they got worse. Never knew what my complexion really was. It was always blue, yellow, and green, so I worked mostly the night shift."

Pregnant again at seventeen, Connie said she thought this might improve her relationship with her husband.

"It didn't. If anything, he resented it," she said, describing how when she was 7½ months along he kicked her in the stomach with his steel-toed boots and by eight months had even shot at her.

At the hospital for the birth of the baby, fate dealt her a kinder hand. She was cared for by an elderly physician who seemed to understand the situation and was determined to help.

"I was scared to death, didn't know what was going on or even what was supposed to go on. In the middle of labor I just yelled 'Stop. I don't want it!' "

" 'This is one thing I can't stop,' the doctor answered gently, then asked, 'Do you know how babies are born?'

"And I said, 'No.' "

The doctor found a book with pictures and showed Connie step by step what to expect. While he could have called someone else to replace him, he knew she was terrified, and stayed with her for twelve hours, until the baby was born.

"Finally the doctor announced, 'I think this baby wants out— now!' " Connie said. "So they took me to the delivery room. Five minutes and it was over! I didn't yell, and I didn't actually cry during labor. He coached me the whole way, and when he laid my son in my arms, I forgot all the pain."

After Daniel was born she stayed with a sister who had five children of her own and "knew what to do," but later she went back to her husband and stayed for about six months. It was the same thing all over again, so she divorced him.

A single mother, with a small child, Connie went back to live with her parents so she could work as a private duty practical nurse to support her child. But two years later she was pregnant again.

As it turned out, Connie was highly anemic, and her infant daughter, Blanca, did poorly, couldn't hold food, had a bad rash, lost weight, and was kept at the hospital to be fed intravenously.

As Connie was crying on the front porch of her house one day shortly after leaving the hospital, one of her neighbors, an eighty-nine-year-old Mexican woman, asked about her trouble. Hearing the story of her infant, the woman said, "Go get that baby, and bring her back here now!"

"After all," Connie continued, "the doctor had told me she couldn't last more than a week at best, and this way at least I could hold her."

Using ingredients from her own garden, the neighbor made an herbal tea, and directed Connie to give it to the baby. She insisted on other feedings, and they all worked wonders. Within three days, Blanca had gained four pounds, had no more rash, and was sleeping well. But on the fourth day, a public health nurse appeared with orders to take the infant back to the hospital.

"You're gonna have to kill me first!" Connie declared. But she managed to persuade the woman to weigh the baby and compare its present condition to what it was before leaving the hospital. In the end, Blanca was allowed to stay with her mother, since there was no doubt about her improvement.

Not long after, Connie met another man, this time seventeen years older. "Seems funny to me now," she said. "My first marriage was a disaster, and then I went and did it again.

"I married Tony in 1980, and he was a replica of Leon as far as emotions and reactions went. I saw him as kind, considerate and loving until we were married and then—same as the other—total change!

"Both men were hard workers, I will say, but from the day we were married it was slosh city. First thing in the morning 'til he came home at night, it was booze, drugs, and beatings.

"Got so I didn't feel anything when he beat me up—didn't feel anything at all—until he started on Daniel. When I saw my son sitting there, looking like he'd had air blown into his cheeks—well—that was the end. The breaking point for me came when he began to touch my kids. Later, counseling helped."

Connie and her two children came back to Bethel, since distance was the only defense between her and her former husbands. She was also determined to find a better life, at least for her children.

"I'm not afraid to express myself now, but when I first came back here I was so used to having someone tell me what to do that I was scared to do anything. I worried about upsetting other people and was afraid of getting into more trouble. I didn't want to see anybody—didn't want them to see me."

She got an Aid to Needy Families with Children (ANFC) grant and found a low-income apartment. Once she found it, she stayed inside and sent the kids to the store, or to the library to sign out books she tried to read.

"The kids were my outposts, and the biggest thing I did was to register them in school, and then run home—drenched in sweat. I sat in my apartment for 1½ years, and I know what it's like to stay hidden in the closet."

An important change began in her life as the result of a visit she made to someone she'd known years before, a woman living in the section for the elderly of the Depot apartments. Connie happened to visit at the same time as an adult tutor who was working with her friend. He talked to her about what a GED (General Education Diploma) was, and how Adult Basic Education (ABE) tutors worked with people.

"Do you have your diploma?" he asked her.

"No," she replied.

"Would you like to get it?" he continued.

"I'm twenty-eight—isn't it too late?"

"It's never too late," he answered, explaining that this program was provided by the state, and if she decided to do it, he would go to her house for one hour each week to help her.

"That was my beginning; I really lived for that one hour a week when somebody I trusted came in," Connie recalled.

Another change took place when she became friends with Sandra Kenny, a single parent with children who lived in the same building. Kenny began looking out for her.

"Sandra said, 'You're not doing anybody any favors by locking yourself up this way. You're certainly not doing anything for your children.' "

Partly because of Kenny's scolding and partly because the government grant required that she spend some time working outside her home, Connie was accepted in the WIN (Working Incentive Network) program and assigned to a school librarian at the high school.

"It got me out of the house," she chuckled, "but imagine putting someone without an education to work in a library."

However, the librarian was helpful and took the time to talk to her about other possibilities. She questioned her about things she would be interested in doing. When Gonzalez said she'd like to be a cook, the librarian told her about a vocational school not too far from where Connie lived. She explained that since Connie hadn't yet received her high school diploma, the courses there would be free.

"I started taking culinary arts one January and finished in the same month the following year.

"It was perfect for me, got me over being scared. And I didn't need baby sitters all that time because I got home every day before the kids."

The average age of the other students in her classes was sixteen, and she was twenty-nine. They all called her "Mom" and she loved it.

"I learned a lot, not only about cooking but about myself and about other people. Getting my GED and the year of culinary arts at the vocational school were the first two things I ever started—and finished—because I wanted to."

The following summer was spent cooking at a snack bar, but it was only seasonal work. By that time, her friend Sandra Kenny had become a supervisor at the Central Vermont Community Action Center; she needed help in the office, and she thought this would also be a good work experience for Connie. She talked her friend into helping in a six-month training program that provided outreach to low-income people.

"Working with these people was an eye-opener for me," Connie said. "It was really interesting, and the kind of work that lets you know that no matter how bad things are for you, there's always somebody worse off. Also it's a wrong idea that everybody who comes in here wants somethin' for nothin'. That's not true—maybe ten percent—but ninety percent, no!"

She believes that in the past six months she's gained half a lifetime of learning. Now, if someone's in a jam, she knows how to help, who to call, and what do, and this has increased her own self-confidence.

"The people we saw are the ones who fall through the cracks, the ones with no other place to turn. Many low-income people are afraid, don't know their rights or how to find out about them. Many are illiterate and can't read the forms they have to complete for the help they need. Also they're used to getting looked down on. Community Action tries to give them back some pride, some control over their lives."

For Connie Gonzalez the future has brightened. She has her GED, a culinary arts diploma, and the last six month's experience with different human service programs. Now that she's working with VISTA, she can take prepaid college courses that coincide with the work she's doing with children. Some of her work experience can also be turned into college credits, and she looks forward to having developed a solid resumé by the end of the year.

In VISTA, Connie will be working with a group of Barre children between the ages of six and fourteen. Children from underprivileged families with problems, they've been referred by social service agencies, school counselors, juvenile parole and other agencies. So far there are close to sixty signed up. It is called Special Friends, and an important aspect of the program is matching children with adult volunteers willing to be role models and friends.

"I'm even learning to work with a computer now, in connection with my work," Connie said proudly.

Connie Gonzalez has been through a lot, done a lot, seen a lot and learned a lot. And once she catches on, she's a fast learner and she's anxious to spread the message.

"You have to give people some pride—put them back into some sort of control over their own lives. The worse mistake is to feel 'it ain't fair' and let it go at that."

"I used to feel that way myself," she added. "But now when somebody says that to me I say, 'No, it ain't fair, but show me the day it ever was? So what are we going to do about it? You have ideas, you have hopes and you don't have to do it alone!'

"I want my own kids to have a better education than I had. And I want to see the kids I'll be working with have some challenge, too. Many of them have never had that—have never had somebody say 'I care what you do.' I see this work as helping take them out of darkness into a little bit of daylight, and believe me, I know the daylight is there."

PATSY ST. FRANCIS

*N*o one could be seen at the St. Francis house in Swanton. A small hound peered through the screen door. He seemed hospitable so I opened the door, walked in and "Hallooed."

The room was dominated by a table that, along with the number of chairs around it, could accommodate a large family or a middling group. There was a kitchen at the other end, and the whole space conveyed a sense of arrested vitality, of having been caught napping between normal activities. A box of doughnuts at one edge of the table within easy reach of a chair, a coffee thermos circled expectantly by cups, and the chairs themselves, partially pushed back and awaiting their next occupants, all reinforced this feeling.

"Lots of people stop in here—our doors are never locked," Patsy St. Francis said as she emerged smiling from her back yard a few minutes later.

As is often the case with preconceived notions of what another person will be like, Patsy St. Francis was different from mine. I anticipated a larger woman, stolid and perhaps difficult to engage in conversation about herself. So much for preconceptions. I found her instead to be a small, trim, pretty woman with curly, dark brown hair, expressive brown eyes and an easy, warm smile—obviously accustomed to being with people and just as obviously, to enjoying them.

"The wife of a chief can be hectic at times," she said in an understated way, explaining that, as Abenaki chief in Swanton, her husband, Homer St. Francis, is in touch with everything concerning the Abenakis in their community. "People come all the time, and I love it."

"If any problems come up, they call Homer, anytime or any hour," she said matter-of-factly.

Later, sitting at lunch with Homer and Patsy around their hospitable table, the character and controversial position of Homer St. Francis within and without the Abenaki community was perceptible. He would traditionally have been considered a war chief, and today battles past and present mistreatment of the Abenakis by federal and state governments. He is outspoken and implacable about his concern for Abenaki rights as well as the potential for regaining them, and there are those who oppose him. When Patsy St. Francis was recommended as an important woman to interview, the same person declared, "Any woman who can live as long as she has with Homer St. Francis has got to be strong."

Patsy is proud of her husband's commitment; she is also involved. She explained that the Abenakis here first began organizing in 1975, and that she had served several years on the board of directors of the Abenaki Self Help Association.

"When they first started organizing, we had meetings here. Since then we've worked out a youth program. We're also working with job development, and we've been able to get some grants. I've seen a lot of changes in people's attitudes since that time. Our people here are proud, and they're determined to hold on."

Since the Abenakis never had a treaty with the United States government, they have legal difficulties in pressing their demands. Several years ago, with the help of the American Civil Liberties Union, a great deal of work was done to get the state of Vermont to recognize the Abenakis as a tribe. This was accomplished under Governor Salmon, but rescinded by Governor Snelling.

"One of the big things for the Abenakis is free hunting and fishing licenses, a part of our tradition," she said, explaining that they've had three illegal fish-ins in an attempt to get the state to recognize their status.

"Nothing happened at the first two, but the game wardens were notified when we had the October one, and they gave us citations for fishing without a license. I understand the governor has hired an expert from Massachusetts, so this time I expect it'll go to court, and maybe there'll be a decision in our favor."

Patsy explained that the St. Francis Indians are only one branch of the Abenakis and that this area was once one of the strongholds of the Abenaki federation of seven nations. The Abenakis today are primarily Catholics because of the Jesuit priests among them in the early eighteenth century.

"The history text in the schools used to refer to the St. Francis Indians as 'bad people and bloodthirsty.' We got after them, and that text was revised. The schools are coming around now, but it was a bad history six or seven years ago."

In the morning, she took me to visit the old, rambling, converted railroad depot where the Abenaki Self-Help Association is located. It serves as the center for many ongoing projects, as well as for intensive planning for the future. Homer St. Francis, much like the mayor of a small town, is always accessible there or at home.

"Homer would like to have a museum here, a place to display the many Abenaki artifacts that have been found on the land around here. He's working on that—also a craft industry and an arts and crafts shop," Patsy said. "Most Abenakis around here did a lot of baskets, and there are still one or two people left who know how to pound a log to get strips for baskets."

With unemployment in the area severe, she and four other women drive thirty miles daily to jobs on the night shift of the Champlain Cable Company in Winooski. They are employed at the factory to make wire.

After visiting the Self-Help Association, we drove to a monument outside Swanton, erected approximately where the first church built in Vermont had stood.

The road ran beside the Missisquoi river, through land recently acquired for a high-priced housing development called *Hideaway Paradise*. Since this is being built on the oldest and largest Indian burial ground in Vermont, the irony of the new title has not been lost on the Abenakis. We passed a few expensively built homes before reaching the St. Francis monument on a diminutive plot of land overlooking the river.

Patsy pointed toward a grove of trees along the riverbank, and recalled that this had always been a favorite fishing spot for her and her husband since the time they were in school. A fence near the new ranch house across from the monument now makes it inaccessible for fishing. Our presence at the granite monument was noisily and continuously challenged by a chained dog outside the new house.

A plaque informed us: "Near this spot stood the first church erected in Vermont, about 1700 by the Jesuit Fathers to the Glory of God Almighty for the mission of the St. Francis Indians . . ." The Mission on the Missisquoi was built by the Jesuits westward on the riverbank.

Here was the region's oldest and largest Indian settlement. First it served the Abenakis driven from Maine in the 1600s. Lasting until 1775, it became the longest–lived of the French settlements in Vermont.

Patsy explained that when a swimming pool behind one of the development homes was excavated, the bones of ancient Abenakis were discovered. Their authenticity was confirmed by the University of Vermont, where they were sent for examination.

"They'll be sending them back, and the Abenakis would like to bury them near the old burying ground, but we don't own any of the land. It's expensive real estate now. Homer is trying to get a little land for this."

Driving back, she pointed out the house, behind which a swimming pool of brilliant, blatant blue existed as an unmarked and unintended memorial to the Abenakis buried there. A woman in shorts was washing the picture window at the front of the house, and I couldn't help wondering about coexistence between the spirit of the past with the triviality of the present.

That day at lunch, Homor St. Francis commented, "If I were to do to a white cemetery what the whites have done to Indian cemeteries—I'd be put in jail right away."

Close family ties are important to Patsy and Homer, even though all the children now live away from home. They have three boys and two girls; the daughter living farthest away is no more than fifteen miles from them. There are three grandchildren and another on the way. Many framed family photographs hang on the living and dining room walls.

One was a particularly arresting profile of a young man with straight dark hair that seemed to symbolize the characteristics of strength and resoluteness associated with young Indian warriors. Noting my interest, Patsy said that the photograph was of their youngest son, taken just before his graduation from high school.

"The teachers tried to get him to cut his hair before graduation, but he refused. And when he went up to receive his diploma, he got a standing ovation.

"I am Abenaki through both my father and my mother's family, but the line is stronger on Homer's side," she said. "It's very direct from generation to generation. He was also raised to hear the stories told by the old people. They remembered many things, and kept them alive. Homer has always been aware—and proud—of his background, and he passed it on to his children.

"My husband was born in this house, right in our bedroom," she said, eyes sparkling. "His great grandfather built the house on one side of us, and his grandfather built the house on the other side, and there've been St. Francis people living there ever since."

"When UVM [the University of Vermont] was doing a dig at Highgate I had a job working there for awhile, it was on-the-job training. We found a lot of pottery, arrowheads, and stone tools. There are a lot of things that were left here by our people and we want a museum to keep those things together."

She explained that as a child she wasn't brought up to think much about her Abenaki connections. She and her family lived on a farm in Highgate until she was twelve and her father died. "When he got sick we had to sell the farm and move to Swanton," she said.

"Then my mother and Homer's oldest brother started going out together and were married." There were thirteen children in Homer's family; he was the youngest. There were ten in Patsy's family.

"They had a daughter who is now my half-sister and also my niece," Patsy continued with a smile. "Homer and I were married when I was seventeen."

Homer is a carpenter and has been a construction worker. He spent time in the Navy, the Marines, and the National Guard and has an honorable discharge from all three. He has been working with the Abenaki Self-Help Association for twelve years.

"I've worked at Champlain Cable for the last four years," Patsy said. "Worked at Head Start as a cook when our youngest child was five years old and I could take him with me, but I didn't work until the children were old enough for me to leave. I was always at home while the kids were growing up."

With obvious pleasure, she brought out some photographs to show me of a camp she and her husband have recently bought at Berkshire, about a forty-minute drive east of Swanton. There were shots of the view from their front door, the peaks of Madonna Mountain and Mansfield, off in the distance, and a little creek not far from the door.

Then, after the silvery little laugh that is one of her characteristics, and almost as an admission Patsy said, "I love to go squirrel hunting, too. I have a double-barrelled rifle that all my kids want when I've finished with it."

In another picture she pointed out an old wood stove in the room. "I love that stove. The building isn't much, but there are things about it. The view is wonderful, and it's quiet—away from everything, and no phone. That's why I love that camp. We all get together there every weekend."

Her family means a lot to Patsy St. Francis. She also shares a vision with her husband. Looking off into the distance she said softly: "There've been a lot of newcomers and a lot of changes in the last few years and some of our dreams seem harder.

"But the work we do is mostly for our children and our grandchildren, so they'll know the traditions, so they can feel proud of who they are, and maybe things will be better for them."

LIZ BLUM

*I*t's O.K. to be critical, but not cynical," Liz Blum said. This energetic, committed political activist, former manager of Jesse Jackson's Vermont presidential campaign in 1988, and co-chair of the Rainbow Coalition of Vermont has frequent opportunities to test her own maxim.

"I happen to feel that women's issues are also important, and I try to do things to further them. One of the ways is to be a role model. Women are still insecure about speaking in public, and because of the things I believe in as an activist, I've been forced to speak. I think this helps other women overcome their hesitation."

Liz Blum combines several strong and somewhat divergent interests, but her motivation springs from a basic interest and compassion for human beings. Her emphasis on women's issues is a key to understanding how the human family—the world family—could shed its differences, concentrating instead on preserving life on the planet. Even her gardening, which she does well, is her celebration of the possibilities presented to us by Earth, ones that should be recognized and acted upon.

She believes that problems experienced by women, disabled people, minorities, working people, older people, and poor people are all related.

"Too often it's in the interests of people in power to keep these groups separate, make them distrustful of each other," she said. "That's why I worked for Jesse Jackson and the Rainbow Coalition: Jackson was the first person speaking to all the issues. The Rainbow Coalition doesn't just mean colors, it means a lot of different issues being considered together."

A traditionalist in her concept of family, Liz maintains, "Being a mother is the hardest job I've ever had, and it's also the most rewarding. But women are lucky to be mothers. I think that in a way men are more oppressed than women. They're not expected to do childcare, and this is one of the big differences. Men would have different—and better—attitudes about human beings if this were part of their experience."

"The role models haven't changed very much," she continued. "I'm convinced that we would have a better society if everybody could do childcare."

Because of her belief that society needs to show more active concern for all children, including those with special problems, she has been for several years the Orange/Windsor County coordinator for the Surrogate Parent Program, which does parent advocacy for children who need special education. She is also the occupational therapist in the two elementary schools at Thetford and Chelsea.

About her work in the schools with children, she said: "I think of it all as education. I don't like to think of it as *special*. I don't like to see children divided up into groups and labeled. We all have more to learn from each other than we realize.

"Everyone is allowed an education, but there are lots of segregated classrooms. Disabled people in our society are often discriminated against. In schools we separate people called mentally retarded, but the purpose of the mainstreaming law is to get people to accept more differences, and it has to start when we're young. The values we place on things and on people become too rigid later."

She is a member of the Development Disabilities Council for the state of Vermont, an independent agency administered by the Agency of Human Services, and she was formerly on the Special Education Advisory Council for the State Education Department.

"I'm mainly interested in working at schools, one on one with children needing this kind of help, and I spend two days a week with children who have motor deficiencies. Problems in planning how to move their bodies, pretty much automatic for many of us, take a lot more cerebral effort for others."

She mentioned several well-known people with severe learning difficulties, among whom were Nelson Rockefeller, former governor of New York, who needed to have all written material read to him; and Albert Einstein, the physicist, who was late in learning to talk.

"All of us are always learning, but we learn differently," she said. "I don't think anybody is stupid, but too often schools only accept as proper what's been decided by the state.

"Sometimes just moving a pencil across the page takes so much energy and concentration that the person can't be bothered with the meaning of the words they're trying to write."

Liz Blum was formerly married to Marty Tucker, and they have two children, Yami, thirteen, and Pallo, nine. From 1972 until 1987, they lived in Chelsea, but recently moved to Norwich. Marty has a successful furniture manufacturing business, Work Space, Inc., that he and his partner developed in Chelsea more than a decade ago.

Liz has always been involved in her community; one example was the Chelsea Playschool, which she was instrumental in starting eight years ago. It is still functioning.

Their first child, Yami, had a mild form of epilepsy, *petit mal*, which has been successfully treated by drugs, but Liz believes that a proper diet with mineral and vitamin supplements had the greatest effect. She takes the raising and preparation of healthy food seriously, hence her involvement with organic gardening. She has also served on the board of NOFA (Natural Organic Farmer's Association), and thinks that the Vermont Department of Agriculture could do more towards encouraging the diversification of agricultural products raised in the state.

"Just think of it, eighty-five percent of all the food consumed in Vermont is brought in from out of state. Much more of it could be produced here, and think what that could do for our local farm economy—not to mention the fact that it could make better and fresher food available to us all.

"Our state government values farmers for their landscaping, not for what they produce," she added emphatically.

"The first thing I did when we moved over here was to find a woman in the rototilling business. I hired her, and then planted lots— I mean lots—of bulbs; garlic, shallots, and other things."

Liz feels fortunate in coming from a middle-class background on Long Island. Her parents were able to provide the family with many cultural and educational opportunities.

"I was always influenced by my parents, and they were also progressive. They did well with a family business, but they believed that their responsibility to society didn't stop with their own good fortune.

"They believed in lasting social change, and that one should act on his or her beliefs. And they brought me up to feel that I could accomplish anything I set my mind to."

Her parents were both active in the civil rights movement, and Liz feels this was important to her as she grew up. Later, she was involved with civil rights on her own.

Her mother was the first woman civil engineer graduating from

Cornell University. "She graduated in the thirties and suffered a lot of discrimination, but this was all part of breaking ground for the women of my generation," she said firmly. "I was brought up to think that traditional roles for women were not necessarily to be expected—or followed.

"She was superintendent of Public Works in Roslyn, Long Island when I was growing up. And I remember when we passed a particular curve on a bridge, she'd say with pride, 'That's my curve, that's one I worked on.'

"My mother also interested me in the women's movement. She had to balance being a more traditional parent and wife with being a professional woman, and she understood the problems that women face."

Liz graduated from Bennington College in 1964 with a B.A. in literature. She spent her junior year studying in Paris.

In 1982 she went back to school, receiving an associate degree in occupational therapy. Every day for two years she drove back and forth to Claremont, New Hampshire, where the school was located, and she used her time in the car to study Portuguese on tapes.

"I love languages," she said, adding that she's also fluent in French, Italian and Spanish. "I've also studied Russian."

As Jackson's campaign coordinator for Vermont, Liz concentrated on fund-raising. "This is one thing that's been weak among progressives," she said. "They haven't been good fund-raisers, but I love it. It makes people feel more committed, more a part of what's going on, and it's a way to keep in touch. The people in Rainbow have worked closely together for a long time, and there's a level of trust. We know what each of us does well, and what we don't do well.

"The Rainbow Coalition also has broad goals for women; one of the things that keeps me going is the supportive relationships with other women. I think sometimes of my good fortune in having gone to a women's college. I was never in competition with men.

"I don't feel bitter about men," she continued. "I feel it's more important to develop alliances with women than to spend time being bitter about men.

"There are so many things men don't understand the importance of, like decent childcare, and the burden that's on women now more than ever. More women are heads of households and have the responsibility of childcare as well as for the support of the family."

She pointed out that a problem with having her time so filled today is that there's not much opportunity to do the kind of cooking she loves. But she's happy about their present location because there's more land and it has a southern exposure. "I've already started my garden," she said, the light in her blue eyes underscoring the pleasure she felt.

"I make a definite effort to spend time with the kids," she added. "I still feel more responsible for them than Marty does. Whatever else I'm doing, I'm always home for dinner. What comes first for me is my kids.

"With Marty, the kids are on a totally equal basis with his work. He's off now on a six-day business trip. I wouldn't feel like doing that."

There's no question about the intensity of purpose behind everything Liz Blum does. It is accompanied, however, by an open friendliness that makes her accessible. She shows little evidence of personal judgmental barriers, and though she has a lot to say, she also knows how to listen.

"The women's movement has helped me become more comfortable with myself, enabled me to disregard barriers," she said. "Another thing, as an activist I have no fear of taking an unpopular position. If I believe in something—am committed to it—I'm not afraid to speak out.

"I've been outspoken about South Africa and the need to divest funds from that country. I've also publicly criticized Israel. I believe they need to give back territory to the Palestinians, but they need their own state, too.

"I have respect for humanity and the earth," she said, "and my burning desire is to live in a world where there's justice." There was a pause while she seemed to be looking a long way off. "But if I didn't feel optimistic, I couldn't operate the way I do."

F<small>AIRE</small> E<small>DWARDS</small>

"Y ou need to live a long time just to get exposed to many important things in life," Faire Edwards said during the afternoon we spent talking together in the living room of her small apartment in Montpelier.

Vibrantly healthy plants decorated the bay window facing out over the street, framed photographs of family and friends hung on the walls, a nice old rug covered the floor, and comfortable furniture completed the room's fittings. Its most salient feature, however, was the stacks of books, newspapers, magazines, and letters on every otherwise horizontal surface. Swiftly moving a pile from each of two chairs, she invited me to use one while she took the other.

There appeared to be every publication possible on the subject of aging and current events. Books in the process of being read were flattened to hold their places, spread out with covers on top to reveal their titles. Notes had been scribbled over the faces of periodicals, providing easy identification of topics needed for reference, and during our conversation, her hands moved with assurance into any stack of papers for easy retrieval of necessary material. I sensed that these piles of publications were stored only temporarily so they could be read, digested, and disposed of to clear the way for the next influx of information.

Faire Edwards is moderately tall and slender, with soft white hair framing a face that wears an often amused but always intent expression. Lying a little askew, her glasses reveal the humor lurking beneath the surface of any conversation. Her hands looked unusually large, capable, and strong.

As an astute and experienced observer of the human scene, she has recently been featured on WDEV, the local radio station, for two minutes early every morning.

"People are beginning to recognize my comments," she said with a small show of pride.

Faire is a senior activist, a good example of how women—often without the support of earlier vocational training—have pulled their experiences, interests, and dormant talents together to find paid work outside the home when additional family income was needed.

"I guess you could say I was raised with upper-middle-class values," she said, "but I always liked to work. So when our living standards no longer matched our financial situation, I was ready to work at anything that would help support us."

Over the years, she became an experienced freelance writer. She worked as a stringer for several Vermont newspapers and wrote copy for commercial advertising agencies and for various public agencies and causes in which she believed. She worked with the Bread and Law Task Force, was a field representative for the Cancer Society, and worked for the State Office on Aging in getting the Retired Senior Citizens Volunteer Program (RSVP) started.

Her influence in building an aging network in Vermont has been substantial. She organized for the Gray Panthers, did publicity for the state Council of Senior Citizens, and lobbied effectively for many related causes. One of these was the Older Women's League and Displaced Homemakers.

"I realized that women were in worse trouble than men, all the way to the grave, and since women live longer, they're in worse trouble longer."

Many women widowed when they are relatively young have a particular problem, she explained. Even though they've gained management skills in the unremitting job of caring for their own families, often with limited resources, they're too often perceived as having no saleable skills when the need arises later for them to look outside the home for an income. In actuality they have a long record of responsibility, experience in management, flexibility in dealing with people, and innovative ideas concerning waste—all skills that could conceivably benefit government, education, and business.

"And yet," she continued, "these women say, 'I'm only a housekeeper, I have no saleable skills.' Society in general places little value on what they've spent years learning."

She pointed out that many of them were left with only the bankrupt estate of a husband who died after a long, expensive illness, and if they're under sixty and a widow with no dependent children, they're not eligible for any welfare program.

"The turning point for me came at Bill's death, January 10, 1971. Our children were grown, and I remember thinking, just after he died, 'Nobody needs me any more.' "

"There's a certain liberation in widowhood," she added with a slight smile, "but there are other things, too, like loneliness and the excessive frugality required to live.

"Soon after Bill's death, in working with the aging, I was in contact with a widow who had only one hundred dollars a month to live on. The thought struck me then, 'Here's somebody who really needs me.' "

Over the years, Faire has focussed on gathering information about ways to make elderly people's lives more liveable, hence more useful, to themselves and to others. She has also used her communication skills to spread this information to those who could benefit from it.

Born in 1912 in the valley of the Genessee River in upper New York, she remembers that as a child she loved looking across the river into the valley.

"I still like to look out over things, preferably over a valley. I like to see the way things fit together."

Her family moved frequently while she was growing up. Her father worked in organic chemistry, sometimes teaching, sometimes in research laboratories, and later as an executive in a large papermaking company.

"He was very excited about Pasteur's discoveries and the new science of bacteriology that grew out of them. He talked a lot about this to me," she said, explaining that for nine years she was an only child.

"We were often in new places without friends, so I had the chance to spend a lot of time talking with my parents about all kinds of things. I think this developed my habit of thinking about things taking place around me. I also learned to observe and to question, and I read a lot."

She pointed out that the Pasteur Institute, with its new science of bacteriology, could be used as a milestone for the demographic revolution, for the lengthening life span that has taken place in this country. Accompanying this science was the new availability of electricity, and its long-term effect on general health as refrigeration of foods and better access to heat became commonplace. Electricity had great impact on women's work in the home.

"It's a battle between the generations to understand the sequences of what went on. Did you realize that the fastest-growing age group within our population today is composed of those aged eighty-five?" she asked. "And within this group, there's a striking predominance of women, the majority of whom live at poverty level or below?"

She underscores what the lengthening of life expectancy means in a society that idealizes youth and equates aging primarily with debilitation. Better planning on a national, as well as a state level, will be necessary in order to dignify, and therefore use, the quality of wisdom that only experience in living can provide.

"We need better communication between the generations, and we also need better transportation for the elderly."

Faire emphasized that better planning is also necessary for meeting the increased need for physical care that accompanies aging. For the growing segment of our population, this could be done in ways that are both more accessible and more humane.

"The people in greatest danger are women—living alone, and over eighty-five, and it's a group that's growing," she said, explaining that currently there are 1,738,000 women age eighty-five or over compared to 728,000 men, and that the ratio of women to men in this age category is still increasing. Also, the wide differential that has always existed between women and men in wages paid during their active working lives follows the women into their aging years.

Even though education was stressed in Faire's upbringing, she wasn't raised to follow in her father's footsteps as far as a future vocation went. College, while regarded as an advantage, was not considered essential in preparing her for adulthood.

"I never completed a bachelor's degree. Started at Oberlin, got sick, had to drop out, and then later went for a while to the Traphagen School of Fashion in New York. Much later I got an associate degree at the Community College of Vermont."

"People didn't rush to get married in the thirties," she recalled. The depression spread an air of uncertainty about the future, and young people were not anxious to make commitments they were uncertain of being able to fulfill. Faire worked as a saleswoman in two New York department stores, and later, after her marriage and before the children were born, at the Singer Sewing Machine Center in Stamford, Connecticut, where they lived. "I got eighteen dollars a week for a forty-eight-hour week and a small commission on sales."

Her plan was to become a fashion writer, so she also worked as a stringer for the Fairchild Business Papers and had regular bylines in Women's Wear Daily.

"I knew I wouldn't have to argue with a man in this field," she added with a grin. "There was no competition with men in fashion writing then."

Six children were born to the couple while they lived in Connecticut, which gave precedence to family responsibilities over her vocational ambition. Nonetheless, the writing experience stood her in good stead some years later after the family moved to Vermont and her husband's illness made income-producing work outside the home a necessity.

The Edwards family moved to Vermont in 1954, after having bought a "bargain-price," old house in Bristol. Bill Edwards had the opportunity for a lucrative job in the area and planned to combine this with badly needed work on their bargain house. In Connecticut they couldn't afford a place big enough for eight people to live comfortably; the children were growing up, and their needs and demands were growing along with them.

"Our overall prospects seemed great," Faire said, "but then Bill got sick. We sold the old place and bought another house in Middlesex that was more liveable, but those were three rugged years; the doctors were trying to find ways of alleviating his rheumatic disorder, and I was trying to find a way for us to live!"

Her youngest child was then four years old.

"There was no fashion writing to speak of here, but there was a little work as a stringer for the *Times Argus* and the *Burlington Free Press*," she said.

She grimaced slightly as she added: "I also started working at the Vermont Motor Vehicle Department. It was very old fashioned at the time, and when the supervisor came by, there was a feeling that all the clerks should get up and curtsy.

"They gave a test of ability before they hired anyone looking for work, and the position should have gone to the ones who failed. It was a terrible job!

"Then for five years I was the whole copy department for an advertising agency in Burlington. And that was fun! It was a five-person agency, and I did the copy for radio, TV, and newspapers."

She often used pictures from old magazines in setting up ads and spoke of a particular problem that arose during the Christmas holidays: "I had horizontal and vertical spaces to fill with Madonnas, and I can tell you a lot about the shortage of horizontal Madonnas."

From there she went to the Bread and Law Task Force, "A love child between Legal Aid, the Office of Employment Opportunity, and Community Action." Its purpose was to stimulate greater use of federal funds already allocated for bettering conditions among the aging.

"We knew the nutrition program of the Older Americans Act was coming through, and that this included the possibility of having meals served to elders. Of course, this was good nutritionally-speaking, but we knew it would also give them something to look forward to and create social contacts that alleviate depression.

"There was real urgency in getting information about the program out to residents in rural areas around the state," she continued. "I wrote the copy, found an ad agency that would put it together, and we got a mailing ready. Someone else scratched around for the postage money, one of the legislators enlisted her daughter and her friends to stuff envelopes, the League of Women Voters and the Ecumenical Council also helped out, and we were able to reach people in time for the program to have a real effect."

Snow covered the ground on the winter afternoon I visited Faire Edwards. It was a cold, gray day, but in response to my touch at the downstairs bell, she waited for my approach at the top of the stairs leading to her apartment, and her greeting was cordial. An aura of warmth surrounded her. A woman of abundant intellectual vitality, humor, and personal independence, she fits no stereotype and probably never has. Her priorities appear to have been carefully developed and thoughtfully tended.

The combination of Faire's particular temperament, her present location, and all the circumstances that shaped her life seemed symbolized by her apartment on the top floor of an old Victorian house on a steep hill. It seemed fitting for the woman who lived there now and who had since childhood "loved to look out over things and see the way they fit together."

ANN DARLING

When the man I was living with threw hot tea in my face one day, I knew what was coming and I threw him out of my life," Ann Darling said. But not only was she confronted with the pain of separation but also an unwelcome insight about herself.

"It registered instantly that I'm no different from the women who come here."

As director of the Women's Crisis Center in Brattleboro, her impulse was to feel shame at having gotten herself into the same kind of situation as the women she's there to serve. "But I got out of it. I had no doubt about what to do and I did it. I realized there could be no trust in the relationship with this man.

"The workers here were supportive, and they didn't make me feel bad. But this discovery about myself pushed me into taking steps to learn more about my abuse and about myself. I discovered from that experience, and the therapy following it, that I was more dependent than I realized. Now I know.

"I've been a feminist since I was sixteen; economic forces were not the issue then but independence was."

With short red hair, alert blue eyes behind gold rimmed glasses, and quick movements, she creates an impression of controlled intensity. Her manner is direct and pleasant; one senses that she's searching—but not for easy answers.

Ann has been the director of the center for 3½ years. The purpose of the Women's Crisis Center in Brattleboro is to help survivors of domestic and sexual abuse in Windham County and southern Vermont. She also chairs the agency through which state funds are dispersed for all the rape crisis centers in Vermont and in Lebanon, New Hampshire.

On the day I visited Ann, the pleasant old house on a residential street was having its exterior painted by a Bahai group that had volunteered the work as their contribution.

Inside, three women were hanging drapes at the bay window of the living room. A few toys were scattered about, there were small children in the background, and it might have been a room in the home of any extended family. However, the outside doors at every entrance to the house are kept securely locked. If women come during the day, the front door is answered, if at night, or over the weekend, a phone call must first be made to the center.

Ann explained that the crisis phone line is answered twenty-four hours a day, every day of the year. A volunteer coordinator answers the crisis line during the day and supervises the twenty volunteers who cover the phone continuously. Volunteer backups answer primarily at night, one night a week, and a staff person is always on hand who can be contacted immediately if advice is needed in handling a situation.

"We talk to women on the phone who've been battered or are in danger, and let them know we're here to help in whatever way the situation calls for," Ann said, describing some of the decisions that might be involved. There's the question of immediate danger, whether the woman, and children if she has any, have a safe place to go; whether she needs to come to the shelter. In some cases, someone might have to meet her at the police station or the hospital.

The average stay for women at the center, with or without children, varies between a few days and a month. In addition to women, during the past year, eighty-two children have also been sheltered along with their mothers.

In her basement office, Ann talked about the arduous task of keeping an organization of this kind running well. While her work as director doesn't allow her much time with the women using the center, she stays in touch with all its activities through staff meetings.

In addition to the director and the volunter coordinator, a case manager works with the women in the house, doing advocacy, and holding group meetings. A full-time children's advocate does individual as well as group counseling with the children and works with their mothers on parenting. There's a full-time counselor for residents, as well as for women coming from the outside. In addition there's a childcare worker/house manager, an administrative assistant, and an overnight staff person.

"Everything is done in consultation with the staff; we work closely together," Ann said.

"We have regular case conferences and staff meetings, and since the case manager has been here longer than I, her judgment is important to me. I also provide support for her.

"Each person on the staff is more or less responsible for carrying out her own work. I don't give directives, we discuss everything ahead of time. I'd get hell otherwise. I figure that we're all adults, and we're all accountable for our own work."

Each crisis center depends for funding on about twenty different sources: foundations and private benefactors as well as state and local contributors. For Ann this means that, although a trained community organizer, she must spend a large proportion of her time writing grants and making reports. This leaves her with too little time for other important things.

"There should be more community education going on as a support for what we're doing," she said, giving as examples the need for more networking with the police and with hospital personnel.

"Too often they don't have the victim's perspective. This is true of probation and parole as well."

Funding is more difficult to secure in Vermont. In Massachusetts, for instance, the state supports two-thirds of the amount needed to run each center. This support means that a funding core is assured and makes more of the director's time available to develop educational programs within the community. Ann believes that there could be considerable progress in this direction if the Vermont legislature provided a larger proportion of the center's funding. The state's share is presently thirty-one percent.

She would also like to see crisis center funding become a line item in the state budget; this would allow monies to be used for the center's work that has been allocated to other state programs with a direct bearing on domestic violence and sexual assault. As an example she cited alcohol or substance abuse programs, pointing out that in about fifty percent of the abuse cases alcohol has been a factor.

Another problem faced by crisis centers is that crisis workers can be subpoenaed.

"This jeopardizes our relationship with the people who come to us for help," she pointed out. "The workers here have no confidenciary privilege, so we can't keep any records, can't have anyone's name on file. It compromises the quality of our service because we can't look back on anyone's history except through memory, can't make recommendations or develop plans for them based on what's happened before."

"Most of the women coming to these centers are poor," she added. "Battered women with money can go to a psychiatrist or a doctor; those professions have confidenciary privileges; they can't be made to divulge confidences in court."

Crisis centers have requested extension of the privilege but the Senate Judiciary Committee has held up the bill for two years.

Ann is clear about the purpose of her work. "As a feminist I want to work with and for women. It was not my choice to push forward in a male-dominated system, to push against the male hierarchy and achieve that kind of success. But I don't judge negatively the women who elect to do things differently. I'm glad they're there."

She describes her background as middle-class. "My parents were both professionals; a librarian and an engineer." Ann is the third child, and she has three brothers.

Her childhood was spent in Connecticut, but her family lived in a suburb of Washington, D.C., during her last two years of high school. This was during the late sixties and she was involved in a number of civil rights and anti-Vietnam demonstrations. She credits sensitivity training at a church camp for developing new insights about herself.

"This impressed me, convinced me that feminism is my particular route to self-respect, even to spirituality," she said.

Marlboro College originally attracted her to Vermont. She received her B.A. degree from there in 1976 and later received an M.A. in social work in Boston, where she lived for seven years before returning to Vermont.

"I had a very influential mentor in Boston and could have become involved in city hall," she said, "but I chose to come back here."

An immediate drop in salary, from twenty-five thousand dollars to sixteen thousand dollars, had to be weighed as a result of this choice but didn't change her decision. She now makes a little over twenty thousand dollars.

She spoke about her own therapy and what it had meant to her: "I have very little memory of my childhood, only a few images. Through therapy I've sort of recreated my youth, and I'm learning personally what I need to know."

Ann looks back into the history of her family for examples of integrity and independence. "My great-grandmother was one of the first Montessori teachers; she had a great knack with children.

"My great-grandfather had a big farm in Pennsylvania during the Civil War. He hired everyone he could find to come and work for him and paid women the same as men. When the men objected he said, 'If they do the same work they get the same pay!' And that's the way it was."

"My heritage is important to me," she added.

Through therapy she is understanding some of the difficulties within her immediate family, and problems that are related to growing up female in a male-dominated culture.

"My parents were sincere, good-hearted people, not heavily into material wealth. Social justice and caring for other people were part of the ethic I was raised with.

"Still, while my mother is very independent and a seeker of truth in her own way, she is emotionally dependent. And one of the important things feminism has taught us is how many women have the need for developing a stronger sense of personal independence."

She explained that some of the women who come to the center for counseling are part of a couple who are trying, with help, to work things out. Some of them are allowed out of their homes by their husbands or boyfriends for a short time. Counselors can only talk to others over the phone.

"A counselor might tell someone, 'You're still in a battering situation. What are you going to do the next time you think he's going to kill you? What about the kids?' It's a step at a time, but based on their previous experience, we try to get women to give thought to ways they can meet their next emergency."

In addition to her job, Ann sings with an amateur choral group directed by Blanche Moyse, a musician famous for her work with the Marlboro Music Festival.

"Blanche Moyse has been kind of a mentor to me, as a woman of discipline and strength, but also a person who understands compassion. A lot of people with progressive ideas can spout the rhetoric, but they have no real sense of compassion for individuals.

"Singing is important to me as a spiritual, as well as a musical challenge, and that is vital to me in my own search for independence," Ann said.

The pleasant old house on a residential street in Brattleboro doesn't disclose its private concerns, but then what home does? Nonetheless, the Women's Crisis Center in Brattleboro represents a haven for women, often with small children, often in a situation of extreme danger with no place else to turn. And like all real homes it offers nurturance, compassion, and safety to those requesting shelter.

GOVERNMENT

MOLLIE BEATTIE

*T*en years ago there were only three women foresters in Vermont," Mollie Beattie recalls. "It was an ongoing joke that when the first one of us walked through the door at a professional meeting, the registrar would ask, 'Are you Lynn, Jane, or Mollie?'

"Forestry is traditionally male dominated, but it doesn't have to be. It's a wonderful field, and it certainly requires no outstanding physical strength," she said. Mollie is proving the truth of her own words as Vermont's first Commissioner of Forest, Parks, and Recreation. Nationally as well, she's the first woman to hold an equivalent position.

Seemingly out of the blue, a couple of years ago she was asked to send her resumé to the governor's office. Later, she was called for an interview. When she asked what it was all about, she was told she was being considered for the position of forest commissioner. Only then did she go out and buy a dress.

"I literally didn't own a dress at the time," she said. In her job as a working forester, there wasn't really any need.

A tall woman with a steady gaze, warm smile, forthright and optimistic manner, she traded her boots, jeans, and days alone in the forest for office garb and management of a chunk of the state's bureaucracy. Her philosophy in either job is much the same. In her view, traditional forestry and politics both lack sufficient awareness of what lies ahead.

When forest management is pursued for short-term economic gain, consideration of factors like future productivity, wildlife habitat, soil fertility, and watershed preservation are problems often pushed aside for someone else to deal with later. Since eighty percent of Vermont is covered by forest, and ninety percent of the forest is in private hands, the long-term consequences are immense.

"A big part of my job is overseeing the management of forest land in private hands," she explains. "Since this is not controlled by law, we've got to educate, persuade, and use other kinds of inducement to change people's attitude about the land, to help them understand the nature and magnitude of this precious resource."

Much of this work is carried out by the county foresters, whom Mollie describes as being deeply involved in helping Vermont's seventy-three thousand landowners with farseeing management.

"I keep in close touch with the foresters," she said. "Most are friends I've worked with for years."

She also works with loggers and representatives of the timber, wood products, and maple industries. An ongoing part of her job is also regular contact with legislators, politicians, and her counterparts from other states and Canada.

Her department manages all state-owned and public lands, including the forty-eight state parks. For the parks, it provides all types of coordination and planning for outdoor recreation as well as for conservation education.

The traditional system in forestry, she pointed out, was designed by males, reflecting forms of leadership and power that permeated everything. It had a great deal to do with the way forest land was managed.

"For a long time it meant building roads and hauling timber, with the value of the forest figured by the net worth of each tree. A coercive view," she said.

In her approach to forestry, economic goals are not achieved by heavy-handed manipulation for monetary gain that can leave the system in a weakened or disordered state. "The nontraditional approach to forestry," she says, "asks how you can best imitate the forces of nature while still achieving some of the same goals. It asks what can be learned by watching, by adjusting the system in relation to these forces. Substantive social change in politics must be handled in much the same way."

She explained that forestry has, until recently, been ninety-one percent male and ninety-eight percent white throughout the country, but that within the last few years, many more women have been added.

"The way you approach both management and leadership of any enterprise has to do with whether you accept the traditional hierarchical system of power vested in the position rather than in ideas, or a nontraditional approach," she said.

Coming from a childhood in the wealthy Connecticut suburb of Greenwich, the product of a proper Roman Catholic convent school with even a brief stint as a fashion model, Mollie Beattie might seem an unlikely candidate for forest visionary.

"I did have a grandmother who tried to go to forestry school," she recalled. "In her day, this was not considered a possibility for a woman, but she had a passion for trees."

After a degree in philosophy, a move to Vermont in 1968, and several years as a newspaper reporter, her life was changed by a three-week visit to Colorado.

"I went to Outward Bound as a student in 1973, and spent my first night outdoors. I loved it." She was offered a job and returned for the next three summers, finally becoming a mountaineering instructor at the age of twenty-seven.

During this stint she visited the forestry department at the University of Vermont to ask about a course in tree identification. The professor brought up the subject of forestry, and told her about a program recently developed at the University of Vermont (UVM) to encourage more women to enter this field. At the same time, she was offered a position as newsperson on WCAX-TV in Burlington.

"When it came to a choice between television news broadcasting and forestry, I chose forestry," she said.

After receiving her degree, she had a series of jobs working in forest management. These included developing an environmental impact statement on a proposed wood-burning plant in Maine and research on techniques to enhance wildlife management on small tracts of land. For two years, Mollie taught forestry to landowners around the state for UVM's Extension Service. She also co-authored *Working With Your Woodland: A Landowner's Guide*, published by the University Press of New England in 1983 as a "middle way between overuse of the forest and not using it at all."

Having developed land management programs for the Windham Foundation in Grafton, Mollie was hired as full-time forester in charge of their two thousand acres of land. The Windham Foundation is a private entity created to revitalize the historic structures and the economy of the town of Grafton and to study statewide Vermont issues. Mollie was encouraged to pursue the idea of a series of conferences where participants grappled with ideas and ways for meeting critical growth pressures affecting such basic aspects of life within the state as: open lands, employment, housing, agriculture, education, and women's issues.

"Try to think of ideal solutions in the best of all possible worlds," she urged the twenty-five participants at each of these Grafton Conferences.

"It was a way to get people thinking in fresh ways about new and old problems," Mollie said.

While forestry is her central interest, she believes that this is only one of the major issues the state faces today. By nature as well as by training, she is also a careful observer of the details of a situation or problem, but she manages as well to maintain an awareness of its broader outlines.

"Too often we see laws passed that only nibble at the edge of large problems. They create the illusion that someone at the top knows what's going on and will see to it that it all turns out right. We've got hierarchical systems with power vested in the position rather than in ideas, and usually nobody's really in control," she said.

"Politics is too important to be left to traditional politicians," she continued. "We need a lot of people who don't look at things in the usual way and we need them soon."

She believes that women can be even more resistant than men to new ideas, but that this has more to do with the nature of power than with the nature of women.

"You have to keep in mind that what we're trying to accomplish is often dominated by old-school vision where the definition of power is less leadership than coercion. The circle of elective politics in America is very much a sort of jousting field, with everyone shining their own armor.

"As a woman trying to lead in a nontraditional direction, the loneliness is intense. You need a support system unless you play by the old rules. You need people who are like-minded to support you.

"What we've gained, as women in any field, is fragile and needs to be guarded and supported."

Mollie Beattie has vision, and she intends to protect it. Given the range of her background and the depth of her interest in the environment, it's not surprising that she's concerned about the danger of working indoors for too long. Even her sporty red car with an "I Brake for Trees" bumper sticker can't erase the two-hour drive from her office and midweek apartment to the 142 wooded acres that she and her husband, Rick Schwolsky, call home.

"It's a segmented life," she says. "Different clothes and different people—but on weekends I get back to the woods."

"I can only see myself doing this kind of job for a few years," she added. "If you're working in natural resources, it's critical to go back to where it all began, where your inspiration got its start. That's what keeps your fires lit."

MADELEINE KUNIN

*H*ow did I get into this?" Madeleine Kunin asked musingly, in response to my question. As the first female governor of Vermont, also one of only two in the entire country today, it was a question she had faced frequently. I assumed her answer could always be further mined for general truths, applicable to other quests made by women, and I was right.

"There are no easy answers," she began, "all are most general, but basically I suppose it's curiosity that leads you to take the next step—and the next—exposing oneself to the fears and rewards of growth."

Her background is one of which stories are made. The immigrant child from overseas, coming to a new country, new customs, and a new language, growing up to become the highest official in her state. However, the gender factor could be the most significant.

Sitting opposite me, on the governing side of the desk, Madeleine seemed both formidable and gracious. Tall and slender, graying hair combed softly away from her face, and always smartly dressed, she carries easily the dignity of high office but adds to that an expression of amused camaraderie with her audience, of one or of many. She also has a gift for bringing focussed and thoughtful attention to what another person is saying.

Describing her position, she said, "The most exciting part for me is stepping into new areas. The discovery that in the process I continue to develop and to change."

Looking off for a moment, she added emphatically, "It has a lot to do with being responsible for your own life.

"It means that you are aligning yourself with the protectors and caretakers out there, the ones who are in charge. In the end, political action means having the certainty that you can have an effect on things around you."

Her active participation in politics began when she ran for, and won, a position in the state legislature. That was 1972, and she lived in Burlington, with her husband and four young children. Sixteen years later, what she acknowledges would have been unthinkable then has become a fact.

"I started in the state legislature," she recalled, "and sort of grew up politically as my children grew up. I feel very fortunate in my timing. I worked my way up the political ladder with no thoughts of becoming governor. And if it weren't for the gender factor it would have been pretty typical."

But her odyssey is atypical in more ways than one. Not only as a Swiss immigrant, arriving in this country as a small child with her brother and widowed mother, refugees from a Europe divided and torn by Nazi domination, but also as the third Democrat since the Civil War to hold this job in the state of Vermont.

Gender is highlighted by the fact that she is also one of only seven women governors in the history of the United States.

"There is still something very hostile about politics. It is not the way women are brought up to behave," she told the Forum for Women State Legislators held in San Diego a few months ago; and later pointed out to another group in Maine, "It is simply a question of numbers—a matter of getting more women into office—making it more ordinary and less extraordinary."

Because of the uniqueness of her position, there's been a change of style in the executive offices. As an extension of her ease in working with people, she has no difficulty with first names, her own or the person's speaking with her. This also seems to be policy followed by her office staff, so that a visitor to these offices is routinely addressed by her or his first name, hence placing the visit within a context of informality.

In talking with other women around the state, I've been struck by the number who give examples of personal experience with Madeleine's graciousness. That she puts people at their ease helps account for her popularity, and it is tempting to associate this particular quality with the fact of her being a woman. No small part of this, however, stems from her genuine interest in people; but as a woman, her background has provided her with an innate understanding of the difficulty many other women have in expressing themselves easily to an authority figure.

For many who know her there's a sense that Madeleine's empathy springs from her own experience in overcoming doubts. They see in her the results of a strengthening confidence that could also be attained in other areas.

Evaluating the effect that her former career as a journalist has had on her political life, she said, "They both take intellectual curiosity, problem solving, and a desire to live life fully. I can see a definite connection between writing and government."

She places importance on role models for women, and without hesitation said, "In my own case, if an observer was looking down from a distant Mt. Olympus trying to distinguish between role models—who knows? My father died when I was three and I grew up without a father. I sometimes think this made me more conscious of my mother's role—and also of mine later.

"Mother was a strong woman, moving to a different country and bringing up two children on her own. I sometimes think that if she had lived in more recent times, she would have been more involved outside the home. But she lived in a time when this would have been hard to carry out.

"It was almost like a warning to me. I have four children, one girl and three boys, and I went through periods of conflict when they were little; but I've had lots of encouragement about my career in politics from my family."

She also cited other women who have attained high-level political positions and have helped to create a climate, as well as role models, that make this kind of success more possible. She included Ella Grasso, former governor of Connecticut; Dixie Lee Ray, of the Nuclear Regulatory Commission; and Martha Layne Collins, a former governor of Kentucky.

Madeleine was born in Zurich, Switzerland, in 1933. Her father was a shoe importer. Her mother, Renee May, decided in 1940 to flee Nazi-era Europe and immigrate to the United States with her two children, Edgar and Madeleine. The family settled in western Massachusetts, and she graduated from public high school in Pittsfield. From there she proceeded to the University of Massachusetts in 1957 and earned a B.A. in history. This was followed by an M.A. in journalism from Columbia University. Later, after her move to Vermont, she received an M.A. in English literature from the University of Vermont (UVM). She has since been awarded numerous honorary degrees.

Offered a general assignment position at the *Burlington Free Press*, she moved to the state in 1957; the region is frequently compared to her native Switzerland. Two years later, she married Dr. Arthur

Kunin, a kidney specialist, who teaches at the University of Vermont.

"I took about ten years off to be home with the children while they were small," she said. But she was active in community affairs, as well as in academic work on a second master's degree from UVM.

Her interest in, and understanding of, the increasing importance of daycare for women was evidenced recently when she spoke at the opening of the state's first employee daycare center at the Brandon Training School. There was experience behind her comment, "More childcare is an issue in which everyone wins. The reality is that everywhere in Vermont, everywhere in the United States, as more families are two-income earner families, daycare is a necessity. Businesses are helped too, since employees can feel good about going to their jobs, and they are more productive."

Madeleine gives much credit to the support given her by her husband and children. "The children have been positive about my political career, and my husband has been downright enthusiastic," she said. Dr. Arthur Kunin's active role in assuming practical and continuing responsibility for the children after her involvement in politics is legendary.

"When I resolved to become governor, I gradually realized that I was capable and that there were things I wanted to achieve," the governor continued.

Her priorities have been clear from the very beginning, and she is proud of what has taken place during her years in office. The state is in an enviable fiscal position, with one of the lowest unemployment rates in the country. However, she is a strong advocate for an educational system that would prepare more residents to work at jobs with better than minimum wage earning potential. Minimum-wage jobs presently account for much of the increased employment.

Governing a state precariously poised between the proponents of heavy growth and development and those urging greater protection of the environment, takes a balancing act of some skill. Madeleine has attempted to meet this challenge by providing public forums around the state on such issues as growth and effective local control, leading up to legislation which would allow more residents to become involved in the planning process. On May 19, 1988, she signed Act 200, the Growth Management Act of 1988, developed as a result of these meetings.

As chairman of the National Governor's Association Committee on Energy and Environment, she has placed global warming at the top of the committee's agenda for the coming year. The scientific community has reached broad agreement that the global warming trend threatens the world environment, and Vermont co-sponsored an international conference on global warming with two other states in February 1989. On a recent television program, she stressed the necessity of developing a stronger environmental ethic among the public.

As might be expected, Madeleine has been in the forefront in appointing women to cabinet-level positions, and she has given significant support to the Governor's Commission on Women.

Leadership by a woman, within a traditional and predominantly male structure, requires an interesting combination of strengths. The usual style within this hierarchy is authoritarian, but Madeleine, while acting from a position of power, also combines it with what is considered a more feminine response, that of listening to other opinions in arriving at decisions. During her first term of office, she was consequently criticized for lack of leadership, a charge that she has successfully disproved.

She admits to the harsh pain of losing one campaign but points out philosophically, "Campaigning is a fairly rigorous exercise. You have a goal and you want to get there, so it's just something that has to be done. The hardest thing to me was losing in 1982, and running again in 1984."

Of the fulfillment she feels in her career, she said, "There is, of course, the loneliness of a high position, of having the ultimate responsibility, hour by hour; but there is also the reward of personal growth in meeting these responsibilities.

"This takes a certain zeal for life itself," she continued. "But each victory builds confidence, and it's a lack of confidence that holds many women back; they've shielded or shackled themselves.

"Events change, so I try to keep some perspective, to put things into context. I know that if things get worse, they will improve. You have to be resilient, be able to recover from setbacks, and willing to try again. It's the scientific method."

LYNN HEGLUND

We structured the Women's State Fair organizational chart in the form of a circle," said Lynn Heglund, executive director of the Governor's Commission on Women.

"It was more like a wheel with a center point, from which spokes radiated out from the hub to other essential components circling around it. This made the flow of information possible in two directions, both to and from the center, to share power and responsibility."

To illustrate, she spread across her desk a large chart that was used in organizing the highly successful Vermont Women's State Fair in Barre last year. It was, she pointed out, a more typically female approach to organization, a power-with model.

"The hierarchical, or power-over, structure that traditional organizations tend to use is generally a pyramid with vertical descent from a top control point. The bottom line is wide and far from the governing point, and the flow of information is often in one direction, from the top down."

Coordinated by talented entrepreneur Christine Donovan of Stowe, the Vermont Women's State Fair drew more than four thousand women from all over the state and established something of a record, not only in numbers attending but in the organizations and programs, workshops, and exhibits it brought together. Participant response was invited and suggestions welcomed for the next fair.

"We needed sixty-five thousand dollars to do this for one day, and we started with twenty-five thousand dollars. It took us nine months to organize, and although we had extra staff from June until September, we were all working a sixty-hour week."

Operating somewhat as the center of a network, the Governor's Commission on Women maintains close touch with women's organizations throughout the state. With a staff of only three, Lynn pointed out that one of the virtues of this size is flexibility. "Because we're small, we also need to be multi-skilled."

Included in the Commission's host of charges is the responsibility for development and implementation of statewide policies affecting women's legal, social, economic and political status. It also provides planning assistance to the executive and legislative branches of government and state agencies on public policy affecting women.

As an example of difficulties still encountered, Lynn mentioned the defeat of a parental leave bill in the 1987-1988 legislature. "You'd think that getting this bill passed would be easy in a country that is said to honor the mother, but in point of fact, there's no real economic reverence for mothers or for the stretched and struggling family and its caretakers," she said firmly.

"The question now is, how do we get those values established in a system that doesn't hold these values?"

She pointed out that another example of the Commission's work is the administering and evaluating of statewide grants programs to Women's Battering and Rape Crisis Services.

"The women who started and continue these programs are a testimony to dedication and selflessness," she said. "As a grants agency, we provide most programs with less than a quarter of the funds they need. They work hard in their own hometowns to raise the rest and provide critically needed services to women and children."

On the economic front, a 1987 study found that while women make up half the state's work force, eighty percent of them are employed in low-paying service and clerical jobs. The Commission and the Department of Education will be funding jointly a study on the sexual stereotyping that seems to still be operating both inside the classroom and outside in business.

Lynn described the role she and the Commission play: "Within a male structure, we operate as a kind of door between two systems. But as a door, it has to swing both ways and sometimes one gets hurt when people from both systems become impatient, when people from each side see the Commission as representing the system on the other side. Operating as an open door so ideas can pass back and forth is tough sometimes, but I can't really complain if we are sometimes misunderstood in the process."

We talked in Lynn's office, just one flight up in a pleasant old Victorian house next to the State Office building. Her room was filled with books, papers, notices, posters, periodicals, paintings, and plants and created a lively, comfortable, and friendly feeling. The other four rooms that are part of the Commission's space also contributed to this impression. A new library and meeting room are now available to the public.

"It's important for women to develop friendships and support systems," Lynn said earnestly. "My own primary support has come from the sisterhood I've had with other women. They've been mentors for me and have helped me to find my work. I think when women say with pride that they've done it all alone, it's an admission of weakness."

Lynn Heglund grew up in Minetonka, a suburb of Minneapolis, Minnesota. "It was the home of Tonka Toys," she said with a fleeting smile, "a relatively middle-class suburb where there was nothing much to do. The main diversion was shopping. There were no real differences between people either; they all seemed pretty much alike. I was dying on the vine and I had to get out."

After high school she spent some time at the University of Minneapolis as an art and language major, an institution with more than fifty thousand students on campus. Somewhere along the way she heard of an "amazing" school in the East called Goddard, and since she had already made a decision to pass through New York City during a job she had as an interpreter, she decided to first visit Plainfield, Vermont, and have a look at the school.

"I thought Goddard was about an hour from New York. My seat companion on the bus was a Mexican man, and the only thing he could say in English was "Plainfield" and the name of a woman who lived there."

This chance encounter led her to a Goddard faculty member, June Edson, a woman who was to become important in Lynn's development and direction. "The Mexican was looking for her daughter, and I found June almost as soon as I arrived on campus. She is still my mentor and guide."

From the age of ten until her arrival at Goddard, Lynn expected to become an artist. During most of high school and her early college years she studied painting and art history and was also a special art history student at the Minneapolis Institute of Art.

After making the decision to remain at Goddard to study, she switched from painting to politics because the instruction in political science there appealed more strongly to her. The college also furnished the possibility of a work-study internship at the American Civil Liberties Union (ACLU) in Montpelier. From 1972 until her graduation in 1975, she was there as an intern.

"David Harrison was the ACLU director during those years, but in 1975 he was planning on leaving." An expression of disbelief spread over her face as she recalled, "He asked me why I didn't apply for the position, and I replied, 'I can't, I'm just a girl,' or something to that effect."

She was persuaded to try by some women board members and was subsequently hired, as the new director, right out of college. At the same time, she registered for a paralegal course at the Woodbury Association, now Woodbury College.

"Law is like learning a new language. It's a different way of think-ing—in a different language, not like ordinary English—it's a long language-learning and value-shifting process."

She believes the road to power for women is not just a question of philosophy, but a matter of the right tools.

"There has to be an understanding of the language of the system you're in, and much of ours is primarily legal and technological. I could see that an important part of my job was understanding legal language and translating it to people who have been disenfran-chised."

Later, Lynn was persuaded, almost on a dare, to apply to the Kennedy School of Government at Harvard. David Harrison recom-mended her and she was accepted. She was surprised and pleased to be accepted, but her decision to attend had to be postponed for a year; she needed to save the tuition money, and there was also illness in her family. She spent the next year working for the attorney gen-eral's office as a civil rights specialist investigating discrimination cases in employment.

"But when I went to the Kennedy School, it was one of the rougher years of my life," she recalled. "To begin with, my father, who had been terminally ill, died the week before school started. For another, I left all the friends I'd made here, to go down there. It was too expensive to live in Cambridge, where most of the other students were, so I commuted every day from Jamaica Plain, and most of my time was spent studying and commuting.

"People were at the Kennedy School to learn how to manage, to become quantitative analysts, to operate within the male system, and I learned how to do that. But to me it lacked a certain ethical center."

She pointed out that there was only one woman professor out of a staff of eighty or ninety and that women made up less than one third of the student body, minorities were ten percent.

"It was male-dominated. Even Harvard grad students who make less than a B average are asked to leave. From the self-directed, relatively organic learning process at Goddard, I went to a male-dominated hierarchy with a narrow concept of success."

She graduated but was depressed about the experience and decided to give up all thought of going into politics, heading instead back to Minnesota.

"I was there for about eight months, and I supported myself with a job making doughnuts," she said with an engaging smile.

"I needed time to digest what all that had meant to me, and I decided to become a writer. Later, as I was planning to go to New

York, my mother gave me a going away present, a copy of the *New York Times*. Reading through it, I saw a job offer in the classified section for a manager at a writer's colony in Dorset, Vermont, so I applied and got the job.

"I told the director very little about my past, and I was there for a year and a half managing the writer's colony. There were writers in the winter and actors in the summer, and somehow they discovered that I knew how to raise money. I had to come clean about my organizing past, and I worked for a short time as a development consultant to the Dorset Theater Festival."

But law and its possibilities continued to intrigue her. From Dorset she went to the law office of Judge Ellen Maloney, recently appointed the first woman superior court judge in Vermont. "I ran her office for a year and a half—basic legal research and management."

Judge Maloney was also on the board of the Governor's Commission on Women, and when the position of director became vacant in 1984, she said to Lynn, "This is something you must apply for." Lynn smiled and added, "So I did, and I've been here ever since."

Like many other women, setting out to discover where their personal talents and inclinations can take them, Lynn has made digressions and detours, dropped stitches and picked them up later.

"I stopped painting after I left Goddard but from the age of nine had always thought of myself as an artist." During the twelve years between 1975 and 1987, she had no chance to paint, but made sketches and worked as she found the time, on the same piece of embroidery. "That's how I sustained that part of myself, and I called the finished piece *Diploma*.

"I started painting again in 1987 because I had to. It's a direct response to this need to create a feminine image. This image keeps coming back in my painting. I'll think I'm away from it—and there she is again. Sometimes I'll say, 'Stop it, I don't want all these complicated feminine forms.' But I understood that this was something I needed to keep in my life, something necessary to nourish a different part of myself."

Lynn helped co-found the North Branch Studio Association. Banding together, she and eighteen other central Vermont artists were able to have shared studio and exhibit space. Lynn worked steadily, three nights a week and one day over the weekend and built up a body of work that she is beginning to be pleased with.

"My painting is an attempt to give this power source in myself more recognition. I'm paying my dues to the thing that was important to me for so long." She also helped organize the early Women's

Caucus on Art in 1979 in the belief that it could provide more solidarity with other women artists around the state. "It's a case of breaking the isolation, the same as in the women's movement," she said.

"It's important for women to find support—people who have experienced similar problems. I don't know where I'd be today if it weren't for help from other women."

"Power is a gift," she continued. "It's something one both earns and already has inside. There are right ways and wrong ways of using it, effective uses and wrong uses—and that's why you need a mentor, someone who personifies and uses it, not as a selfish tool, but as a reverenced gift."

She pointed out that the first generation of women to use personal power and obtain political power in significant numbers was just one short generation ahead of her. She believes that without their work, there wouldn't have been the kind of job she has now. Much of the opportunity for affecting change, so necessary and so nurturing for our society, might not have existed.

I thought of the two charts Lynn used as an example of the difference in male and female structures. There is a vast gap between the linear mold characterizing masculine thought and the circular configuration considered to be more typically female. The latter attempts to embrace, include, and work with a variety of qualitatively different aspects of life, all with necessary parts to play.

With no hesitation Lynn Heglund concluded: "I'm lucky that within a male structure I'm now able to work with others as a translator of female values. Women's voices help keep me honest; I wouldn't want to do it alone."

ELLEN LOVELL

I'm in charge of the whole operation here. The traditional title of this position is administrative assistant, but there's a trend towards changing it officially to chief of staff." Ellen Lovell spoke of her work in Washington at the office of Vermont Senator Patrick Leahy.

She chuckled as she explained, "If I'm traveling with the senator he always introduces me to military men and other dignitaries as his chief of staff—otherwise they would assume I was his secretary.

"There are some very skilled women in Washington doing this kind of work now. However, because the person holding this job is seen as a political advisor to the senator, it's been traditionally perceived as a man's job."

Ellen is the first woman to fill this position for Senator Leahy. He was elected in 1974, and when she joined him in Washington, he was replacing his third chief of staff. Currently there are about fifteen other women, out of a possible one hundred, filling these senatorial positions.

Formerly the director of the Vermont Council on the Arts (VCOA), Ellen was invited by Senator Leahy to go from there to his office in Washington. She joined the staff in the middle of his second term.

"It was a very unconventional route to the Senate. Most of the chief aides have run senators' campaigns, have done more work in politics and have more political experience," she said.

"Senator Leahy was looking for a new chief of staff, but he also wanted a Vermonter. The man preceding me was a lawyer and left the job to go into practice."

"Leahy was willing to take a big risk. Though I asked a lot of questions, I really didn't know how big a job and how complicated it was or how keenly I would feel the responsibility."

But while there were new aspects to this work, Ellen is not a novice at many of the political skills necessary to its performance. At the Arts Council, she lobbied hard with successive governors and with the legislature to get money for the arts, so she is knowledgeable about state government. And since the Council may accept private, in addition to public funding, she was also accustomed to working with individuals at high levels within some of the large corporate enterprises that have moved to the state.

Having earlier forged a good relationship with the National Endowment on the Arts, she was also not a total stranger to the way some things worked in Washington. "I've always felt very strongly about what I do. I've always felt the arts affected people's lives in a very important way—and obviously the same is true of government.

"I could have continued my work with the Vermont Council but I saw this as an opportunity to learn—to affect larger systems—and I jumped at it. I make judgments and give advice to the senator. I've always been something of a generalist, and I like looking out over the whole picture."

Explaining some of the inherent complexities of her position, she pointed out that the work demands an understanding of the senator's responsibilities within an important arm of federal government. These operations and decisions must also be seen in a context that includes their effect upon the rest of the world as well as their impact upon Vermont. A broad overview is vital, but an understanding of the details making up the whole is also essential.

"Work days have a funny kind of pattern, and I'm usually working on a few things," she offered by way of extravagant understatement.

Ellen emphasized her need for a great deal of background material, but said that much information comes from talking to people in the nation's capital.

"There are experts all around us, and there's usually somebody who knows a lot more than I do about any specific area. Communication is a large part of my job, and I do this by phone, by meetings, or by just walking around to where my informant is. We also have a good computer system.

"We're now involved in the annual planning process, and the entire staff is working on this. Consideration is given to what was accomplished the year before, and looking ahead we try to recognize the pitfalls and opportunities that may occur. We study legislation that must come up and try to map all that out."

She emphasized that every act of the senator's demands tremendous preparation, and enumerated a few of the things that must be accounted for within the limits of finite time: his agenda, for the day, week, month, or year; information Vermonters need about things taking place in Washington with significant bearing on the state's affairs; briefing for the senator before he chairs one of his frequent hearings; background material for upcoming press interviews; overseeing speeches that are due; summaries for committee meetings; and mailings to constituents, as well as the newsletter sent to them regularly.

"A lot happens automatically and there's a high level of trust among those who work for the senator; people fulfill their responsibilities. For instance, a speech writer will have a speech three days ahead of time so there's plenty of room for reaction, instead of bringing it in at the last minute," she explained.

"One of the things I like about the Leahy operation is the teamwork that was already established by him. He gets the credit for setting the tone, for the high level of staff morale.

"My responsibility is that of a trouble shooter. He counts on me to kick in when anything goes wrong, so I need to be in touch with just about everything taking place."

Overall, she focuses on how the influence Senator Leahy exercises in his committees affects the folks back home, what conflicts or pressures will be created from things that may be good nationally but are not good for Vermont. Ellen needs to know enough about the matter to make connections with Vermont and what is good for the state, as well as how it affects what the Senator has stood for historically.

"I haven't really had a vacation in two years, but I've had some marvelous trips. There were 3½ weeks in China with the senator around the end of August, and one to the Mideast only recently."

Ellen has been in Washington for over five years. She left the Vermont Council on the Arts in November 1983. She described attending a testimonial dinner in Windsor on her last night, after which she threw some things into a bag and left on a plane for Washington.

Her husband, Chris, and son, Evan, stayed in Vermont for three years, moving down in the fall of 1986. Chris is presently in a Ph.D. program at American University, with a fellowship in education. Evan is now a student at the University of Vermont.

"Most of my conscious hours are spent living my work," she said. "I'm not home often before eight in the evening, although it's sometimes ten or eleven. Washington is the most workaholic place in the world, and there's no social life. I may occasionally collapse over a weekend, or Chris and I may go for a run or take our canoe out on the Potomac.

"We have a little brick house in suburban Washington and sometimes I take the Metro to work, but I usually drive, and it takes me about thirty-five minutes. I have public radio on in the car going to work, listening to the news, and then look over all the newspapers after I get into the office."

Ellen is forty-one, relatively young for a woman attaining a position of this importance within an area that is predominantly male. She is moderately tall, and slender, and her style has a definite elegance about it. There's a quality of graciousness as well that in no way interferes with her basic firmness of purpose.

We spoke of her background, and it's clear that there was parental support for the ambition she exemplifies.

"I come from a middle-class, suburban family. There were three kids, all girls. My mother didn't work, but she was very busy with volunteer activities, PTA, American Field Service, things like that.

"There was no real precedent for my working, except that our father was determined that all the girls have a good education and my mother always encouraged me to think of a career. Both parents were consistent in encouraging us to find our talents and try them out. They were not actively political, but my mother was a strong Democrat and my father a committee Republican.

"I grew up in a lot of different places," she added, explaining that her father's business required a certain amount of traveling. In her junior year she was selected for an American Field Service Program and went to Brazil as an exchange student.

"I went to school there for a year, learned Portuguese, and returned to Connecticut to finish my last semester in high school. From there it was two years at Connecticut College, but I chafed under it. So instead of continuing, I had a semester at the Gujarat Institution in India and was there for five months studying Hindu Esthetic Theory.

"I came back, transferred to Bennington College, and that's how I got to Vermont. I was a philosophy major there, took as many art courses as I could, and married in my senior year. I had expected to head into education."

"I was twenty-one when I married," she continued, "and my son, Evan, is now nineteen."

Ellen began working when Evan was three months old; she's grateful that her mother never remonstrated that she was leaving Evan at too early an age. When she found a daycare center that she felt good about, she was ready to go to work.

"It was 1970 and the Arts Council was five years old. They'd had a few years of giving grants for educational kinds of things, needed somebody to evaluate those grants, and I was hired. I was there thirteen years and director for eight," she said.

"Starting my career in Vermont had the advantage of smallness," she continued. "It was easier to be effective with people in a small state. Of course, I ran into some of the conventional attitudes: when I went places with Frank Hensel, the former director of VCOA, people always assumed I was his secretary."

We spoke about her goals now, after five productive years in a position of political importance, and what she might see ahead.

"Now, in my early forties, I find that my goals are more personal," she said. "I want to maintain a relationship with my son, and I want to resume singing. I've had to abandon my writing, but I'd like to get back to it."

Ellen is a first soprano in the Capitol Hill Choral Society. "I made a decision to go to the Choral Society, and this involves a 2½-hour rehearsal once a week. But once I felt my job was under control, I was determined to do it. This means that at least one night a week I have to leave work by 7:15.

"Work in Washington is out of control in terms of people's lives," she continued. "But on the other hand, it's extremely gratifying to feel you're in the middle of important events and decisions. Still, many feel that Washington is remote from the rest of the country.

"Working for the Arts Council, I would bring things like Alvin Ailey and his dance group to Vermont for four performances. And I could see people enjoying them, could see how they have been affected by it. Whereas, work in Washington can seem tremendously removed from the immediate lives of the people you are supposedly working for."

On the other hand she smiled as she quoted what another person had said about the advantages of working in the nation's capital. "At least you get to read about what's happening in *The Washington Post*, the day before it happens."

I questioned Ellen about some of the advantages, as well as the problems, a woman might face in this kind of career.

"In general, it's tougher for women to compete because they pay more attention to relationships," she said.

"This has to do with the quality of communication between me and the people I work with. I'm disturbed if there's dissatisfaction, and I can't settle down until I've gotten things back on track.

"I've always felt that the way I conducted myself is what matters. I never wanted to do my job the way men would do it, and I've thought about the way other men did it before me, but I try to stay true to myself. I don't want to lose my qualities as a woman. Women often understand relationships better than men—they want to know how people do *it*, as well as how *it* does."

Regarding spiritual values she said, "I've been a churchgoer all my life, but I want to learn more. I want to put the spiritual into my daily life more consciously, work out my own relationship to God."

We spoke of marriage in general, and its effect upon a woman's career. "It's something I've thought about from time to time. Most women have lots of other responsibilities, in addition to their jobs, but I'm fortunate in being married to a marvelously supportive man. And often as not he has dinner waiting when I get home at night."

Ellen's answer to my question about the origin of her confidence was also direct: "I would call it courage rather than confidence. I've always had a lot of self-doubt, but acting in the face of that takes courage."

GLORIA
DANFORTH

*P*ig is tacky, *cop* is alright," Sergeant Gloria Danforth said, somewhat ruefully, "but it does make me feel bad to hear people express
surprise when we've been helpful to them."

It's an occupation that most, if not all, would agree is necessary
for keeping any sort of order in our puzzling society, but not all of
us are in agreement as to how it should be regarded.

At a time when growth is the buzzword everywhere we turn, it's
surprising to find one important area where there's been so little of
it.

"The Vermont force has about the same number of people as when
I first came on in '76," Sergeant Danforth continued, pointing out
that while burglar alarms feeding into police barracks have increased,
along with traffic, homes, businesses, shopping centers, and many
other areas over which the state police must assume some responsibility, the strength of the force itself has remained more or less the
same.

However, the addition of women to the active ranks of the Vermont
State Police is one area of change. Gloria explained that after a hiring
freeze from 1974 to 1976, it was decided, for the first time, to fill some
of the vacancies with women. Height requirements were eliminated,
and she, along with one other woman who has since quit, became
the first two women troopers in Vermont. They went through the
same training as the men.

"It's changed a lot since then," she said, admitting that the State

Police training school in Pittsford was a "man's academy." A "make-do" women's wing was pulled together, but the customary regimen was followed: the use of fire arms, first aid, intensive physical training, a small amount of criminal investigation, regimentation, and discipline.

"All the fixtures in our room had been painted over, but the "overkill" inspector knew there was brass under those fixtures, so we were required to scrape off all the paint and shine them to within an inch of our lives," she said, noting that this was not done in the men's quarters. Nor, for that matter, was scrubbing the large hallway on their hands and knees in the evening, after a full day's participation in the regular training program. And even though they harbored some resentment at this effort to discourage the first female recruits, they kept at it.

"We were so stitched for time that we started sleeping on the floor so we wouldn't have to make up our beds in the morning," she added. "But we were hurting, so that didn't last too long. Sounds funny now, but it wasn't then."

The other difficulty, encountered in those early days, was clothes. "Nothing fit," she said simply. "Everything was cut for men, Marine style, too large, including the combat boots. And they hurt my feet. I looked funny and I walked funny and so many troopers transferred from the barracks where I was working that I almost had an identity crisis.

"Now I have boots that fit, and female shirts, with a different tie clasp from the men. Everything necessary to complete the uniform is now cut for women," she said.

Sergeant Danforth is a trim, tailored woman who wears her uniform with style. She stands at five feet, four inches but seems taller. She also carries thirteen pounds of weight around her waist—her revolver and holster. Her manner projects efficiency and authority, but there is warmth and responsiveness as well.

"It's training in life," she said with conviction, speaking about her career, and she gives the impression that, despite its obvious difficulties, she finds challenge and purpose in her work.

"What keeps me going is that every once in a while I can really help someone out," she said. "I can also tell people where to go in situations where I can't step in—sexual harassment, for instance. And people can ask for me by name if they'd feel more comfortable speaking with me."

Since Gloria has made her way in an occupation not primarily associated with women, I was curious about what motivated her and why. That she has lasted 11½ years and received promotions indicates there was more than whim behind her choice.

"At first I wanted to become anything that would help get poor people out of jail," she said, "but my viewpoint has changed. I understand that there has to be punishment, and at some point, people have to be rehabilitated."

Gloria was raised in North Pownal, just north of the Massachusetts border. "My grandparents were immigrants from Poland, and from Ireland, hard-working people. Both my parents dropped out of high school to go to work."

"I was Perry Mason growing up," she continued with a grin. "They were the only books around the house, and I read them all.

"So I grew up wanting to be a lawyer. Went to Castleton State College but somehow got into their cooperative education program. As a result I worked part-time as a correction officer at the Woodstock Correctional Center when it was operated for both men and women."

She also worked part-time for probation and parole, both in Massachusetts and Vermont, and later as a law clerk in the state's attorney's office in Rutland. Though the experience was invaluable, the remuneration was limited. After graduation from Castleton, she obtained a job at better pay working as a guard for a security company in Springfield, Massachusetts.

"But I missed Vermont," she said without hesitation.

About that time her mother sent her a newspaper clipping of an interview with a captain of the Vermont State Police. According to him, Vermont had no women on its force because none qualified. Gloria made up her mind to go back to Vermont and try for it.

She applied to the Department of Public Safety, and the first test was an investigation of her background, both in Massachusetts and in Vermont. She was unaware of this during the process, but she passed. Next was a written examination, which she also passed; then a successful physical examination, followed by a lie detector test.

"It was intimidating," she said, "and I still blush to think about the questions they asked."

After a final hearing before three officers, and a thirteen-week training period at the Pittsford Police Academy, she was sent to the Middlesex barracks and from there to the Chelsea Outpost.

"On road work, as a woman, there's no special consideration and only a single person in the cruiser," she said. "The back-up is the same as for a man, and we all face a lot of potential for danger. I know what it feels like to need somebody there to assist."

She mentioned domestic quarrels as one of the most frequent ways police officers get killed. "We're not primarily involved with radar traps as some people seem to feel," she said. "You've got to watch what you say. You can't go in there and be a tough cop if you can't back it up. And you don't make promises you can't keep."

She described her present position as sergeant and the ranking process within the force. The first step is a recruit, who later becomes a trooper second class. This covers the first year on the job, when a trooper can be fired if there's a question of performance. The next stage is trooper first class, and then, after five years, promotion to senior trooper. After that the first real promotion is to the rank of sergeant.

Sergeant Danforth is also supervisor of the Bethel Barracks, the highest-ranking woman in the state police. She pointed out, however, that of approximately 270 state troopers only 8 are female, and 4 have been recruited since last year.

A lieutenant, the next highest rank, is in charge of all office operations that involve uniformed personnel.

Promotion procedures are based on tests every two years, written and oral, as well as a yearly evaluation.

Gloria's present rank of supervisor includes, among other things, trooper assignments, crisis situations, untimely or suspicious deaths, special units such as search and rescue, accidents in which there are one or more fatalities, federal grant programs, the child protection team, and making sure that alarm files are up to date.

"As supervisor I'm half administrator and half trooper," she said. "Technically I'm in charge of just about anything that goes down on the shift."

And within a paramilitary organization, she finds that men sometimes find it hard to have a female in uniform telling a male trooper what to do. However, she maintained that the troops are generally trained to accomplish tasks on their own, but if an order is necessary she feels competent to give it.

"All in all, the macho types who feel defensive are a minority, and there are men within the ranks who don't mind being identified as your friend.

"But the uniforms and other trappings that go with the job tend to set us apart in the public's mind. It makes us realize that we're not considered as a friend or even friendly. I'd like to be, but then, we're not supposed to ask questions, just do the job. I'm sensitive to that issue, the importance of the job I already know."

She pointed out that the public doesn't always understand how specific criminal law can be in limiting what law enforcement officers are allowed to do. "People call and want us to do something, but unless the law's been violated there's not much we can do. We can't arrest somebody because we think something's going to happen. But you get creative after awhile, you learn to talk, and that can help."

She noted that Vermont's pay is not comparable to other state police and police organizations. "It's a job that's difficult to sell because other areas are safer and pay more money. But I think it takes a special person to be a cop."

Working hours are four days on with two days off. Four shifts of night duty, back to days and then nights again. The usual shift covers nine to ten hours, although during the winter, this is increased to eleven. When Gloria first joined the force, there was no overtime, but that has changed. Stress is an undeniable part of the job, and constant changes in tours of duty are hard on family life.

"Still, women coming on now are more interested in combining this work with a family. I didn't think it was possible to do both when I started, but the fact that it's being done now is a sign of progress."

Nonetheless, it's a demanding, difficult and dangerous job, and the question about how the rest of us would survive without it is real. But it's also a job that has a hard time presenting its best side to its public, because its best side is its worst to a perpetrator, and few among us smile as a trooper writes us a ticket for speeding.

"I came into this, not only as a woman in a new field but as someone interested in the whole area of law enforcement," Gloria said. "It's a fascinating field."

"I'm also working on my M.A. in administrative management at St. Michaels College, and I like it. It's nice to deal with people other than cops for a change," she added with a wry smile.

"Police often feel removed from the general public because of their occupation, and a female police officer tends to be further removed because of her gender. But I think there's a tendency for all troopers to feel like social outcasts some of the time."

Sergeant Gloria Danforth surprised me. I had expected someone with a stronger appearance of severity, but there was a simple friendliness about her. She was approachable and pleased to talk about her work, its rewards, problems and possibilities.

"I think one of the greatest rewards for me has been in helping somebody during a tragedy and then, years later, running into them and having them remember my name," she said.

[Sergeant Danforth is now assigned to the criminal division of the Vermont State Police where she develops training for troopers investigating child abuse.]

MARY JUST SKINNER

I first became a senator in 1978, and I find senate work more satisfying and broader than the principally one-on-one aspect of a law office.

"Still, I practice law because I like to, and I like the blend possible between law and politics. Now I spend four months in the senate and have eight months for legal work."

Senator Mary Just Skinner, recently reelected for her sixth term in the Vermont Senate, is currently one of the six women to be elected to this august body. We spoke at the end of a long working day, and the lights in her Montpelier office were among the few still visible at that hour. She has been concerned with women's issues since college and also places importance on matters that concern low-income Vermonters.

"I made women's issues my priority when I first worked for Vermont legal services, because I was very aware of the inequities that existed.

"When I first began to practice here in 1971 there were not that many women practicing law. Those that were worked mainly in legal services or for the state, but there were no women in private law firms."

"That has changed considerably," she added.

Regarding the involvement of women in politics or in other issues of importance, to them and to their families, she believes that in a small state like Vermont there are countless ways for a woman to make her opinions known. She makes a distinction between the possibilities that exist here, and those within highly populated areas.

"There are so many ways to get involved here, to volunteer, and to make a difference in what happens—the school board, Scouts, church organizations, town selectmen, parent's groups, town commissions, women's groups—I've never seen a place where energy can be channeled so well.

"Also, the cost of running for office here is so much less than in other places. You can start with small resources; you can't just buy your way in, which is a great incentive. Finances are not yet a problem and it's very exciting."

(After the last election, however, she warned that the competition for votes was driving up prices, and that a new era in this respect seemed to have been ushered in.)

"One wonderful thing about campaigning for office is that there's a lot of sharing. You talk to many different people, find out what they do, about their businesses, their churches, and their dreams.

"And once I became a senator, I realized that my interest in running for public office paid off. Every day we're in session we're charged with making decisions that affect lots and lots of people."

Mary Just Skinner was born in Indiana, grew up in the suburb of Oak Park, outside Chicago, and attended public schools there. She graduated from Barnard in 1968 and received her law degree from the Columbia University Law School in 1971. Married to Scott Skinner, another lawyer, they came to Vermont a year after her graduation from law school.

Following her graduation from law school, Mary received a Reginald Haber Smith fellowship. The program was run through Howard University and was awarded to 120 people with a demonstrated commitment to work with low-income people.

"It was an extremely competitive program, and I felt fortunate to get picked to stay in New York and work for the South Bronx legal services. It was a remarkable experience."

When her husband was offered directorship of the Vermont Public Interest Research Group, she was able to transfer her fellowship to Vermont Legal Aid. "It was a different demographics of poverty," she said. She explained that they already had a weekend house here and both loved Vermont.

While with Legal Aid, Mary represented a pregnant Marine who was discharged automatically because of her pregnancy. On appeal to the Second Circuit Court of Appeals, the court ordered the Marine Corps to consider each pregnant woman on an individualized basis to determine whether pregnancy would actually interfere with the kind of work she was doing. This was the first case in which the

Marine Corps was sued for a policy already established in other branches of the military.

On the subject of combining her professional work with the demands of raising two children, she smiled as she recalled: "I used to be the only lawyer in the state with a bassinette in the office. I'm now forty-one, and I started having children at thirty-three. My kids are at the point now where they're able to manage much more for themselves." Her sons, Justin and Wilson, were eight and five years old respectively at the time of our interview.

She kept each infant with her for the first three months but was fortunate in the availability of excellent childcare near her office in Montpelier. This continued until the children were old enough to attend public school near their home in Middlesex. In her recent election, Mary identified responsible after-school childcare programs throughout the state as one of her priorities. She understands the importance of this to women as well as to their potential employers.

Continuing on the subject of mixing work and family, she emphasized two things of importance to her: the emotional and practical support of her husband and her own inclination for hard work.

"I function best when I'm busy. I also have a husband who is very supportive and takes an active role in our family. We generally try to stagger things during the week, as far as night meetings, so that one of us is always home with the kids, and we're almost always home weekends."

"We live only seven miles from Montpelier so that by 5:30 every day, one of us is at home."

There's a quality about Mary Just Skinner that seems almost old-fashioned. A few decades ago the descriptive phrase might have been well-bred. Tall, slender, and pretty, she dresses with tailored femininity. Her manner is conventional and there is nothing startling about her general demeanor. By contrast, she has an unselfconscious and vigorous commitment to working for people in the most vulnerable positions within our society, and her motivation seems to spring from strongly moral sources.

Success has followed in many areas, and there have also been setbacks. She is proud of having reported the proposed state Equal Rights Amendment on the floor of the senate in 1982 and worked for its passage. She advocated the Rape Shield Law, strengthening domestic abuse statutes, as well as increased penalties for abuse of the elderly.

As special assistant to the attorney general she represented low-income Vermonters in utilities litigation before the Vermont Public Service Board and the Vermont Supreme Court; "Electricity and telephone are necessities of life for everyone, and this is certainly true of low-income Vermonters," she said.

Later, as a freshman senator, Mary litigated the case that resulted in retention of the ten-cent phone call when an attempt was made to increase the rate from public phones. "This would have hurt poor people most," she said.

"On a pro bono basis, I represented the Governor's Commission on the Status of Women in its petition to the Vermont Public Service Board to gain dual listings in telephone directories. Vermont was the first state in which this was required."

She was the minority whip several years ago, and more recently the chair of the Senate Judiciary Committee. "It's a committee that affects lots of people's lives, and on my personal agenda, this is just where I want to be—how we deal with domestic abuse statutes, criminal statutes affecting the elderly, as well as the need for more streamlined child support guidelines," she said. "Also there is a review of court procedures for more efficient delivery of service, as well as criminal laws which reflect society's views on unacceptable behavior."

At the time we spoke, before the last election, she pointed out that Vermont has a tradition of having only three or four women in the senate. "Never more. I don't know how far back this practice goes, but there are lots of women in the house." The tradition was broken in the last election, however, and five women were also elected.

Since her recent reelection to the senate, Mary has become chair of the Senate Finance Committee. "Within the past fifteen years there has been no other woman on this committee," she pointed out. Senator Elizabeth Ready of Addison County also serves on this committee.

Some control over Vermont's future growth interests her. "Growth should be targeted to the extent it can be," she said, "and places designated where growth is appropriate. The legislature is also dealing with statutory mechanisms so that communities have more say in the way growth occurs. We need more coordination on a regional level: the towns need to work together to create the right ingredients for their own areas. Another tough area is going to be keeping taxes low, regardless of what legislation we pass."

Affordable housing is another priority. She is also convinced that within the next five years, unless there are effective safeguards, there will be large numbers of federally subsidized housing that could, in short order, be turned into high-priced condos.

"There needs to be a way of making sure that regulations are in place for keeping this housing available and affordable, of making sure developers can't get federal money for starting low-income units and then after several years be able to prepay mortgages and convert them into higher income units, thus further drying up affordable housing. Putting together solutions for this situation won't be easy, but it is vitally important."

While waiting in the small reception room outside her office, I admired a quilt hanging behind the secretary's desk. In the senator's office there were two others displayed; and to me this was a promising sign because they symbolized Mary Just Skinner's own efforts to create a more comprehensive design out of the disparate human material existing within the state.

Summing up her personal experience and attitude towards work, she said: "Gender hasn't seemed to affect my career, partly because I've always been recognized for hard work. But as long as I can remember, I've always felt I've had more advantages, and I've always wanted to help people without them.

"I also understand some of the difficulties faced by women who've had far less accessibility to education than I've had, who've been less fortunate in other ways.

"They've had much less access to the tools they need for controlling their own lives, and I have an interest in helping them."

LOLA PIEROTTI AIKEN

What I tell the young women at Champlain College when I talk to them is, 'I know you want the best, but if the best is not available, keep on going.'

"Take what's available but keep going, even if it means going out of state, which a lot of young women don't want to do," Lola Aiken, Senator George Aiken's widow, added, blue eyes twinkling. (She is a member of the Champlain Board of Trustees and often invited to speak to students there.)

She described her own doubts when in 1941, as a young, inexperienced clerk working in the Vermont secretary of state's office, she was offered a secretarial job in Washington. It was in the office of a newly-elected U.S. Senator and former Governor of Vermont, George Aiken.

"At first I thought 'No.' But I went for advice to a friend who had been a secretary to a United States Senator from Vermont. When I spoke to him about it he said, 'Lola, if you go down for six months, or a year, it would be a great education and you'd never regret it.'

"I was concerned, because it would leave my mother alone, but I went. And he was right—I've never regretted it."

"I didn't know my husband when I first went to work for him," she added, recalling that at that time she was the lowest-paid worker in his office.

Lola spoke easily about herself, her background, and the professional, and later personal, life she shared in Washington with "the Governor," as she always refers to him.

He was a man who epitomizes, possibly more than any other, before or since, many of the qualities most admired by Vermonters: integrity, independence, and an unfragmented scale of values. The work in Washington was a team effort, and Lola's contribution, starting as an inexperienced secretary, gained steadily in importance over the years. In 1972, the Senator decided not to run again for office, and he and Lola moved back to Vermont. Since his death in 1984, she's maintained the kind of busy schedule that has always been her lot. Her work is volunteer now, and includes membership on seven boards.

I visited her in her home, high on a hill overlooking Montpelier. In a spacious living room, I chose a comfortable chair at one end of a large wooden coffee table. She sat in a corner of the couch nearest me.

Large and expressive blue eyes are one of her dominant features, and since she is petite, one could make the mistake of expecting her to be retiring, if not a little shy. But Lola Aiken has spent years working with all manner of people and situations, decisively and sympathetically, leaving no room for affectation that could dull her response to the person or matter at hand. Her manner is vivacious, her enthusiasm for living is like a small locomotive.

The wood paneled living room had an imposing brick fireplace at one end and large picture window at the other through which one could view the city below.

"I'd like to open the view of Montpelier a little more, but the Governor always hated to see trees cut," she said, a little pensively.

On the walls were oil and watercolor paintings and photographs that had strong associations with other places and people. She pointed to a watercolor that included both the United States Capitol and the United States Senate office buildings. This painting was made into prints for invitations to a party given on one of the Senator's birthdays while he was still in Washington. The party was given by Senator Margaret Chase of Maine. "The Governor had nominated her for the Presidency in 1964 at the Republican Convention, the one at which Barry Goldwater was nominated," Lola said.

This celebration took place at the capital; President Lyndon Johnson, Ladybird Johnson and their daughter Luci came, preceded by a contingent of Secret Service men, with one of them bearing a box full of gifts for the Governor. "LBJ was a great one for gifts," Lola said, smiling. She showed me a pair of handsome gold cuff links with the presidential seal, and several sets of playing cards with the Air Force One insignia.

Referring to her life now, away from the bustle of the nation's capital and transplanted back to the relative quiet of Vermont, she said, "I was born in Montpelier and I've always loved it. People ask me if I miss Washington and I say 'No, I only miss people.' "

She laughed gaily as she continued the story of her work in Washington. "At first I didn't like the Governor. He was the kind of Vermonter who didn't want to waste time. When I went into his office to tell him something, he wouldn't even look up from the newspaper he was reading to answer my question. But while he didn't look up, he heard everything I said."

But the months passed into years, and Lola remained, becoming an important part of Senator Aiken's staff. After he was appointed as a delegate to the United Nations by President Eisenhower, Lola accompanied him to New York as his secretary.

"He had a room in the United States Mission," she recalled, "and I was given a desk just outside the door. He insisted that it be moved inside. 'It made more sense,' he said.

"He also wanted me to have a pass to go from one section of the building to another, but it didn't happen. He knew there would be times when he was in another part of the building and would need to call his secretary. He didn't want to have to go through the formalities every time, he wanted me to be able to move freely."

"So he told the administration, 'I've asked for a pass for Lola, and I've never received it. If I'm sitting in the U.N., I need to be able to call her down.'

"When it was explained to him that secretaries were not allowed to have a pass he said, 'All right, if a secretary isn't acceptable how about an administrative assistant?' and I received my pass."

And to Lola he said, "You've been doing the work for many years, you might as well have the title." And so it became official that she was the Senator's administrative assistant.

In another instance concerning form and procedure at the U.N., Lola told the Governor that women who worked at the United States Mission in supportive positions were never invited to any of the U.N. parties, whereas men of equivalent status were included. Senator Aiken again went to the authorities and remonstrated. "Before I leave here, I want every woman working here to be invited to at least one function," he said, and his suggestion was followed.

Prior to Jack Kennedy's election as President, he and Senator Aiken enjoyed neighboring offices in the Senate building for eight years and got to know and respect each other. Later, when President Kennedy started the first Commission on the Status of Women, Senator Aiken was invited to join, which he did.

Lola told another story illustrating the Governor's impatience with arbitrary gender distinctions. He went on a fact-finding trip for the Foreign Relations Committee of the Senate to several South American countries, and as his administrative assistant, she accompanied him.

Shortly after arriving in Caracas, he inquired about the evening schedule. When she told him that it was a stag dinner, he blew up and said that he wanted all the wives, or any other women involved in the delegation, to be there. The dinner was reframed to include the women who were part of the mission, either through office or marriage.

"The Governor always said that I could get more information out of people than he ever could," she continued. "I love people, it's my Italian background. When I was growing up our house was always full of people. In high school we always had at least two tables of bridge every Sunday, boys and girls. My mother wanted to know where we were so she liked having things take place in our house.

"She was from a little village west of Florence. I always wish I'd asked her how she got to the boat in order to come here. My father was working in the stone shed, and after my mother got to this country she couldn't speak any English, but she managed to get on the train in New York. She kept asking the conductor how far it was to Montpelier, and he kept saying, 'Soon,' so she didn't take her coat off for the whole fifteen hours, afraid she'd miss the station.

"She had a four-year-old child, my sister, with her, and a suitcase with everything she'd brought along. When she got to the [Montpelier] station, the cablegram she had sent to my father hadn't reached him so she had to walk all the way from the station, with a child, a suitcase, and no English. She came in 1904 and couldn't understand the dialect spoken by the Italians here.

"My father was a granite cutter. He'd go off every morning at 7 A.M. whistling, and he'd come home at night still whistling. My mother used to say, 'Look at him—the secret is to be happy.' He was a wonderful man. Italian men are wonderful. Very family-oriented," she said.

Lola Pierotti had just graduated from high school when her father died from the dreaded white lung of granite workers. She was grateful that he was only sick for a month.

"My memories from childhood center on my mother and the big, black cookstove in the kitchen. She'd have us pull up a chair in front of the woodstove when we got home from school on a cold winter day, and she'd open the oven door so we could prop our feet up in front of it to warm them. There'd also be hot chocolate to go along with it.

"I have a clear memory and a strong feeling, even as an adult, about opening that front door, calling out, 'Mom,' and finding her there."

Because she recognizes the importance of her own early years in preparation for a different kind of fulfilling work, Lola stressed the significance of family life to society.

"The most important job in the whole world is the family. We need more public attention to the importance of family life and help for those women who want to stay home with their children."

Reflecting later on how few women, relatively speaking, become politicians, she observed, "It's a hard, hard job to get started in. A lot of women have families and they just can't devote the time to it.

"Madeleine [Governor Kunin] was lucky to have Arthur. He really took care of the kids, and I remember telling him at some function or other, 'She's damned lucky to have you.'

"Still, women are better at this [politics] than men; they're better with people." And as an illustration she used Margaret Chase Smith who, at a memorial dinner given for her when she was ninety-one, shook hands with five hundred people and had a different greeting for each one.

"But I wouldn't run for anything," Lola concluded firmly.

"The last time the Governor ran for office he spent $17.09. We'd get up in the morning, go to a diner in some little town and sit up at the counter. He always loved diners. He'd ask, 'What's going on up here?' and believe me they'd tell him.

"He couldn't win that way today," she added, shaking her head slowly, then forcefully when, as an important afterthought, she said, "Yes, he could have!

"I married him on June 30, 1967, and there was a special reason for this date: it was the end of the fiscal year. But I was off the payroll as soon as we were married; the Governor didn't want any hint of nepotism."

Nonetheless, she continued in her old position, and the two of them went to the office every day at 7 A.M. as usual.

"We'd have breakfast later with Mike Mansfield: this had gone on for years. It started when Mike was new to the Senate and looked as though he didn't know anyone. I asked him if he would like to eat with us. Afterwards we had breakfast together every morning we were in town for the next twenty-five years."

"Mike didn't like to have anybody else join us," she added, eyes sparkling. "Arthur Goldberg sat with us a few times but Mike discouraged him. And the press never tried to pump us about any of the things we talked about."

When Senator Aiken was eighty-two, he decided against running for office again. He was unwilling to discontinue his active participation in life, however, so he lectured at the University of Vermont.

"They gave us an apartment at the Living and Learning Center, but we had most of our meals in the main dining room. We sat at a big table there, and he enjoyed the kids who joined us.

"The Governor always said, 'Give kids responsibilities and they'll rise to them.' He believed in them and they knew it."

Senator George Aiken died when he was ninety-two, on November 19, 1984. "It will be four years next month," Lola said. "He didn't want a political funeral, family only. We were planning it at the hospital. I said, 'I'll give the eulogy,' and he said, 'Make it funny.' He told the minister that, also the priest.

"I kept mine funny, too, and prayed that I wouldn't cry. When I was trying it out, I would break down at a certain word, but when I got up at the funeral I went right over it. I knew the Governor would be pleased.

"I wanted lunch served afterwards, but it was Thanksgiving and they couldn't do it at the Putney Inn, so the inn's owner and four Knights of Columbus put it on. They did everything. The next day we stood around the grave with the family and talked about the Governor with the children.

"I sometimes have the strongest urge to talk about my husband. Since his death I often need to talk about him with someone I can trust. But I have a sister in Connecticut who I can call when I feel that way. I'm lucky."

"There are times when I think that what everybody in the world needs most is someone to talk to," she continued, summing up briefly and with the wisdom of compassion, a simple human need, too often overlooked.

Lola Aiken has had and continues to have a full and eventful life. Although she's had to change directions since her husband's death, she remains involved on her own terms, allowing the past to add warmth, humor and purpose to her future.

"There's a lot of good going on in the world," she concluded softly. "I'm an optimist, and the Governor was definitely an optimist. I'm a Catholic; I'm also a believer, and we had a wonderful life together."